If God Made
the Universe

WHO
MADE
GOD?

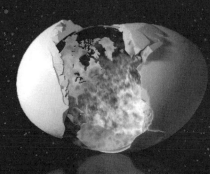

If God Made
the Universe
WHO
MADE
GOD?

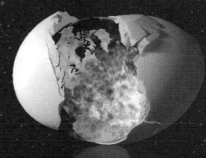

130 ARGUMENTS FOR CHRISTIAN FAITH

HOLMAN
REFERENCE

Nashville, Tennessee

ISBN: 978-0-80549-580-5

Printed in the USA
1 2 3 4 –14 13 12
DP

TABLE OF CONTENTS

Section One—Apologetics: Introductory Issues

Section Two—The Existence of God

Section Three—The Scriptures: Their Origin, History, and Accuracy

Section Four—Jesus Christ

Section Five—Theology

Section Six—Science and Faith

Section Seven—Ethics

Section Eight—Heaven, Hell, and the Spiritual Realm

Section Nine—Cults and World Religions

Section Ten—Evangelism

SECTION 1

Apologetics: Introductory Issues

What Is Apologetics?

Kenneth D. Boa

A pologetics may be simply defined as the defense of the Christian faith. The simplicity of this definition, however, masks the complexity of the problem of defining apologetics. It turns out that a diversity of approaches has been taken to defining the meaning, scope, and purpose of apologetics.

The word "apologetics" derives from the Greek word *apologia*, which was originally used as a speech of defense. In ancient Athens it referred to a defense made in the courtroom as part of the normal judicial procedure. After the accusation, the defendant was allowed to refute the charges with a defense (*apologia*). The classic example of an *apologia* was Socrates' defense against the charge that he was preaching strange gods, a defense retold by his most famous pupil, Plato, in a dialogue called *The Apology*.

The word *apologia* appears 17 times in noun or verb form in the NT, and can be translated "defense" or "vindication" in every case. Usually the word is used to refer to a speech made in one's own defense (Lk 12:11; 21:14; Ac 22:1; 24:10; 25:8,16; 26:2,24; 1Co 9:3; 2Co 12:19). The idea of offering a reasoned defense of the faith is evident in Philippians 1:7,16; and especially 1 Peter 3:15, but no specific theory of apologetics is outlined in the NT.

In the second century this general word for "defense" began taking on a narrower sense to refer to a group of writers who defended the beliefs and practices of Christianity against various attacks. These men were known as the *apologists* because of the titles of some of their treatises. But apparently not until 1794 was *apologetics* used to designate a specific theological discipline.

It has become customary to use the term *apology* to refer to a specific effort or work in defense of the faith. An apology might be a written document, a speech, or even a film. Apologists develop their defenses of the Christian faith in relation to scientific, historical, philosophical, ethical, religious, theological, or cultural issues.

We may distinguish four functions of apologetics, though not everyone agrees that apologetics involves all four. Such opinions notwithstanding, all four functions have historically been important in apologetics, and each has been championed by great Christian apologists throughout church history.

Vindication **or** *Proof.* This involves marshaling philosophical arguments as well as scientific and historical evidences for the Christian faith. The goal is to develop a positive case for Christianity as a belief system that should be accepted. Philosophically, this means drawing out the logical implications of the Christian worldview so they can be clearly seen and contrasted with alternate worldviews. The question of the criteria by which Christianity is proved is a point of contention among proponents of various kinds of Christian apologetic systems.

Defense. This function is closest to NT and early Christian use of the word *apologia,* namely defending Christianity against the plethora of attacks made against it by critics of varying belief systems. This involves clarifying the Christian position in light of misunderstandings and misrepresentations; answering objections, criticisms, or questions from non-Christians; and in general clearing away any intellectual difficulties that nonbelievers claim stand in the way of coming to faith.

Refutation. This function focuses on answering the arguments non-Christians give in support of their beliefs. Refutation cannot stand alone, since proving a non-Christian religion or philosophy to be false does not prove that Christianity is true. Nevertheless, it is an essential function of apologetics.

Persuasion. By this we do not mean merely convincing people that Christianity is true, but persuading them to apply its truth to their life. This focuses on bringing non-Christians to the point of commitment. The apologist's intent is not merely to win an intellectual argument, but to persuade people to commit their lives and eternal futures into the trust of the Son of God who died for them.

How Apologetics Changed My Life!

Lee Strobel

S kepticism is part of my DNA. That's probably why I ended up combining the study of law and journalism to become the legal editor of *The Chicago Tribune*—a career in which I relentlessly pursued hard facts in my investigations. And that's undoubtedly why I was later attracted to a thorough examination of the evidence—whether it proved to be positive or negative—as a way to probe the legitimacy of the Christian faith.

A spiritual cynic, I became an atheist in high school. To me the mere concept of an all-loving, all-knowing, all-powerful creator of the universe was so absurd on the surface that it didn't even warrant serious consideration. I believed that God didn't create people, but that people created God out of their fear of death and their desire to live forever in a utopia they called heaven.

I married an agnostic named Leslie. Several years later she came to me with the worst news I thought I could ever get: she had decided to become a follower of Jesus. My initial thought was that she was going to turn into an irrational holy roller who would waste all of her time serving the poor in a soup kitchen somewhere. Divorce, I figured, was inevitable.

Then something amazing occurred. During the ensuing months, I began to see positive changes in her character, her values, and the way she related to me and to the children. The transformation was winsome and attractive. So one day when she invited me to go to church with her, I decided to comply.

The pastor gave a talk called "Basic Christianity," in which he clearly spelled out the essentials of the faith. Did he shake me out of my atheism that day? No, not by a long shot. Still, I concluded that if what he was saying was true, it would have huge implications for my life.

That's when I decided to apply my experience as a journalist to investigating whether there is any credibility to Christianity or any other faith system. I resolved to keep an open mind and follow the evidence wherever it pointed—even if it took me to some uncomfortable conclusions. In a sense, I was checking out the biggest story of my career.

At first, I thought my investigation would be short-lived. In my opinion, having "faith" meant you believed something even though you knew in your heart that it couldn't be true. I anticipated that I would quickly uncover facts that would devastate Christianity. Yet as I devoured books by atheists and Christians, interviewed scientists and theologians, and studied archaeology, ancient history, and world religions, I was stunned to find that Christianity's factual foundation was a lot firmer than I had once believed.

Much of my investigation focused on science, where more recent discoveries have only further cemented the conclusions that I drew in those studies. For instance, cosmologists now agree that the universe and time itself came into existence at some point in the finite past. The logic is inexorable: whatever begins to exist has a cause, the universe began to exist, and therefore the universe has a cause. It makes sense that this cause must be immaterial, timeless, powerful, and intelligent.

What's more, physicists have discovered over the last fifty years that many of the laws and constants of the universe—such as the force of gravity and the cosmological constant—are finely tuned to an incomprehensible precision in order for life to exist. This exactitude is so incredible that it defies the explanation of mere chance.

The existence of biological information in DNA also points toward a Creator. Each of our cells contains the precise assembly instructions for every protein out of which our bodies are made, all spelled out in a four-letter chemical alphabet. Nature can produce patterns, but whenever we see information—whether it's in a book or a computer program—we know there's intelligence behind it. Furthermore, scientists are finding complex biological machines on the cellular level that defy Darwinian explanation and instead are better explained as the work of an Intelligent Designer.

To my great astonishment, I became convinced—*by the evidence*—that science supports belief in a Creator who looks suspiciously like the God of the Bible. Spurred on by my discoveries, I then turned my attention to history.

I found that Jesus—and Jesus alone—fulfilled ancient messianic prophecies against all mathematical odds. I concluded that the NT is rooted in eyewitness testimony and that it passes the tests that historians routinely use to determine reliability. I learned that the Bible has been passed down through the ages with remarkable fidelity.

However, the pivotal issue for me was the resurrection of Jesus. Anyone can claim to be the Son of God, as Jesus clearly did. The question was whether Jesus could back up that assertion by miraculously returning from the dead.

One by one, the facts built a convincing and compelling case. Jesus' death by crucifixion is as certain as anything in the ancient world. The accounts of his resurrection are too early to be the product of legendary development. Even the enemies of Jesus conceded that his tomb was empty on Easter morning. And the eyewitness encounters with the risen Jesus cannot be explained away as mere hallucinations or wishful thinking.

All of this just scratches the surface of what I uncovered in my nearly two-year investigation. Frankly, I was completely surprised by the depth and breadth of the case for Christianity. And as someone trained in journalism and law, I felt I had no choice but to respond to the facts.

So on November 8, 1981, I took a step of faith in the same direction that the evidence was pointing—which is utterly rational to do—and became a follower of Jesus. And just like the experience of my wife, over time my character, values, and priorities began to change for the good.

For me, apologetics proved to be the turning point of my life and eternity. I'm thankful for the scholars who so passionately and effectively defend the truth of Christianity—and today my life's goal is to do my part in helping others get answers to the questions that are blocking them in their spiritual journey toward Christ.

How Should We Handle Unresolved Questions About the Bible?

Paul Copan

B ecause God is truthful, we can expect His written self-revelation (in the original manuscripts) to be truthful in what it affirms. But not everything in Scripture is perfectly clear. The Apostle Peter admitted that Paul's writings are hard to understand in places (2Pt 3:15-16). Besides sophisticated theological material, historical distance and cultural differences exist between the biblical world and our own. What was apparent to Israel and the early church may appear less clear to us today. Yet lack of clarity doesn't equal "discrepancy."

Some critics cite numerous "contradictions," which actually turn out to be resolvable upon examination. Because the Bible is both divinely inspired *and* a human work, we can expect to find (1) different writing styles and personalities and (2) authors' utilizing earlier records/documents and extra-biblical writers (cp. Jos 10:13; 1,2Ch; Lk. 1:1-4). We shouldn't require that biblical writers cite OT passages verbatim; they can generalize or summarize without being exact (e.g., what was said at Jesus' baptism; Peter's confession of Jesus; the placard on Jesus' cross). And we don't have the exact *words* Jesus spoke (which were mainly Aramaic, not Greek), though His *voice* does come through.

When faced with more challenging passages, there are six things to keep in mind as you proceed:

Clarify a passage by examining its context. Taking note of the context, including examination of other Bible passages that are clearer, can resolve many difficulties. For example, context reveals that "justify" and "works" in James 2 mean something different than they mean in Romans 3. Also, the epistles' teaching can help us distinguish between historical descriptions in Acts and what's normative for church life.

Absence of evidence isn't evidence of absence. Skeptics may mention biblical cities that haven't been discovered—though lots *have* been!—and conclude that Scripture is unreliable. But in the past "absence of evidence" arguments were used to deny the factuality of Abraham's camels, the Hittite people, and the Davidic dynasty. But with new discoveries in archaeology, the skeptics were proven wrong and Scripture was confirmed.

Be charitable towards the author. Proverbs 26:4-5 advises (1) *not to answer* a fool according to his folly and then (2) to *answer* him! Skeptics call this a contradiction, but surely we should give the text the benefit of the doubt: the wise compiler of Proverbs recognized that sometimes answering a fool is appropriate, while other times silence is best.

What the Bible describes is often different from what it prescribes. Many bad things are described in Scripture, but that is not the same as bad things being prescribed. For instance, Scripture describes Jephthah's rash vow (Jdg 11) but in no way prescribes it as morally right.

Precision is not always the author's concern. The author may be utilizing a literary strategy, making a particular theological point, or just making a casual observation. For instance, Matthew chapters 8 and 9 cluster miracles together thematically; this should not be taken as an indication that the miracles are chronologically linked. In another example, Matthew highlights

Peter's importance and does not mention his blunders that are recounted in other Gospels; this does not mean Matthew denies Peter made the blunders.

We have to live with some unanswered questions. Although there are many fine evangelical commentaries and books dealing with the questions and challenges we find in Scripture, much will remain hazy to us in this life; we see through a glass darkly.

What Is a Worldview?

Ronald H. Nash

A worldview is the total of answers people give to the most important questions in life. The five most important questions any worldview must answer are God, ultimate reality, knowledge, ethics, and human nature. Every human being has a worldview, even though many people are uninformed about the nature and content of worldviews and the power that worldviews have over the way we think and behave.

Worldview thinking is an important tool to help Christians understand, explain, and defend the Christian faith. Instead of viewing Christianity as a collection of theological bits and pieces to be believed or debated, we should approach it as a conceptual system, as a total world-and-life view. Once people understand that both Christianity and its competitors are worldviews, they will be in a better position to judge the relative merits of these competing systems. The case for or against Christian theism should be made and evaluated in terms of total systems, not individual issues within the worldview.

The reason some people reject Christianity is not due to their problems with one or two isolated Christian beliefs; their dissent results rather from the fact that their fundamentally anti-Christian worldview leads them to reject information and arguments that support the Christian worldview. Opponents of the Christian worldview disagree with Christianity because they hold to competing worldviews. Obviously people can and do change their worldviews. Saul of Tarsus was one of early Christianity's greatest enemies. He was fanatically committed to a system that seemed to rule out any possibility of his change or conversion to the Christian faith. Saul's conversion encourages us that even the most intractable people may be capable of changing their conceptual systems. People who used to be humanists, naturalists, atheists, or followers of competing religious faiths have found reason to turn away from their old conceptual systems and embrace Christianity. Conversely, some people who used to profess allegiance to Christianity reach a point where they feel they can no longer believe. It seems unlikely that a single set of necessary conditions will always be present when people change a worldview. After all, many people remain unaware that they have a worldview, even though the sudden change in their lives and thoughts resulted from their exchanging one worldview for another. In many cases, the actual change is triggered by a significant event, often a crisis of some kind. But in other instances, an event or piece of new information led them to think in terms of a conceptual scheme that was totally different for them. Quite unexpectedly, these people saw things they had overlooked before, or they suddenly saw matters fit together in a pattern that brought meaning where none had been discernible before.

People change their minds on important subjects for a bewildering variety of reasons (or non-reasons). When faced with a choice among competing worldviews, we should choose the one that, when applied to the whole of reality, gives us the most coherent picture of the world. Helping people in this comprises one of the most important tasks of apologetics.

How Should a Christian Understand Postmodernism?

Douglas R. Groothuis

The term *postmodernism* means many different things. However, postmodernist philosophy, generally understood, claims to leave behind modernist (or Enlightenment) commitments to the objectivity of truth, the universality of reason, and the inevitability of progress. Instead of attempting to fashion a rational worldview, postmodernism opts for lesser goals by cobbling together various ideas, practices, and goals for pragmatic purposes. As postmodernist Walter Truett Anderson puts it, "Truth isn't what it used to be." Postmodernism embraces a cluster of ideas, most of which contradict the Christian understanding of truth, authority, and rationality. (One positive note is that postmodernism tends to deflate overly optimistic accounts of human reason and progress based solely on human ability.)

Postmodernists claim that the quest for a comprehensive and authoritative worldview is forever out of reach, and that to claim otherwise is an arrogant pretext for dominating those with whom one disagrees. For example, claims for the objective truth of the Christian worldview are unwarranted and lead to the oppression of non-Christians. Such "metanarratives" (Jean-Francious Lyotard) must be abandoned. No worldview holds any objective or rational authority over any other.

Thinkers such as Jacques Derrida "deconstruct" texts in order to abolish their authority. Texts do not possess any knowable or rational meaning that is established by the author or discernible by the informed reader. Their meaning is variable and open-ended. The text has no authority. The reader contributes decisively to the meanings (plural) of texts. Thus deconstruction undermines the truthfulness of any text (including the Bible), since no text contains a single meaning that may correspond with objective facts. Ironically, deconstructionists decry "misinterpretations" of their own writings.

For postmodernists, "truth" is fundamentally a social, linguistic construction devised for a certain purpose. Various cultures have their own "maps" which describe reality differently. However, we cannot determine which "map" connects more closely with reality, since we cannot press beyond our own cultural conditioning. There is no objective reality apart from our languages and concepts. Various communities determine their own truths. There is no God's eye view of anything and thus no objective truth. As Friedrich Nietzsche declared, "There is no truth, only interpretation."

Against these claims, Scripture claims to be an objectively true revelation from God, which is authoritative on whatever it speaks (Rm 3:4; 2Tm 3:15-17). Only God knows reality comprehensively, but humans may attain partial knowledge by attending to God's revelation and by using their minds in wise ways. The Bible—and most philosophers—claim that a true statement is one that corresponds with reality. Social customs or personal opinions do not create truth. Hence the Bible's condemnation of idols as *false* gods. The statement, "Jesus is Lord," does not merely express the cultural language and tradition of Christians. It is a truth-claim about objective realities. Moreover, good apologetic arguments may rationally verify the objective truth of this statement.

Postmodernist claims are logically flawed. First, their pronouncements on truth contradict themselves. Their statements claim to be applicable to reality itself, not merely to one's culture. Yet this is just what postmodernists claim cannot be done. In rejecting all objective authority, they end up asserting their own authority and the truth of their own meta-narrative. This is contradictory and false. Secondly, sane people judge certain acts—such as the terrorist attacks on America on September 11, 2001—as objectively evil, and not as merely relative social constructions. If so, the postmodern view of contingently constructed morality cannot be defended. Postmodernism emphasizes the diversity of truth claims, particularly in pluralistic settings, but it provides no method to test these claims against reality. Instead, it succumbs to a kind of intellectual indifference—the enemy of moral progress and spiritual virtue.

Although no major religion adheres to the postmodern view of truth, this mindset has affected how many people view spirituality, particularly in nations with significant religious freedom. Many think that religion is a matter of choice, taste, and preference. One seeks a designer religion that suits one's taste, or one is born into a religion that defines who one is. One may even mix and match elements from several religions. Debating whether a religion is true or false is pointless. All are "true" in the postmodern sense because they give meaning to people's lives. This perspective contradicts the Christian's apologetic duty to address the falsity and rational inadequacy of alternative religions in order to present Christianity as true, rational, and pertinent (2Co 10:3-5).

How Should We Treat New Challenges to the Christian Faith?

Gary R. Habermas

I t happens every year in the popular press. Usually the Easter season is the designated time to break the bombastic news that Christianity has been proven untrue. Amid the twists and turns of the plot, expect the story to emerge in a similar manner—often as a news flash promising exciting new evidence, scholarly opinion, and perhaps even photos or DNA tests. In recent years, the questions have included: Was Jesus married to Mary Magdalene? Did Jesus father one or more children? Was Mary supposed to be the appointed leader of the church, only to be denied that right by male leaders? Was Judas Iscariot not really the betrayer of Jesus, but Jesus' key disciple and hero? Were Jesus' bones discovered in His family's burial tomb?

Besides books and media presentations, these questions arise in other formats as well. We see them in emails, posted on the web, and hear them discussed over coffee. Many Christians are unbothered by these questions, responding by rolling their eyes and commenting on the current state of prejudice against believers. But some Christians react fearfully, afraid their faith might prove unfounded. We will propose some general suggestions for evaluating challenges made against the Christian faith.

Divorce our emotions from the challenge. It is unwise to respond with immediately elevated emotions, because it often turns out that the emotions were completely unwarranted in terms of the data. Give it a few days or weeks, and likely you will find that everything has calmed down and returned to normal. A great many sensationalistic claims have been made over the years, but how many of them have truly proven to be devastating? That such claims regularly arise, cause a brief storm, and are then dissipated teaches us to be reserved in our response.

Even if it initially appears like there may be some substance to a claim, there is still no reason to connect one's emotions to the issue. Many researchers have noted that this sort of emotional quandary is linked not to the challenges themselves, but to the things that we say to ourselves *about* the challenges. For example, if we tell ourselves such catastrophic things as, "Oh no, what if my faith is misplaced?" or "What if the Bible is wrong?" such statements will often cause strong emotions and cloud objective assessment. So we need to begin by calming our thoughts.

Know the basis for Christian Theism. Before jousting with the various challenges to faith, we must know at least the basic reasons that undergird our belief structure. Too many Christians attempt to counter critical views without having done their own homework, only to become part of the problem.

Part of knowing the basis for Christian Theism involves working from the center out. In other words, the closer a given doctrine or practice is to the center of Christianity, the more important it is to defend it. Correspondingly, questions that lie on the periphery do not need to be treated with the same sort of diligence. After all, Christians differ with each other on matters lying at the periphery! But it is no coincidence that our cardinal doctrines are also the best-grounded beliefs, often established by multi-faceted evidences. We must remember that since the center holds firmly, we can rest securely in our faith.

Think through each critical premise in light of an overall strategy. When we respond, we should think through each portion of our opponent's argument, giving the most weight and attention to the areas of the opposing position that are the most crucial. For instance, which of the opposing premises, if successfully challenged, would count most heavily against the entire critical thesis? Another relevant, though somewhat less important question, concerns which assertions are the most open to counterattack.

After learning the basis for Christian Theism, we should also learn the basic principles of critical thinking. Some scholars exhibit an almost uncanny knack for dissecting opposing arguments and exposing their most crucial weaknesses. This trait can often be learned and should thus be cultivated. One way to do this is to study the tapes and writings of those who debate or dialogue well. The experience can be similar to studying a chess match. What overall strategy is being pursued? Why were certain moves made? Were there still better arguments at their disposal? In short, there is no substitute for knowing the data and then being able to use it effectively.

Again, we want to defend most clearly those areas that are most central to our own thesis. It is at this precise intersection of challenging our opponent's chief arguments as they most impact the heart of Christian theism that we make our strongest stand. This is where we pour on the relevant data and employ the best argumentative techniques.

Restate the total case. When we are finished with our critique, we should put the pieces back together. In discussions of this nature, many people lose focus on the most crucial elements and often feel that they have lost contact with the real points being made. Therefore, we can encourage everyone involved by restating and clarifying the chief points in favor of Christian Theism, as well as the best critiques against the opposing position.

In sum, divorcing critical challenges from our emotions is a prerequisite to treating the actual questions. Then, there are no substitutes for knowing our own position and for having the basic tools involved in digesting and dissecting an argument. This provides the basis upon which we build our counter-challenge, aiming for the most crucial and vulnerable premises of our opponents' position. The result should be a carefully-reasoned, final case that clearly showcases the truth of Christian Theism.

Can Something Be True For You and Not For Me?

Paul Copan

" **I**t's all relative. . . . That's true for you, but not for me. . . . That's just your reality. . . . Who are you to impose your values on others?" You've heard statements like these before. They fit with the relativist belief system, which says truth functions more like *opinion* or *perspective*, and that truth depends upon your culture or context or even personal choices. Thus evil actions by Nazis or terrorists are explained away ("We don't like it, but they have their reasons"). Relativism, however, is seriously flawed.

Relativism cannot escape proclaiming that truth corresponds to reality. "The moon is made of cheese" is false because it does not match up with the way things are. As Christians, we claim the biblical story is true because it corresponds to the actualities of God's existence and His dealings with human beings. Truth is a relationship—a match-up with what is real or actual. An idea is false when it does not. But what of those making such claims as "Reality is like a wet lump of clay—we can shape it any way we want" (a relativistic idea known as *anti-realism*)? We can rightly call such statements into question. After all, these persons believe that their view corresponds to the way things are! If you disagree with them, they believe you are *wrong*! Notice, too, that they believe there is at least one thing that is not subject to human manipulation—namely, the unshakable reality that reality is like a wet lump of clay that we can shape any way we want to! So we can ask: "Is that lump-of-clay idea something you made up?" If it applies to everyone, then the statement is incoherent. If it doesn't, then it's nothing more than one's *perspective*. Why take it seriously? And if there's no objective truth or reality, how do we know that our beliefs are not delusional?

Relativism is self-contradictory. If someone claims to be a relativist, don't believe it. A relativist will say that your belief is true for you, but his is true for him. He defends this by saying there is no objective truth that applies to all people. The only problem is that *this* is an objective truth that the relativist means to apply to all people! (Even when he says "That's true for you, but not for me," he believes his view applies to more than just one person!) To show the self-contradictory nature of relativism, we can simply preface relativistic assertions this way: "It's objectively true that 'that's true for you but not for me'" or "It's true that 'there is no truth.'" The bold contradiction becomes apparent. Or what of the line that sincere belief makes something—Buddhism, Marxism, Christianity—true? We respond by asking: Is this principle universal and absolute? Is it true even if I don't sincerely believe it?—that is, what if I sincerely believe that sincere belief does not make something real? Both views obviously cannot be true.

The basis and conclusion of relativism are treated as objectively true. Ask the relativist why she adopts the relativist view, and she'll probably say, "Because so many people believe so many different things." The problem here is that she believes this to be universally true and beyond dispute. Furthermore, she believes that the logical conclusion to draw from the vast array of beliefs is that relativism must be the case. The relativist doesn't believe these are a matter of personal preference. The basis for relativism (the variety of beliefs) and the conclusion that relativism obviously follows from it turn out to be treated as objectively true by the relativist. So even the relativist believes in the inescapability of logic.

Relativism is always selective. People usually aren't relativists about the law of gravity, drug prescription labels, or the stock index. They're usually relativists when it comes to God's existence, sexual morality, or cheating on exams. But try cutting in line in front of a relativist, helping yourself to his property, or taking a sledgehammer to his car—and you find out that he believes his rights have been violated! Rights and relativism don't mix! But if it's all relative, why get mad at anyone?

Relativism is usually motivated by a personal agenda—the drive for self-control. Atheist philosopher John Searle uncovers what's behind relativism: "It satisfies a basic urge to power. It just seems too disgusting, somehow, that we should have to be at the mercy of the 'real world.'" We want to be in charge! Now, pointing out one's motivation is not an argument against relativism; still, it's a noteworthy consideration. Truth often takes a back seat to freedom. But clearly when a person shrugs off arguments for the inescapability of objective truth with "Whatever!", he has another agenda in mind. Relativism makes no personal demands upon us—to love God, to be people of integrity, to help improve society.

How Should a Christian Deal With Doubt?

Gary R. Habermas

D oubt may be defined as uncertainty regarding God or our relation to Him. Questions arise in many forms, including factual or philosophical issues, assurance, suffering, or unanswered prayer. Few subjects are characterized by more misunderstandings than doubt. Contrary to popular opinion, doubt is not always sin. Neither is it necessarily the opposite of faith or the product of weak faith. It is experienced by many believers in Scripture such as Abraham, Job, David, Jeremiah, and John the Baptist. And almost all believers, as well as unbelievers, experience doubt at times. As strange as it seems, it can produce positive results, and many doubters are very much in love with the Lord.

Doubt may be divided into three general varieties. *Factual doubt* usually raises issues regarding the truth of Christianity. *Emotional doubt* chiefly concerns our moods and feelings, often posing questions pertaining to assurance of salvation. *Volitional doubt* is a category that ranges from weak faith to a lack of motivation to follow the Lord.

Factual doubt. The answer to factual doubt is the facts. In other words, questions concerning God, Jesus, the Bible, or the resurrection are answered by the data. No religion can claim the factual foundation upon which Christianity is based. A frequent mistake made by factual doubters is to confuse disputed areas among Christians (for examples, sovereignty and free will, the age of the earth, the sign gifts, or eternal security) with the question of truthfulness of the Christian faith. If we know that the deity of Jesus Christ, His death, and resurrection are true, the truth of Christianity is established. When we respond with a faith commitment to these truths, salvation results. If this center is true, other major doctrines, some of which are less verifiable, will also follow. This firm basis satisfies our most essential factual questions.

Emotional doubt. This is the most common as well as the most painful variety of doubt. Frequently, these persons repeatedly wonder if they are saved, while exhibiting signs of their obvious love for the Lord. They often tell themselves that what they most desire is just beyond their grasp, hence their pain. Here the chief issue is not what is being said, but the emotion in the background. The remedy is to treat the latter. Many passages in Scripture command us to address our unruly emotions (cp. Ps 37:7-8; 39:2; 42:5-6,11; 55:4-8,16-17,22; 56:3-4; 94:19). The chief tactic is to shift our focus from our worries to God's eternal perspective. For instance, in Philippians 4:6-9, Paul tells us to replace our anxieties with prayer and thanksgiving. The apostle promises peace for those who do so (vv. 6-7). Then he commands us to explicitly change our worrisome thoughts to God's truth (v. 8) and to model ourselves after his pattern, again promising the result of peace (v. 9). The best response every time a doubt arises is to weed out and correct the improper thought by forcefully dictating to ourselves God's truth in place of the wrong belief.

Volitional doubt. This covers a wide range of uncertainty. The more extreme versions are often characterized by formerly committed believers who now seem not to care anymore. Perhaps they even appear to live no differently from unbelievers. This is probably the most dangerous species of doubt, since the individual may be in danger of turning away from the Lord. But how do we motivate someone who does not wish to be energized? Friends and loved ones must get involved.

Any biblical means of stirring the dying embers may be helpful here. In Scripture, probably the most frequently prescribed methods are being convicted of sin (Heb 3:12-13) or being challenged by the truth of heaven. Everyone experiences the lure of living forever (Ec 3:11). Believers more specifically seek heaven (Heb 11:16,35; 13:14). Dozens of times we are challenged to pursue our eternal home, applying its truth deeply to our lives

(Mt 6:33). After all, everything we do for the Lord after our salvation determines the capacity to which we will enjoy eternity (Mt 6:19-21; Mk 9:41).

Perhaps the key is to assist the volitional doubter in charging their spiritual batteries. What could be worse than failing the God of the universe, and falling short of His Kingdom? Conversely, what could be better than living with Him and our believing friends and loved ones for a truly blessed eternity? We need to drive these truths home to those who waver, by the power of the Holy Spirit (Jd 20-23; Jms 5:19-20).

Doubt can be a positive incentive to change and grow. But other times, intervention is necessary. The body of Christ needs to be alert and sensitive, helping each other focus on the Lord and His Kingdom.

How Does One Develop a Christian Mind?

J.P. Moreland

" I want to develop a Christian mind, but I don't know how." This attitude is both common and understandable. That we are to develop our minds as Christians is not in doubt. We are admonished to love God with our minds (Mt 22:37), be transformed by its renewal (Rm 12:2), and give thoughtful answers to questions about the faith (1Pt 3:15).

A mature Christian mind has two aspects to it. First, it is a mind that has formed the habit of being focused on God constantly throughout the day. It is a mind preoccupied with God and directed regularly towards Him in prayer and meditation (Ps 16:8; Is 26:3; Lk 18:1; Ro 12:12; 1Th 5:16-18). But how can one do this and still perform one's daily tasks? Fortunately, people can do more than one thing at the same time. While driving a car or centering one's attention on some other task, one can still be aware of God in the boundaries of one's attention. And one can bring God to the center of prayerful focus at various times throughout the day. There are two habits that facilitate focusing on God constantly. First, memorize four or five Bible passages that really speak to you. Now make it a practice to pray these passages to the Lord all throughout the day. As you pray through a passage phrase by phrase, use it to pray about things of concern to you. Second, regularly ponder these passages or other scriptural readings, thinking of what they mean, of how you can internalize them, and of how you can promote them to others.

The second aspect of a mature Christian mind is one that sees all of life in light of a Christian worldview and is growing in intellectual excellence. A worldview is the sum total of the things one believes, especially in regards to reality, truth, knowledge and value. A Christian worldview is a biblically grounded set of beliefs about all of life, from work, recreation, and finances, to God, life after death, and morality. One tries to think of all of life in light of the teachings of Holy Scripture and, more specifically, of the Lord Jesus.

There is no secular/sacred separation in such a mind. All of life is an occasion for discipleship and worship for a mature Christian mind. Further, an intellectually excellent mind is one that is informed, that makes important distinctions when a less mature mind fails to do so, and that develops deeper and deeper insights into issues of importance. To develop such excellence, one must regularly read and expose oneself to excellent teaching. Try to read books that are a bit challenging to understand. One must also be willing to engage others—believers and unbelievers—in conversations about important worldview issues. Such regular practice, if combined with a growing ability to listen nondefensively, will bring motivation and opportunity for regular growth in intellectual excellence.

How Should a Christian Relate to Culture?

Charles Colson

O ne writer in a psychological journal pondered what makes humans distinct from beasts. After discarding several possibilities—tool usage, language, ability to think—the author concluded that humans seem to be the only creatures who care about what makes them distinct.

On the surface, the outstanding trait of humans is culture, but not everyone agrees. Some claim even beasts have cultures: chimpanzees "harvest" termites with a "tool"—a stripped tree branch wrought by their own hands; termites cultivate mushrooms for consumption; birds create species-specific nests; whales sing. But such simple, largely instinctive practices (which neither change nor improve over time) hardly compare with humankind's achievements. Beasts haven't any arts or technologies, scientific institutes or historical archives, philosophers or physicians. Apparently, culture is a distinguishing mark of humankind.

But what makes humans creatures of culture? Why has every recorded human society—however primitive—indulged a level of culture beyond anything beasts might produce? Whence this penchant for culture?

Scripture teaches humanity's attachment to culture derives from two sources. First is *the image of God*. Humans aren't like beasts; we've been created in the likeness of God (Gn 1:26-28). We have a spiritual essence, being made for conscious communion with our Creator. God Himself is a being of culture. He communes within Himself in His triune being (Gn 1:26; Jn 17:5); He fashioned a universe of great wonder and diversity (Gn 1:1; Jn 1:1-3); He continues to sustain that universe in exhaustive detail (Col 1:17; Heb 1:3). It shouldn't surprise us that a creature made in the very likeness of such a God would be drawn toward cultural activities as well.

Second, humans also have a *mandate* for culture, which, along with other works of God's law, is written on every human heart (Rm 2:14-15). God has created people to exercise dominion over other creatures (Gn 1:26-30)—the "cultural mandate." Rather than a license to tyranny and plunder, God intends that humans exercise the kind of responsible stewardship that allows all creatures to realize full potential. Our stewardship should also allow God's goodness, beauty, and truth to flourish. In the process of carrying out this mandate, people create culture—language for communication; families for love and nurture; agriculture for sustenance; resource development for tools and pleasures; governments for social order; procedures, protocols, and practices; things useful and things beautiful—all part of our in-built, God-given drive to order our world and develop the beauty and potential of our environment.

Humans are made to employ hearts, minds, and hands in the creation, maintenance, and propagation of those artifacts, institutions, and conventions by which we define, sustain, and enrich our lives. Culture can be a rich means of bringing honor and glory to God, as God Himself knew in providing a specific and glorious design for His tabernacle and temple; as the psalmists showed in their skillful use of poetry and song; as Solomon demonstrated in government and public works to the astonishment of the world; and as Jesus showed through His powerful use of storytelling.

No human can be indifferent to culture. The key question for the disciple isn't *whether* to be involved in culture, but *how*. Since Christ has been exalted as Lord, all culture must be put to use in a way that serves His interests and promotes His glory. Even down to the mundane details of table manners— "eating and drinking," we might say (1Co 10:31)—all of culture is to be engaged and used for God's glory. The Christian church's heritage includes a vast repository of cultural firsts (hospitals, universities, musical notation); signal achievements (the music of Bach, the paintings of Rembrandt, the poetry of Hopkins); and everyday delights (hymns, books, inspiring stories). Such artifacts, institutions, and conventions—the stuff of culture—are the fruit of patient, deliberate labors of faithful believers who, understanding their duty as image bearers of God, and submitting to their Lord's cultural mandate, point the way for the rest of us to follow obediently in the path of culture to God's glory.

Scripture calls us to engage culture. As the most significant cultural artifact in all of human history, how could we ignore it? And as God's image-bearers, how can we ignore the calling to take every thought captive and offer all that we are and have to God's service and glory (2Co 10:3-5; Rm 12:1-2)?

What Are Self-Defeating Statements?

J.P. Moreland

C hances are you've heard someone say something like this: "There are no moral absolutes, so you ought to stop judging the moral beliefs and behaviors of others!" A crucial flaw in one's views is when one makes a self-defeating (also called "self-refuting" or "self-referentially incoherent") statement.

What exactly is a self-defeating statement? It is a statement with three characteristics: (1) It establishes some requirement of acceptability for an assertion, sentence, proposition, or theory; (2) It places itself in subjection to this requirement; (3) It fails to satisfy the requirement of acceptability that the assertion itself stipulates. A statement is about a subject matter. The subject matter for "All dogs are mammals" is dogs. When a statement is included in its own subject matter and fails to satisfy its own standards of acceptability, it is self-defeating.

Some examples of self-defeating statements are: "No sentence is longer than three words." "I cannot utter a word of English." "I do not exist." "There is no truth." " There are no truths that cannot be verified by the five senses or by science."

In identifying a self-defeating statement, great care must be exercised in making sure that the statement actually refers to itself, that it is a part of its own subject matter. For example, the claim that one cannot utter a word of English is not self-defeating if asserted in French. More importantly, though false, the statement "There are no moral absolutes" is not self-defeating. Why? The statement is a philosophical assertion *about* morality and not a claim *of* morality. To be a claim of morality, an assertion must be a moral rule such as "Do not kill," "Abortion is wrong" or "One ought to be tolerant of others." The statement "There are no moral absolutes" is not itself a moral rule. Like a statement made in English about all French statements (for example, "No French statement is longer than three words"), "There are no moral absolutes" is false. But since it is not included in its own subject matter, it does not refer to itself and, therefore, is not *self*-refuting.

Another important example is "There are no moral rules, so one *ought* to refrain from passing judgment on others." Is this self-defeating? It's hard to tell because the word *ought* is ambiguous and comes with different meanings: A rational *ought* occurs in "Given the evidence, one ought to conclude that the defendant is guilty." A rational ought places an intellectual duty on someone, and a violator is irrational, not immoral. An aesthetic *ought* occurs in "One ought to play this piece with great emotion." This places an aesthetic duty on someone, and a violator is guilty of failing to produce beauty. A moral *ought* occurs in "One ought to keep one's promises." This places a moral duty on someone, and a violator is immoral. The *ought* in "There are no moral rules, so one *ought* to refrain from passing judgment on others" is either a rational or moral ought. If the former, the assertion means "Given all the evidence, there just are no moral rules, so one has an intellectual duty to stop judging that others have violated absolute moral rules when there are none." Though false, this statement is not self-defeating because it is not itself an example of asserting a moral obligation. Rather, it asserts an intellectual duty, and a violator would be irrational, not immoral. Still, if one were to seek a reason for why this is an intellectual duty, one may well find a self-defeating statement lurking in the neighborhood. For example, the advocate may think that there is no evidence for absolute moral rules because he accepts the self-defeating assertion that only claims verifiable by the five senses can be true. If the *ought* is a moral one, then the sentence is self-refuting: "There are no moral rules, so one has a moral duty to follow this moral rule—do not judge others."

Some statements like "2+2=7" could not possibly be true. Others like "There are no dogs" happen to be false but could have been true. Self-defeating statements do not just happen to be false; rather, they are necessarily false. It is impossible for these statements to be true: "There are no truths" (the statement itself says it is true there is no truth), or "Only what is testable by science can be true" (the statement itself is not testable by science). Among other things, this means that no amount of future research will show that a self-refuting statement was true after all. This is important, because a skeptic cannot say there may be no current evidence for its truth, but someday science will advance to the point of proving that it is true after all.

How Can We Know Anything at All?

Garrett DeWeese

K nowledge is crucial in our day-to-day lives. We don't trust a dentist who *believes* he can perform the extraction, no matter how sincere his belief; we go to a dentist who *knows* he can. We don't rely on a friend's *hunch* when wondering whether to take an umbrella; we listen to a meteorologist who has *good reasons* for his prediction. The prosecuting attorney (ideally) doesn't try to get the jury to *feel* angry with the defendant; she wants to establish the *truth* of his guilt.

Similarly in matters of religion, what should matter is knowledge, not merely sincere belief; good reasons for faith, not hunches; truth, not feelings. Christianity is more than ritual or mythology or emotions; it is a knowledge tradition. Christianity claims certain things can be *known*.

Kinds of knowledge. We use *knowledge* (and the verb *to know*) in at least three different senses: (1) propositional knowledge—knowing facts; (2) knowledge by acquaintance—knowing something or someone directly; and (3) skill knowledge—know-how.

Here are some examples. A sports fan may know many facts about last year's MVP, or a historian may know all about ancient Rome, and yet neither person's propositional knowledge constitutes the direct knowledge by acquaintance which the player's teammates or Julius Caesar possessed.

Someone may have the know-how to ride a bike or play pool without having any propositional knowledge about force, inertia, or angular momentum.

Christianity involves all three types of knowledge. Eternal life, Jesus said, is knowing God (Jn 17:3). This is knowledge by acquaintance, and is more than knowledge of Bible facts or systematic theology. (Sadly, it is possible for someone to know a lot about the Bible, a lot about theology, and yet not know God.) Jesus goes on to say that eternal life is knowing Him, for He is God's Son. This involves knowing certain facts about Jesus of Nazareth, and about His mission as Savior. So both knowledge by acquaintance and propositional knowledge are involved.

What about skill knowledge? Since salvation is not by works, no skill is involved in becoming a Christian. But growing in our faith involves learning certain skills: how to study the Bible, how to think Christianly about decision making, how to pray, how to share our faith, and so on.

Propositional Knowledge. All three senses of knowledge are important, but propositional knowledge demands careful consideration. The vast bulk of what we know is propositional, and not by direct acquaintance or know-how. Propositional knowledge may be defined roughly as *justified true belief*. First, obviously, you can't know something if you don't *believe* it. Second, the proposition you believe must be *true* if it is to count as knowledge. Sincere (but false) beliefs, even useful (but false) beliefs, are not knowledge. Third, a true belief must be *justified*; that is to say that you must have *the right kinds of reasons* for the belief. Even true beliefs do not count as knowledge if they are the result of a lucky guess, a hunch, or a passionate wish that things be so. The right kinds of reasons are those which make it probable that the proposition you believe is true. They are truth indicators.

What counts as the right kinds of reasons depends on the nature of the proposition. I believe the sun is shining because I can see it and feel its warmth. I believe I had cereal for breakfast because I clearly remember it. I believe my wife loves me because she tells me so, she shows me in many ways, and she's stuck with me for a number of years. And I believe Tiglath-Pilesar was a mighty king of Assyria who invaded Israel in 743 B.C. because I read about him in the Bible (2Kg 15–16) and in reliable histories of Assyria. In all these cases, the reasons why I believe what I do are truth-indicators. They are the right kinds of reasons to justify those beliefs.

Can We Know Anything Without Using Our Senses? In the examples above, the justifying reasons involved the senses—even beliefs based on memory, for the memories were formed through sensory experiences. It is clear that beliefs based on our senses can be justified (provided, of course, that we are not too tired, the lighting is adequate, our sense organs are functioning properly, and so on). Knowledge based on the senses is called *empirical knowledge*.

The Enlightenment doctrine of empiricism holds that all knowledge of the world is empirical. Today, the spectacular successes of the natural sciences have enshrined empirical investigation as by far the best—and for most people, the only—way to know. But what about things we can't sense? Is nonempirical knowledge possible? The question is crucial, for many important things can't be known through our senses, things such as logic or justice, that we have a soul, or that God exists.

Is empiricism true? No. Notice first that the claim, "All knowledge of the world is empirical," is itself not an empirically verifiable statement. Thus the claim is self-refuting. Additionally, there are good reasons to think at least some knowledge of the world is non-empirical (a doctrine called *moderate rationalism*). Beliefs that certain things exist, which cannot be directly observed, may be inferred from empirical observations. This is how we justify belief in such things as electrons, gravitational fields, beauty, or love. And similarly for belief in God. Further, the analogy between sensory experience and religious experience provides good reasons for the justification of religious beliefs based on religious experience.

Finally, we can know some things without using our senses at all. For example, we can know much about ourselves through introspection (a nonempirical process). We can know that we have minds that think, believe, hope, fear, and so on, and that we are not identical to our bodies. Many ethicists claim moral knowledge is accessible through intuition or conscience or pure reason. Following St. Anselm, many scholars have thought that the ontological proof—a nonempirical argument—establishes God's necessary existence. Moreover, we have nonempirical as well as empirical evidence of God's existence (Rm 1:19-20), what has been called the *sensus divinitatis*. And since our belief in God's existence is justified, we also are justified in believing what God has revealed to us. For all these examples, we can point to the right kinds of reasons which justify nonempirical beliefs.

What Are the Three Laws of Logic?

J.P. Moreland

There are three fundamental laws of logic. Suppose P is any indicative sentence, say, "It is raining."

The law of identity: P is P.
The law of noncontradiction: P is not non-P.
The law of the excluded middle: Either P or non-P

The law of identity says that if a statement such as "It is raining" is true, then the statement is true. More generally, it says that the statement P is the same thing as itself and is different from everything else. Applied to all reality, the law of identity says that everything is itself and not something else.

The law of noncontradiction says that a statement such as "It is raining" cannot be both true and false in the same sense. Of course it could be raining in Missouri and not raining in Arizona, but the principle says that it cannot be raining and not raining at the same time in the same place.

The law of the excluded middle says that a statement such as "It is raining" is either true or false. There is no other alternative.

These fundamental laws are true principles governing reality and thought and are assumed by Scripture. Some claim they are arbitrary Western constructions, but this is false. The basic laws of logic govern all reality and thought and are known to be true for at least two reasons: (1) They are intuitively obvious and self-evident. Once one understands a basic law of logic (see below), one can see that it is true. (2) Those who deny them use these principles in their denial, demonstrating that those laws are unavoidable and that it is self-refuting to deny them.

The basic laws of logic are neither arbitrary inventions of God nor principles that exist completely outside God's being. Obviously, the laws of logic are not like the laws of nature. God may violate the latter (say, suspend gravity), but He cannot violate the former. Those laws are rooted in God's own nature. Indeed, some scholars think the passage "In the beginning was the Word [logos]" (Jn 1:1) is accurately translated, "In the beginning was Logic (a divine, rational mind)." For example, even God cannot exist and not exist at the same time, and even God cannot validly believe that red is a color and red is not a color. When people say that God need not behave "logically," they are using the term in a loose sense to mean "the sensible thing from my point of view." Often God does not act in ways that people understand or judge to be what they would do in the circumstances. But God never behaves illogically in the proper sense. He does not violate in His being or thought the fundamental laws of logic.

What Is Divine Revelation?

Gordon R. Lewis

R evelation is an activity of the invisible, living God making known to finite and sinful people His creative power, moral standards, and gracious redemptive plan.

First, God discloses Himself and His power to everyone by the marvels of His creation—the amazing life-support system of planet Earth. From their paintings, we can discover some things about painters. Similarly in the magnificence of creation, with its microscopic complexities and cosmic expanse, we realize our dependence upon the Creator's powerful existence and intelligent design (Ps 19:1-6; Rm 1:19-20).

Second, God makes plain His moral nature and ethical principles for our well being by implanting *oughts* and *ought nots* in every human spirit. Even people who do not have Moses' Ten Commandments (Ex 20:1-20) feel an obligation to obey those universal principles of right and wrong, and they guilt when they disobey (Rm 2:14-15). The universal principles restrain evil and prompt all to seek God (Ac 17:27). However, left to their own nature, everyone worships and serves the creation rather than its Creator (Rm 1:25; 3:10-23). Our habitual failure to live up to God's laws demonstrates our need for His mercy and redeeming grace.

Third, God made His merciful redemptive purposes known centuries before Christ through mighty acts like delivering Israel from slavery in Egypt (Ex 12) and through the reliable messages of His prophetic spokesmen (Heb 1:1). Criteria by which to distinguish true from false prophets included the logical consistency of their teaching with previous revelation (Dt 13:1-5) and the verification of visible signs (Dt 18:20-22). God promised to send His anointed One to defeat Satan's destructive purposes in many ways. The Messiah would be a son of Eve (Gn 3:15), a descendant of Abraham (Gn 22:18) and David (2Sm 7:12-16), and be born of a virgin (Is 7:14) in Bethlehem (Mc 5:2). Because those who chose the way of sin chose a way that ends in death, without the shedding of blood there is no forgiveness. So believing citizens of Israel pictured Christ's coming sacrificial atonement for sin by offering animal sacrifices and observing the Passover.

Fourth, God made His just and loving plan of redemption known supremely in the life, words, and works of Jesus, the long-awaited Messiah. "No one has ever seen God. The One and Only Son—the One who is at the Father's side—He has revealed Him" (Jn 1:18). To appreciate more fully what God is like, study the life, words, works, and atoning death of Jesus. At Calvary, the guiltless Savior substituted Himself for guilty humanity, defeated Satan, and provided the just basis for His reconciling mercy and grace (Rm 3:25). Then the risen Christ demonstrated His saving power over sin, guilt, death, and Satan (Rm 1:2-4; 10:9-10)!

Fifth, after Jesus' ascension to heaven, God communicated His redemptive purposes through spokesmen called apostles. Jesus taught and trained them for three years and they were eyewitnesses of His resurrection (Ac 1:21-22). Through Paul, an apostle who later saw the risen Christ, God revealed His plan to unite both Jewish and Gentile believers in one body, the church (Eph 2:11-22).

Sixth, the King of kings will be revealed in all His power and glory at His second coming.

Seventh, all the above sources of revealed truth have been preserved for us in the Holy Scriptures.

Writing History—Then and Now

Kirk E. Lowery

I s the Bible "history"? Did the ancient biblical authors write "history" as we moderns understand it? These questions are essential elements of the debate about the trustworthiness and authority of the Bible. In recent years, the usefulness of the Bible for writing history of the Ancient Near East has come under attack as it has not been since the 19th century. And this attack is rooted in the intellectual winds of our time. Since the 1970s people have been questioning whether science or history can tell us anything more than the ideology, politics, and biases of the scientist or historian, either individually or collectively. It is part of the so-called "postmodern" debate about the nature of knowledge. Many postmodernists assert that the meaning of any particular biblical text (or any other literary text, for that matter) cannot be separated from the worldview and ideology of the reader. They deny that the original intention of the author can be recovered.

In order to evaluate the usefulness of the Bible for history and its trustworthiness as a source of both information and judgment on people and events, we must remember that there are two separate points of view—the ancient and the modern. Are we talking about modern ideas of history or ancient ones? Were the biblical writers attempting to write history as *we* understand it? If they were not attempting to write a modern history, just what were they trying to do?

The word *history* is normally understood in two senses: (1) what actually happened in the past, or (2) the telling (or writing) about what happened in the past. The first sense is objective (although some deny even this) and the second necessarily filters those events through the personality of the historian. While the modern historian begins with a chronology and facts, it hardly stops there. He reconstructs facts and events, fitting them together into a tapestry of telling a story. He evaluates his sources for their value and validity, much as a lawyer probes the credibility of a witness. Indeed, the historian is more like a prosecutor than a scientist in his method of work. After that examination, he makes conclusions about people and events, much like a judge or jury. The basic concern is that the Bible asserts certain facts or that certain events happened. Did they happen and in the way the Bible presents it? The Bible also makes judgments on people's actions, attitudes, and deeds. Can we trust its judgment on events we cannot access?

Where did all this radical skepticism come from? There has always been skepticism about the Bible. Marcion (c. A.D. 85–160), for example, rejected just about all the NT except for Paul's writings and a highly edited Gospel of Luke. But modern (and postmodern) views of the Bible are rooted in the period known as the Enlightenment in the 17th century. This was a time where thoughtful persons began to distinguish between knowledge and superstition by using empirical methods. They struggled against state church authorities in their pursuit of truth. They pursued the original texts of not only the Bible, but of the classics of Greek and Roman philosophy and literature. Their struggle polarized them from not just the contemporary church authorities, but galvanized them to regard any religious text as suspect. The 17th century was a time of discovery of what was true and what was superstition or chicanery. In that respect, the skepticism was healthy. Since many chose the cloak of religious authority to pander their intellectual wares, skepticism was a very powerful defense against this abuse. And a healthy skepticism is still useful, for superstition (in pursuit of money or adherents) is still used today against the unwary, that is, against those who uncritically trust whatever they are told. And it is important to remember that not everyone at that time embraced the "scientific" method with radical unbelief. Many of these early "scientists" were trained clergy, most notably Isaac Newton.

The modernist approach to history writing includes establishing events and a chronology, distinguishing between primary (original witness to the events) and secondary (dependent upon another) sources, and arranging those facts in some sort of a narrative. The modernist historian believes there is an objective reality in the past that can be accessed and known today. Critical scholars of the 19th century focused upon supposed "contradictions" and "errors" of fact to be found in the Bible. During the first half of the 20th century, archaeological discoveries supported the presentation of fact found in many places of the Bible that previously had been challenged. At the end of World War II scholars held the Bible to be much more trustworthy than they did at the beginning of the century.

In the past fifty years, the focus has changed. Once preoccupied with "contradictions" in the Bible, and "errors" of fact, now the emphasis is upon how the reader *responds* to the message of the text. One's understanding of the text is inevitably filtered through the previously existing biases of the reader. The original meaning of the text intended by the author is not accessible to the modern reader; indeed, "Truth" is not knowable. This brings us to the late 1980s and early 1990s when a new movement of historians arose to challenge the conclusions of their older colleagues; they have come to be known as the "Minimalists." The controversy is all about *historiography*, the art of writing history. It is an art, not a science. One cannot repeat the "facts" of history in the same way that a scientist can reproduce the same events again and again in an experiment. But writing history is not simply telling a story. It is about the trustworthiness of the sources which one uses for telling that story. Are the sources the historian uses to "prove" his point credible? The historian is much like the lawyer who constructs a tale about a crime (or lack of a crime), and uses witnesses and evidence to support his point of view and conclusion. And then it is the framework (often a story, but it could be a table of demographic facts) that relates all the events to one another. This involves selecting which facts will be included and which will be set aside as not relevant to the point being made.

The Minimalists assert that Israel as depicted in the Hebrew Bible never existed, except in the minds of the Persian and Hellenistic writers who created the patriarchal narratives and the stories of the Monarchy out of whole cloth. They were novelists in the modern sense who wrote fiction. Unless there is independent verification by "extra-biblical sources," they reject the Hebrew Bible's usefulness as a witness to the events written about. The biblical text is held to a higher standard of verification than are "extra-biblical" sources.

They believe that unwritten archaeological remains are more reliable than written documents, because they are "real," whereas the message contained in documents are created by humans with ideologies, misperceptions, lacking complete information, etc. Immanuel Kant (1724–1804), an Enlightenment philosopher, said that reality—the thing in itself—cannot be truly known. The Minimalists explicitly cite Kant as one reason they rate the biblical text so low for knowledge of the past. However, while archaeological remains tell us what the material world was like and the context and constraints under which the people of the past lived, they cannot tell us what decisions people made or explain why people made the choices they made.

Further, Minimalists insist that any assertion by an ancient text must be verified by an independent source. But insistence on a strict verification principle would leave us in the dark about most everything. In point of fact, no one lives this way. We constantly make decisions based upon insufficient verification and make the "likely" choice. Better is the principle of "innocent until proven guilty," that a text is given the benefit of the doubt until and unless grounds for suspecting it are discovered.

How does one answer the Minimalist? Let's take the problem of the conquest of Canaan. Archaeological evidence is lacking for the Israelite conquest and occupation in the Iron Age. The Minimalists conclude it never happened, and certainly not as presented in the book of Joshua. Kenneth Kitchen, a well-known and respected Egyptologist, is famous for his dictum: "the absence of evidence is not the evidence of absence." Also, the biblical text helps explain it: "I gave you a land you did not labor for, and cities you did not build, though you live in them; you are eating from vineyards and olive groves you did not plant" (Jos 24:13). In other words, the Canaanite material culture—cities, farms, vineyards, and orchards—were not universally destroyed by the Israelites. Apparently, total destruction was the exception rather than the rule.

How should we evaluate these ancient texts? We should allow the ancient writers to speak in the manner that they wish. We should try to understand the ancient writers before posing questions of them that are outside of their intention and their worldview. We should "translate" the message of the ancients from the ancient context to the modern. Finally, we must embrace humility:

we do not have all the data, we do not have complete or even certain understanding to answer all our questions. Let us make a virtue of necessity and take what the ancient writers give and be content with that.

So what were the biblical writers doing and what did they expect to accomplish? And how ought the modern reader to understand their literary output? The books of Kings and Chronicles, along with the other "historical" books of the Hebrew Bible, are not books written by modern historians for modern readers. Their literary nature is much different. For one thing, their purpose is *didactic* or *polemic*, that is, the authors are attempting to convince their readers about moral and spiritual principles. Their stories are intended to support this purpose and their various propositions. Second, their commitment to truth does not aspire to modern standards of reporting. What they valued as important and unimportant does not map easily to third millennium A.D. values. For example, the recording of genealogies strikes many modern readers as irrelevant to the story. But it was critical to how these ancient peoples conceived of their identity. Genealogies may have had the function of establishing chronology or the framework for the story being told. It establishes precedence, relationship, and identity. Who are we? How did we get to here?

Allowance must be made for paraphrase, abbreviation, explanation, omission, rearrangement, and other techniques used by the ancient author that might offend modern principles of historiography. This is not to say that the ancients did not write history. To the contrary, they often show sensitivity to the events and corroborating witness to those events. But they also did not make a distinction between the writer's judgment or evaluation of events and the events themselves. They did not have precision—or, at least, modern notions of precision—in mind when they wrote. That does not mean the authors were not trying to tell a story that corresponds to real events! In order to understand the ancient texts, one must mentally and emotionally *become* an ancient and enter into their world. The process is similar to watching a film, where one must grant the filmmaker the premise of the film and even suspend belief in how the world should work before the message of the filmmaker can be perceived. The difference with the ancient writers is that we have much more work to do before we can enter into their world. Only then have we earned the right to form an opinion.

The ancient writer made choices: subject matter (events needing telling), point of view (theological purpose), aesthetics (creative choices). These writers selected their material, glossed over less relevant events, simplified the story to meet space constraints and only included detail that illuminates the significance of the events as the writer understood them. This is true of modern professional historians as much as of ancient story tellers. Consider the painter who tries to depict some real object or scene. If you look closely you may not be able to count the individual leaves on a tree, but see only splotches of color. But as one backs away and looks at the entire canvas, the scene becomes "like" the real object. The painting is only a representation of reality and not the actual object itself. So any telling of a story is a representation of the actual events and not the actual events themselves.

How, then, should we understand the intentions of the biblical writers? The first historians we have evidence of were the Sumerians, for whom history was a matter of personal experience, not the analysis of sources or principles of interpretation. Later, Mesopotamian rulers desired to interpret the present or future in light of the past. Events on earth are controlled by the gods; hence, their decrees have a prominent place in their myths and legends. Indeed, that may have been the cultural function of the myths and legends. The earliest historiographers in the modern sense of the word were Manetho (3rd century B.C., Egypt) and Herodotus (*Histories* c. 440 B.C.) and later, Aristotle (384–322 B.C., *Natural History of Animals*). The biblical writers were something in between: the view of these ancient Hebrew writers is that history has a *planned* goal. History is not the result of forces or great men, but moves forward to an end planned by God. Their purpose in writing history was didactic: to teach the reader about how God acts in human affairs, what are His purposes and the consequences of obedience and disobedience to that purpose.

Has Christianity Had a Bad Influence on History?

Alvin J. Schmidt

C hristianity has not had a bad influence on history. Christian beliefs and practices that are consistent with Christ's teachings have produced countless salutary by-products in history. Evil actions of erring Christians, especially prominent leaders—some probably not even Christian—are regularly recorded in history books, leading many to believe that Christianity's influence has been mostly harmful. Commonly cited examples are the Crusades, the Spanish Inquisition, the medieval witch persecutions, the executions of Hus and Savonarola, and the Roman Catholic Church's silencing Galileo. These acts were sinful and highly inconsistent with Christ's teachings.

Christianity has had numerous positive influences on history. Largely unknown in today's world, even to countless Christians, Christianity elevated the sanctity of human life. In ancient Rome and other pagan societies, human life was cheap and expendable. The early Christians, motivated by the gospel, opposed abortion, infanticide, child abandonment, suicide, and gladiatorial contests—all legal and widely practiced in the Roman era. Fifty years after the legalization of Christianity in A.D. 313, the now-Christianized Roman emperors outlawed these inhuman acts. Infanticide and child abandonment are illegal in most Western countries, and while abortion has unfortunately returned in the West from the pagan era, nobody has yet suggested the gladiators be brought back for popular entertainment.

In the fourth century, Christianity introduced hospitals to the world. Greeks and Romans had no such institutions of compassion. Christians, moved by Christ's words, "I was sick and you took care of Me" (Mt 25:36), built hospices as early as A.D. 325 and hospitals in 369—first in the East and then the West. Names of numerous hospitals still reflect this Christian origin: St. John's Hospital, Lutheran Hospital, Presbyterian Hospital, etc.

Before Christianity appeared, women were practically slaves, having little or no freedom and dignity. Not so in the Christian church! Women were baptized and catechized with men; they communed at the same altars with men. Adultery was no longer defined in terms of a woman's marital status; a married man having sex with a single woman now was also guilty of adultery. Christianity permitted a woman to reject a male suitor and inherit property; she no longer had to worship her husband's pagan gods.

Other positive effects include: (1) Countries where Christianity has had the greatest presence were the first to abolish slavery. Slavery is still present in some Islamic countries. (2) "No man is above the law" originated with St. Ambrose. In A.D. 390 he demanded that Emperor Theodosius repent for wantonly killing 7,000 people. He told the emperor he wasn't above the law. In 1215 the Magna Carta expanded this Christian concept of liberty and justice. (3) Christian teachings resulted in economic, political, and religious freedom. (4) Universities grew out of the church's medieval monasteries. (5) Christian theology—not pagan pantheism—motivated early scientists to explore God's natural world. (6) Christianity inspired the invention of the musical scale and great musical compositions. (7) Christianity's influence is present in many of the West's social institutions, its nomenclature, literature, and education, which shape much of people's daily lives—both Christians and non-Christians.

Is Beauty in the Eye of the Beholder?

David A. Horner

The answer is yes—and no. Beauty involves both subjective and objective elements, both taste and truth, which is why there is often confusion about it. The ability to perceive beauty does involve a kind of "taste" which can be cultivated and trained, or distorted and dulled. Some instances of beauty are perceptible only to those who have cultivated a taste for them, through disciplined practice. For instance, trained musicians hear subtle distinctions of tone that others miss, and painters see additional hues in the sunset. In a fallen world, we can lose our taste for beauty through inattention, self-absorption, and suffering. We can even develop a taste for what is in fact ugly.

Beauty itself, however, is objective, a matter of truth. Tones and hues are real properties of music and sunsets; they are there, whether or not we are sensitive enough to perceive them. The way we experience beauty shows this. We are "struck" by something beautiful. We may even be surprised by it; it takes our breath away. We respond to it with spontaneous expressions of awe, gratitude, appreciation, or reverence. These reactions show we don't really think it is beautiful merely because we think it's beautiful. We are responding to the beauty it has, independently of us. What is truly beautiful merits such a response.

Ultimately, beauty is grounded in the nature of God Himself, the supremely beautiful Person (Ps 27:4), and then in His creation, which reflects His beautiful intentions and artistry (Gn 1; Ps 50:2). The created order is magnificently diverse in its beauty, making room for a wide variety of legitimate preferences and tastes for very different aspects of its beauty (Ec 3:11).

There are deep connections between goodness, truth, and beauty (e.g., goodness is a kind of moral beauty; Php 4:8). The full meaning of the Hebrew word *shalom* conveys the rich biblical picture: more than merely "peace," *shalom* is the uniting and flowering of truth, goodness, and beauty in a flourishing and whole life. However, the breaking of *shalom* as a result of the fall into sin has introduced ugliness into the world. Evil is not only false and bad, but ugly (for instance, pornography is an ugly distortion of God's beautiful created context of sexuality). Thus our experiences of beauty are often distorted and even dangerous when we worship beauty instead of God (Gn 3:6; Rm 1:21-25).

Each of us needs beauty in our lives, relationships, work, and worship. We are made for it, and we long for it. Our hunger for beauty is an expression of our fundamental human longing for *shalom*, most ultimately for *shalom* with God (Rm 5:1).

Beauty has value for apologetics: it is part of the common ground we share with all people, as made in the image of God and living in a God-created world. Beauty points beyond the physical cosmos to the Creator. Like goodness and truth, beauty is not a physical property, measurable by science, and its reality indicates that the physical world is not all there is. The beauty of the world points to the nature of the Divine Artist whose handiwork it is. And the fundamental human longing for beauty, for *shalom*, is a hunger that cannot ultimately be satisfied in this fallen world. It is a clue that we were made for more than this life (Ec 3:11).

Is Logic Arbitrary?

David K. Clark

L ogic involves principles that govern how humans should think and speak. Studying logic means investigating correct reasoning. Traditionally logic is said to begin with three basic laws: identity, non-contradiction, and excluded middle. According to the law of identity, if a statement is true, then it's true. Non-contradiction says if a statement is true, it can't be false. The excluded middle asserts a statement is either true or false. Logic includes such laws, but more as well.

People observe various kinds of laws—moral, natural, mathematical, legal, and logical. Some laws declare *what ought to be*. Moral and legal laws say what a person *should* do, although it is possible to violate them. (People should tell the truth, but often don't). Other laws describe *what actually is*. Natural laws assert what *does* happen under certain natural conditions. Natural laws aren't really violated (although it's possible for a stronger opposite force to overcome a weaker force as in a tug-of-war).

Logic has an *ought* component. This makes logic somewhat like math. If a shopkeeper wants to make a profit and regularly gives $50 in change to customers who pay with $20 bills, she violates logic. But this isn't a moral transgression; it's a logical blunder. She's not acting immorally but irrationally. It's wise to think logically.

What is the ground or foundation of logic? Human logic is patterned after reality. The Creator built logic into the structures of the physical and spiritual worlds. The principles of logic reflect a deep reasonableness that characterizes both God and God's creation. Because the logic of human thought and speech is grounded in God and God's work, logic is not arbitrary.

People suggest in several ways that logic is arbitrary. Some say logic isn't a discovery of the human mind detected in reality, but an invention of the human mind imposed on reality. If so, logic is arbitrary because it's grounded in how humans choose to think.

This position yields a repugnant consequence: it disconnects human thought from reality. It implies that human interaction with the real world fundamentally distorts that world. The human mind recalibrates the input of the real world to fit its own inward configuration. So there's no telling whether human intellection has any connection with reality. That is troubling, for life and action require knowledge of the real world. (In addition, someone stating this position is likely refuting himself. He is probably saying the truth about the real world is that human thinking is imposed on reality).

Others say logic is grounded in culture, not in objective reality. Different cultures have different logics, according to this view. People commonly say logic is a Western invention that Asians successfully ignore. Logic is arbitrary because it's rooted in random cultural habits.

This is a misunderstanding. While people of various cultures may think about different content and begin at varied starting points, the deep reasonableness that governs human thinking is the same across all cultures. Consider an analogy. An African tribesman counts lions. An Inuit with no knowledge of lions counts seals. Both count according to mathematical principles. Similarly, the content of thought obviously differs from place to place, but the underlying reasonableness built into the creation will govern human thought regardless of culture.

Why So Many Denominations?

Charles Draper

I f you look in the telephone directory, you will find a huge diversity in kinds of churches. Even within individual denominations there often exists great variation. Jesus once prayed that His followers would be one (Jn 17). But what we see today is anything but oneness. What are we to make of this disunity? Does this not demonstrate that Christianity is hopelessly divided? Perhaps. Then again, there may be another way of looking at it.

It is important to ask whether denominations are a good thing at all. Denominations generally developed out of churches seeking fellowship with one another and partnership in joint ministry. That is certainly a biblical idea (Ac 11:27-30). Often denominations began as renewal movements in the church. So the Reformed movements of the sixteenth century arose to restore teachings about justification by faith and God's sovereignty in salvation—teachings that had been eclipsed in the church for a long time. Later, some Presbyterians caved in to the pressures of liberalism and newer conservative Presbyterian groups emerged to preserve the traditions. Other denominations had similar experiences. Baptists came along within the Reformed tradition contending that the Reformation principles of justification by faith ought to be applied to the church. In the twentieth century Pentecostals and Charismatics formed new unions based on their view of the Spirit and spiritual gifts.

So is this a good thing or a bad thing? Several points are important. One, it is always vital to avoid false teaching in the church. Often in the NT false teachers were either disciplined or left churches of their own accord (1Tm 1:19-20; 1Jn 2:19). In other cases the early church leaders predicted a future time of apostasy when false teachers would gain great influence (2Tm 3:1-9). In such cases, it might be necessary for genuine Christians to separate themselves from a false church.

That is not to say that all denominational separations have been for the right reasons. The most important thing to do is to examine a church's life and doctrine to see if it is consistent with Scripture. And finally, we have to realize that in this life Christians will not agree on everything. The existence of different denominations allows Christians to worship with those who have a similar stance on important interpretive issues.

SECTION 2

The Existence of God

Can Religious Experience Show There Is a God?

R. Douglas Geivett

The Bible reports many direct experiences of God. Moses comes across a burning bush in the desert, and God commands him to return to Egypt to free His people (Ex 3–4). The Angel of the Lord promised Gideon divine deliverance from Israel's enemy, the Midianites (Jdg 6:11-8:32). In his old age, childless Abram is promised by the Lord he will yet have a host of ancestors, and his aged wife, Sarah, will bear a son who becomes the patriarch of a new nation (Gn 12,28). In 1 and 2 Kings, God appears to kings and prophets with numerous warnings and promises.

In the NT we read of the experiences surrounding the birth announcements of Jesus and John the Baptist (Lk 1:5-38); the transfiguration (Mt 17:1-8; Mk 9:2-8; Lk 9:28-36); Paul's conversion while on his way to Damascus to persecute Christians (Ac 9:1-19); and Peter's decision, motivated by a vision, to take the gospel to the household of Cornelius (Ac 10). There are many other reports of this kind in the Bible. And the record does not end there. Every generation of believers has testified to the immediate presence of God in various ways.

Admittedly, in most cases, these religious experiences occurred in people who already believed in God. The experiences often were intended to impart reliable information or divine guidance, and were frequently accompanied by miraculous confirming events. On the other hand, these experiences confirmed them in their belief in God, led them to testify to the existence and supremacy of the Lord, and emboldened them to act on the information and guidance they received.

This raises the question: Does religious experience provide grounds for believing God exists? It is reasonable to think so, and here's why.

It is a basic principle of rationality that how things appear in experience provides good grounds for believing that is how things are, unless there is at least as good a reason to think that how things seem is actually mistaken. If I seem to see an orange tree in my garden, then, in general, I have good grounds for believing there is an orange tree there. But suppose that, during the past ten years, I've never seen an orange tree there, I did not recently arrange for an orange tree to be planted there, my wife now looks and says she does not see an orange tree there, and I've recently been prescribed medication known for its hallucinogenic side-effects. These considerations make it very unlikely that I am seeing what I seem to be seeing. And thus I have no good grounds for believing an orange tree is in the garden.

While alleged experiences of God do not typically involve the faculties of sensory perception, they do have much the same structure as perceptual experiences of things like orange trees. An entity (an object or a person) is represented as present to the consciousness of some person. So if I seem to be directly aware of God's presence, and there are no overriding defeaters for how things seem, then I have good grounds for believing that God is present, and hence for believing that God exists (since God would not be present if God did not exist).

But now we must ask: would my experience be evidence for others, if I reported my experience to them? Is testimony about an experience of God good grounds for believing God exists?

A basic principle governing the rationality of belief based on testimony is that the testimony of an experience should be trusted, unless there is at least as good a reason to think that it is mistaken. If I report to others that I saw a particular orange tree, then, in general, recipients of my testimony have good grounds for believing I saw it, and hence that particular orange tree exists. But if I have a reputation for clowning around, or telling minor lies, or if I have no idea what an orange tree looks like, or recipients of my testimony have strong independent reasons for denying that there is an orange tree in the garden, then it would not be so reasonable for them to accept my testimony.

Similarly, if I report a personal experience of God, this will be grounds for others to believe that God exists, if what I report is plausible, and it is plausible that my faculties are adequate for such an experience, and I have a reputation for honesty.

In general it seems rational that belief in God may be grounded in an experience of God for those who have had the experience, and testimony about the experience may even provide grounds for belief in God for those who do not have such experiences themselves. In combination with other evidences for God's existence, direct religious experience and testimony about such experience may provide especially strong motivation for believing in God. It should at least provide strong motivation for exploring the other evidence for God's existence.

Does the Existence of the Mind Provide Evidence for God?

J.P. Moreland

Many believe that the existence of finite minds provides evidence of a divine mind as their Creator. If we limit our options to theism and naturalism, it is hard to see how finite consciousness could result from the rearrangement of brute matter; it is easier to see how a conscious Being could produce finite consciousness in His creation.

This argument assumes a commonsense understanding of conscious states such as sensations, thoughts, beliefs, desires, volitions. So understood, mental states are in no sense physical since they possess four features not owned by physical states:

1. There is a raw qualitative feel or a "what it is like" to have a mental state such as a pain.
2. Many mental states have intentionality—*ofness* or *aboutness*—directed towards an object (e.g., a thought is *about* the moon).
3. Mental states are inner, private, and immediate to the subject having them.
4. Mental states fail to have crucial features (e.g., spatial extension, location) that characterize physical states and, in general, cannot be described using physical language.

Given that conscious states are immaterial and not physical, at least two reasons have been offered for why there can be no natural scientific explanation for the existence of conscious states:

Something from nothing. Before consciousness appeared, the universe contained nothing but aggregates of particles/waves standing in fields of forces. The naturalistic story of the cosmos' evolution involves the rearrangement of atomic parts into increasingly more complex structures according to natural law. Matter is brute mechanical, physical stuff. The emergence of consciousness seems to be a case of getting something from nothing. In general, physico-chemical reactions do not generate consciousness. Some say they do in the brain, yet brains seem similar to other parts of organisms' bodies (e.g., both are collections of cells totally describable in physical terms). How can like causes produce radically different effects? The appearance of mind is utterly unpredictable and inexplicable given naturalism. This radical discontinuity seems like a rupture in the natural world.

The inadequacy of evolutionary explanations. Naturalists claim that evolutionary explanations can be proffered for the appearance of all organisms and their parts. In principle, an evolutionary account could be given for increasingly complex physical structures that constitute different organisms.

However, organisms are black boxes as far as evolution is concerned. As long as an organism, when receiving certain inputs, generates the correct behavioral outputs under the demands of reproductive advantage, the organism will survive. What goes on inside the organism is irrelevant and only becomes significant for the processes of evolution when an output is produced. Strictly speaking, it is the output, not what caused it, that bears on the struggle for reproductive advantage. Moreover, the functions organisms carry out consciously *could just as well have been done unconsciously*. Thus, both the sheer existence of conscious states and the precise mental content that constitutes them is outside the pale of evolutionary explanation.

It will not do to claim that consciousness simply emerged from matter when it reached a certain level of complexity because "emergence" is merely a label for and not an explanation of the phenomena to be explained.

Does the Cosmological Argument Show There Is a God?

J.P. Moreland

The cosmological argument starts with the existence of the universe and reasons to the existence of God as the best explanation of the universe. There are different forms of the argument. Two important versions are the Leibnizian and Thomist arguments named, respectively, after Gottfried W. Leibniz (A.D. 1646–1716) and Thomas Aquinas (A.D. 1225–1274). In recent years a third version has become prominent and it may be the most effective of all—the *kalam cosmological argument*. This argument highlights two alternatives for the origin of the universe:

Universe >> Had a beginning >> Was caused >> Personal
Universe >> Had no beginning >> Was not caused >> Impersonal

The defender of the cosmological argument tries to establish one horn of each dilemma and, thus, to argue for these three premises:

1. The universe had a beginning.
2. The beginning of the universe was caused.
3. The cause of the beginning of the universe was personal.

A philosophical argument for premise 1 involves the impossibility of crossing an actual infinite number of events. For example, if one started counting 1, 2, 3, . . . , then one could count forever and never reach a time when an actual infinite amount of numbers had been counted. The series counted could increase forever, but would always be finite. If the universe had no beginning, then the number of events crossed to reach the present moment would be actually infinite. It would be like counting to zero from negative infinity. Since one cannot cross an actual infinite, then the present moment could never have arrived if the universe were beginningless. Since the present is real, it was only preceded by a finite past and there was a beginning or first event!

A scientific argument for premise 1 derives from the second law of thermodynamics, which in one form states that the amount of useful energy in the universe is being used up. If the universe were infinitely old, it would have already used up all its useful energy and reached a temperature of absolute zero. Since there are many pockets of useful energy (our sun for example), the universe must be finite in duration. Therefore, there was a beginning when the universe's useful energy was put into it "from the outside."

Premise 2 is confirmed by universal experience with no clear counterexamples. Alleged cases where something comes from nothing actually involve one thing coming into existence from something else (e.g., lead from uranium; particles transitioning from energy in a partial vacuum).

Evidence for premise 3 derives from the fact that since time, space, and matter did not exist earlier than the beginning of the universe, the universe's cause had to be timeless, spaceless, and immaterial. This cause cannot be physical or subject to scientific law since all such causes presuppose time, space, and matter to exist. The universe's immaterial cause was timeless, spaceless, and had the power to spontaneously bring the world into existence without changing first to do so. (If it had to change before bringing the world into existence, that change, not the act of bringing the world into existence, would be the first event.) Such a cause must have free will and, since only personal beings have free will, the cause is a personal Creator.

If God Made the Universe, Who Made God?

Paul Copan

A theist philosopher Bertrand Russell once mused: "If everything must have a cause, then God must have a cause." But the question of who or what caused God is misguided.

First, science supports the notion that the universe had a beginning and that something independent of the universe brought it into being. The well-accepted scientific belief in the universe's origination and expansion and the second law of thermodynamics (energy tends to spread out) support the universe's absolute beginning from nothing. This sounds remarkably like Genesis 1:1! The chances of a thing's popping into being from literally nothing are exactly zero. *Being* cannot come from *non-being*; there's no potential for this. Even skeptic David Hume called this "absurd"—a metaphysical impossibility.

Second, believers reject the claim "Everything that exists has a cause" and affirm "Whatever begins to exist has a cause." To say "Everything needs a cause" would necessarily exclude an uncaused God. This is "question-begging" (assuming what needs to be proved). It's like presuming that since all reality is physical (which can't be demonstrated), a nonphysical God cannot exist.

Third, why think everything needs a cause, since an uncaused entity is logical and intelligible? Through the centuries, many believed that the universe didn't need a cause; it was self-existent. They did not believe an uncaused universe was illogical or impossible. But now that contemporary cosmology points to the universe's beginning and an external cause, skeptics insist that everything needs a cause after all!

Fourth, a good number of uncaused things exist. Logical laws are real; we can't think coherently without using them (e.g., the law of identity, $X = X$, tells you: "This book is this book"). Moral laws or virtues (love, justice) are real. But none of these began to exist. They are eternal and uncaused (being in God's mind).

Fifth, the question "Who made God?" commits the category fallacy. To say that all things, even God, must be caused is incoherent—like the question "How does the color green taste?" Why fault God for being uncaused? When we rephrase the question to say, "What caused the self-existent, uncaused Cause, who is by definition unmade, to exist?" the answer is obvious.

Does the Design Argument Show There Is a God?

William A. Dembski

S uppose you take a tour of the Louvre, that great museum in Paris housing one of the finest art collections in the world. As you walk through the museum, you come across a painting by someone named Leonardo da Vinci. It's the *Mona Lisa.* Suppose this is your first exposure to da Vinci—you hadn't heard of him or seen the *Mona Lisa* before. What could you conclude? Certainly you could conclude that da Vinci was a consummate painter. Nevertheless, just from the *Mona Lisa* you couldn't conclude that da Vinci was also a consummate engineer, musician, scientist, and inventor, whose ideas were centuries ahead of their time.

The design argument is like this. It looks at certain features of the natural world and concludes that they exhibit evidence of a designing intelligence. But just as the *Mona Lisa* can only tell us so much about its author (da Vinci), so the natural world can only tell us so much about its author (God). The design argument allows us reliably to conclude that a designing intelligence is behind the order and complexity of the natural world. But it cannot speak to the underlying nature of this designing intelligence (for instance, whether this intelligence is the transcendent interpersonal triune God of Christianity).

Nor can it speak to the actions of that designing intelligence in human history. In particular, the design argument is silent about the revelation of Christ in Scripture. It follows that the design argument cannot "prove the Gospel" or "compel someone into the Kingdom."

Christian theologians have long recognized that the design argument is a modest argument. Even so, it is a powerful argument. Perhaps the best-known design argument is William Paley's. According to Paley, if we find a watch in a field (and thus lack all knowledge of how it arose), the adaptation of the watch's parts to telling time ensures that it is the product of an intelligence. So too, according to Paley, the marvelous adaptations of means to ends in organisms (like the human eye with its ability to confer sight) ensure that organisms are the product of an intelligence. The theory of intelligent design, or ID as it is commonly abbreviated, updates Paley's argument in light of contemporary information theory and molecular biology, bringing the design argument squarely within science.

The implications of ID for the Christian faith are profound and revolutionary. The rise of modern science led to a vigorous attack on orthodox Christian theology. The high point of this attack came with Darwin's theory of evolution. Orthodox Christian theology has always been committed to the proposition that God by wisdom created the world. A clear implication of this proposition is that the design of the world is real. The central claim of Darwin's theory is that an unguided material process (random variation and natural selection) could account for the emergence of all biological complexity and order. In other words, Darwin appeared to show that the design of the world was unreal—that science had dispensed with any need for design. By showing that design is indispensable to our scientific understanding of the natural world, ID is breathing new life into the design argument and at the same time overturning the widespread misconception that science has disproved the Christian faith.

What Is Natural Law?

Paul Copan

From a Birmingham jail, Martin Luther King Jr. discussed civil disobedience, noting that "there are two kinds of laws: just and unjust" and that there is a "natural law" to which we are subject. He was right: we shouldn't say we know right and wrong only because "the Bible says so." Romans 2:15 states that God's moral law has been written on the hearts of *all* human beings. This innate awareness is described in C.S. Lewis's *Abolition of Man* (Appendix). There he lists various universally recognized moral laws and virtues—impartial justice, truthfulness, kindness, mercy, marital fidelity, respect for human life. They have been regarded as true for all from ancient Babylon and

Greece to Native America, from Jews and Christians to Hindus and Confucians. Though humans are capable of recognizing basic moral principles, they *may* suppress their conscience, harden their hearts, and become morally dull.

Medieval theologian Thomas Aquinas spoke of certain "laws." He said there is an *eternal* law, which God alone knows and by which God created and governs the universe. Because God created us in His image (as moral, reasoning beings), we are capable of recognizing a self-evident *natural* law, the reflection of God's eternal law in the created order. Everyone can know natural laws apart from the divine law that God has given to us through special revelation (the Bible, Jesus Christ). God has placed within us a disposition to have moral knowledge. Unless we suppress our conscience, we naturally know basic moral truths. General virtues and vices, Thomas Reid wrote, "must appear self-evident to every man who has a conscience, and has taken the pains to exercise this natural power of his mind" ("Of Morals").

Some will respond, "There can be moral atheists. We don't need God for morality." However, atheists have been made in the image of God. Though they deny God's existence, they have still been designed by God to function properly and even to create human law for the good of society—the law that to varying degrees applies the *natural law* placed within us. Atheists ignore the very basis of goodness—God, who created them and who is the highest Good. (See J. Budziszewski, *The Revenge of Conscience* and *Written on the Heart*.)

Does the Moral Argument Show There Is a God?

Paul Copan

Here's a good rule of thumb about morality: *Never believe those who say murder or rape may not really be wrong.* Such people haven't looked deeply enough into the basis for moral belief—and just aren't functioning properly. (Usually, when personally threatened with murder or rape, they change their tune!) Color-blind persons need help distinguishing red from green. Similarly, morally-malfunctioning persons (denying basic moral truths) don't need arguments; they need psychological and spiritual help. Like logical laws, moral laws/instincts are basic to well-functioning humans.

As part of God's general self-revelation, all people—unless they ignore or suppress their conscience—can and should have basic moral insight, knowing truths generally available to any morally sensitive person (Rm 2:14-15). We instinctively recognize the wrongness of torturing or murdering the innocent or committing rape. We just know the rightness of virtues (kindness, trustworthiness, unselfishness). A person's failure to recognize these insights reveals something defective; he hasn't looked deeply enough into the grounds of his moral beliefs.

Philosophers and theologians past and present have noted the connection between God's existence and objective moral values. A moral argument for God's existence goes like this: (a) If objective moral values exist, then God exists. (b) Objective moral values do exist. (c) Therefore, God exists. If objective moral values exist, where do they come from? The most plausible answer is God's nature/character. Even many atheists have admitted that objective moral values—which they deny exist—don't fit an atheistic world but would serve as evidence for God's existence.

We live in a time when many claim everything is relative, yet, ironically they believe they have "rights." But if morality is just the product of evolution, culture, or personal choice, then rights—and moral responsibility—do not truly exist. But if they *do* exist, this assumes humans have value in and of themselves as persons—no matter what their culture or science textbooks say. But what then is the basis for this value? Could this intrinsic value just emerge from impersonal, mindless, valueless processes over time (naturalism)?

An Eastern philosophical approach to ethics is monism (sometimes called "pantheism"). This view says everything is one, which means no ultimate distinction between good and evil exists—which serves to support relativism. A more natural context for ethics is the theistic one—in which we've been made by a good God to resemble Him in certain important (though limited) ways. The Declaration of Independence correctly notes that we've been endowed by our Creator with "certain unalienable rights." Human dignity isn't just "there." Dignity and rights come from a good God (despite human sinfulness).

Can't atheists be moral? Yes! Like believers, they've been made in the image of God and thus have the ability to recognize right and wrong.

Doesn't God Himself conform to certain moral standards outside Himself? No, God's good character is the very standard; God simply acts and naturally does what is good. Universal moral standards have no basis if God doesn't exist. These standards presuppose some cosmic blueprint for how humans ought to live.

Moral values are rooted in personhood. Without God (a personal Being), no persons—and thus no moral values—would exist: no persons, no moral values. The moral argument points to a good God in whose image we're made.

SECTION 3

The Scriptures: Their Origin, History, and Accuracy

Who Wrote the Pentateuch and When Was It Written?

Daniel I. Block

Although Jewish and Christian tradition almost unanimously recognize Moses as author of the Pentateuch, few issues relating to the OT are debated as hotly today, and in few is the gulf between critical and evangelical scholarship so wide. Many conservative scholars continue to believe that Moses wrote virtually all of the Pentateuch with his own hand. So long as critical scholars recognized Moses as an historical figure, in principle his involvement in the composition of the Pentateuch was not excluded—unless, of course he was thought to be illiterate. However, since the middle of the 19th century A.D., especially following Julius Wellhausen, most critical scholars have rejected Moses having a significant role in the origin of the Pentateuch.

The questioning began early with doubts whether Moses recorded his own death and burial (Dt 34), or knew of a place in northern Israel called Dan (Gn 14:14; cp. Jos 19:47; Jdg 18:28b-29), or referred to the conquest of Canaan as past (Dt 2:12). Thus scholars developed an alternative explanation for the origins of the Pentateuch known as the Documentary Hypothesis. According to the classical form of the theory, the Pentateuch is the product of a long and complex literary evolution, specifically incorporating at least four major literary strands composed independently over several centuries and not combined in the present form until the time of Ezra (fifth century B.C.). These sources are identified as J, E, D, and P. J represents a ninth century B.C. (c. 850) document that originated in Judah, distinguished by its preference for the name *Yahweh* (Jehovah). The E source preferred the divine title *Elohim*, and theoretically was composed in Israel in the eighth century B.C. D stands for Deuteronomy, supposedly written around 621 B.C. to lend support to Josiah's reforms. The priestly document, P, assumedly was composed about 500 B.C. by priests seeking to preserve their own version of Israel's history. According to the theory, these sources were compiled and combined in the middle of the fifth century B.C. Nehemiah 8 recounts the moment when

Ezra publicly read the Pentateuch as a unit for the first time. Because Joshua describes the fulfillment of the promises of land to the patriarchs and because of stylistic links to Deuteronomy, Gerhard von Rad added Joshua to the pentateuchal corpus, calling the six books the Hexateuch.

Variations of the Documentary Hypothesis prevailed for more than a century. However, due to advances in literary studies, today the state of pentateuchal scholarship is confused, with new theories or radical modifications appearing often. The new theories push the dates for pentateuchal origin ever later. R. N. Whybray argued that the Pentateuch is a unitary composition written in the fourth century B.C., inspired perhaps by the Greek *Histories* of Herodotus.

The internal evidence suggests Moses kept a record of Israel's experiences in the desert (Ex 17:14; 24:4,7; 34:27; Nm 33:1-2; Dt 31:9,11). Furthermore, many statements in the OT credit the Pentateuch to Moses (e.g., Jos 1:8; 8:31-32; 1Kg 2:3; 2Kg 14:6; Ezr 6:18; Neh 13:1; Dn 9:11-13; Mal 4:4), and the NT identifies the Torah very closely with him (Mt 19:8; Jn 5:46-47; 7:19; Ac 3:22; Rm 10:5). A series of additional features within the text point to an early date for its composition: (1) the forms of the names and many of the actions of the patriarchs make best sense in a second millennium B.C. environment; (2) the narratives suggest a thorough acquaintance with Egypt; (3) Egyptian loanwords appear with greater frequency in the Pentateuch than anywhere else in the OT; (4) the name Moses itself suggests an Egyptian setting for the story; (5) the general viewpoint of the narrative is foreign to Canaan; (6) the seasons are Egyptian; the flora and fauna are Egyptian and Sinaitic; (7) in some instances the geography reflects a foreign viewpoint (e.g., a comment like that found in Gn 33:18, "at Shechem in the land of Canaan" is unlikely after the exile because by then Israel had been in the land for 900 years); (8) and archaisms in the language (like the use of the third person singular pronoun, *hi*, for both genders), all point to an early date.

It is doubtful Moses wrote the account of his death in Deuteronomy 34. Frequently the text provides explanatory notes updating facts for a later audience. One example is Genesis 36:1, where a parenthetical comment lets the reader know that "Esau" is "Edom." In another example, the aboriginal inhabitants of the Transjordan are described for readers living too late to have known them (Dt 2:10-12). Furthermore, the form of the cursive Canaanite script that Moses probably used was still in its infancy when he wrote and was replaced with the square Aramaic script in the postexilic period, and the vowels were added a millennium later. The archaic qualities of the poems (Gn 49; Ex 15; etc.) in contrast to the surrounding narrative suggests the narrative texts may have been updated periodically in accordance with the evolution of the Hebrew language, whereas the poems were left unmodified. This may explain why the grammar and syntax of Deuteronomy in its present form reads much like Jeremiah, who lived long after Moses.

There is no reason to doubt that Moses wrote down the speeches he delivered (Dt 31:9-13), or that when he came down from Mount Sinai, he arranged for the transcription of the revelation he had received on the mountain, if he did not write it all himself. Just as the pieces of the tabernacle were constructed and woven by skilled craftsmen and finally assembled by Moses (Ex 35-40) so literary craftsmen may have composed some bits and pieces of the Pentateuch, submitted them to Moses, who then approved them. When exactly the pieces were put together in their present form we may only speculate (Deuteronomy suggests some time after the death of Moses), but it seems likely that by the time David organized for temple worship, the contents of the Torah were fixed.

Has the Bible Been Accurately Copied Down Through the Centuries?

Norman L. Geisler

The Bible is the most accurately transmitted book from the ancient world. No other ancient book has as many, as early, or more accurately copied manuscripts.

Old Testament manuscript reliability is based on three factors: their abundance, dating, and accuracy. Most works from antiquity survive in only a handful of manuscripts. There are only 7 for Plato, 8 for Thucydides, 8 for Herodotus, 10 for Caesar's *Gallic Wars*, and 20 for Tacitus. Only the works of Demosthenes and Homer number into the hundreds. Yet even before 1890, Giovanni de Rossi published 731 OT manuscripts. Since that time some 10,000 OT manuscripts were found in the Cairo Geniza, and in 1947 the Dead Sea caves at Qumran produced over 600 OT manuscripts.

Further, the Dead Sea Scrolls (DSS), containing at least fragments of all OT books except Esther, all date before the end of the first century A.D. and some to the 3rd century B.C. The Nash Papyrus is dated between the 2nd century B.C. and the first century A.D.

The manuscripts' accuracy is known from internal and external evidence. (1) It is well known that Jewish scribal reverence for Scripture led to its careful transmission. (2) Examination of duplicate passages (e.g., Pss 14 and 53) show parallel transmission. (3) The early Greek translation of the OT, the Septuagint, substantially agrees with the Hebrew manuscripts. (4) Comparison of the Samaritan Pentateuch with the same biblical books preserved within the Jewish tradition shows close similarity. (5) The Dead Sea Scrolls provide manuscripts dating a thousand years earlier than most used to establish the Hebrew text.

Comparative studies reveal word-for-word identity in 95 percent of the text. Minor variants consist mostly of slips of the pen or spelling. Only 13 small changes were discovered in the entire DSS copy of Isaiah, eight of which were known from other ancient sources. After 1,000 years of copying, there were no changes in meaning and almost no changes in wording!

The reliability of the NT is established because the number, date, and accuracy of its manuscripts enable reconstruction of the original text with more precision than any other ancient text. The number of NT manuscripts is overwhelming (almost 5,700 Greek manuscripts) compared with the typical book from antiquity (about 7 to 10 manuscripts; Homer's *Iliad* has the most with 643 manuscripts). The NT is simply the best textually supported book from the ancient world.

The earliest undisputed NT manuscript is the John Rylands Papyrus, dated A.D. 117-138. Whole books (e.g., Bodmer Papyri) are available from A.D. 200. And most of the NT, including all the Gospels, is available in the Chester Beatty Papyri (c. A.D. 250). Noted British manuscript scholar Sir Frederick Kenyon wrote: "The interval then between the dates or original composition and the earliest extant evidence becomes so small as to be in fact negligible, and the last foundation for any doubt that the Scriptures have come down to us substantially as they were written has now been removed." Thus, both "the authenticity and the general integrity of the books of the [NT] may be regarded as firmly established." No other ancient book has as small a time gap between composition and earliest manuscript copies.

Not only are there more and earlier NT manuscripts, but they are more accurately copied than other ancient texts. The great NT scholar and Princeton Professor, Bruce Metzger, made a comparison of the NT with the *Iliad* of Homer and the *Mahabharata* of Hinduism. He found the text of the latter to represent only 90 percent of the original (with 10 percent textual corruption), the *Iliad* to be 95 percent pure, and only half of 1 percent of the NT text being in doubt. The great Greek scholar A. T. Robertson estimated that NT textual concerns have to do with only a "thousandth part of the entire text," placing the accuracy of the NT text at 99.9 percent—the best known for any book from the ancient world. Sir Frederick Kenyon noted that "the number of [manuscripts] of the NT, of early translations from it, and of quotations from it in the older writers of the Church, is so large that it is practically certain that the true reading of every doubtful passage is preserved in some one or the other of these ancient authorities. This can be said of no other ancient book in the world."

In summary, the vast number, early dates, and accuracy of the OT and NT manuscript copies establish the Bible's reliability well beyond any other ancient book. Its substantial message has been undiminished through the centuries, and its accuracy on even minor details has been confirmed. Thus, the Bible we hold in our hands today is a highly trustworthy copy of the original that came from the pens of the prophets and apostles.

Can Biblical Chronology Be Trusted?

E. Ray Clendenen

The Bible is not a book of philosophical or ethical principles, although it contains them. It is a book about how God has made Himself known in history. Its message is timeless in that the nature of God and man has not changed. But the framework of that message, which holds it together and cannot be extracted from it, is the story of what God has said and done in history.

Chronology is the foundation of history; without it, history is a swarm of events floating in space with no relationship to each other or to us. *Relative* chronology places events before or after (or simultaneous with) each other. *Absolute* chronology relates events to us by fixing them on our conventional timeline in terms of B.C. or A.D.

The Bible is full of relative chronology. For example, we are told that Abraham was 100 years old when Isaac was born (Gn 21:5), the Israelites lived in Egypt for 430 years (Ex 12:40), Israel wandered for 40 years in the wilderness (Nm 32:13), Judah's exile lasted for 70 years (Jr 25:11-12). But no absolute dates are given for any of these or other biblical events. Does this situation leave us unable to confirm or deny biblical chronology? This is not the case for two reasons.

First, the Bible's relative chronology can be shown to be internally consistent. Israel's time in Egypt, the wilderness, and the exile, for example, is consistently given in many different places. Chronological differences between Kings and Chronicles have been closely examined and have yielded to reasonable methods of harmonization.

Second, the historical accounts in both Old and New Testaments intersect at various points the histories of surrounding nations such as Egypt, Assyria, Babylon, Persia, and Rome, whose chronologies have been established to a high degree of accuracy. Assyrian chronology, for example, is set according to an eclipse known to have occurred on June 15, 763 B.C.

Problems still remain. Differences between ancient and modern calendars, for example, often necessitate the giving of alternate dates in the form 931/0 B.C. Furthermore, different methods of harmonizing the dates of biblical kings yield slightly different results.

Even conservative scholars do not always agree on how a particular chronological reference should be interpreted. For example, some scholars argue that many numbers in the Bible are figurative, especially 40 and its multiples. These scholars prefer in some cases to give priority to archaeological clues in establishing biblical chronology. Thus the patriarchal period is often dated to the Middle Bronze Age between about 1800–1600 B.C. It is also supposed that the Hebrews migrated to Egypt during the Hyksos period (about 1700–1500 B.C.) when Semitic people ruled Egypt. The exodus is then associated with the reign of Rameses II shortly after 1290 B.C. Following the wilderness period, the conquest of Canaan would have begun about 1250 B.C. Pharaoh Merneptah (1224–1214 B.C.) mounted a campaign against Canaan in the fifth year of his reign (about 1220). In his record of that campaign, he records that, among others, Israel was utterly destroyed. Thus by that date, the people Israel were a recognized group in Canaan.

Assuming a literal interpretation of 1 Kings 6:1, however, the exodus occurred in 1446 B.C., and the conquest period lasted about seven years to around 1400 B.C. Continuing backwards, based on Exodus 12:40, Jacob's migration to Egypt would have been in 1876 B.C. Data regarding the ages of the patriarchs would place their births at 2006 B.C. for Jacob (Gn 47:9), 2066 B.C. for Isaac (Gn 25:26), and 2166 B.C. for Abraham (Gn 21:5). Because the genealogical lists in Genesis are believed by most to be intentionally incomplete or "open," attempts are usually not made to establish historical dates prior to Abraham.

The NT is not much concerned with *when* events took place, with Luke being somewhat the exception. He tells us, for example, that Jesus was 12 when His parents lost Him in Jerusalem (Lk 2:42) and was about 30 at the beginning of His ministry (Lk 3:23). Both references are altogether reasonable. In Lk 3:1 he appears to set the date for John the Baptist's ministry—"In the fifteenth year of the reign of Tiberius Caesar, while Pontius Pilate was governor of Judea, Herod was tetrarch of Galilee, his brother Philip tetrarch of the region of Iturea and Trachonitis, and Lysanias tetrarch of Abilene." There is nothing problematic about this date except the interpretation of Tiberius's 15th year, the determination of which depends on the beginning point and which calendar Luke had in mind.

Due to an error by a sixth-century Scythian monk who was responsible for our current Western calendar, Jesus' birth actually occurred in the B.C. era, perhaps in late 5 B.C. We know that Herod the Great, who was very much alive when Jesus was born, died between March 12/13 and April 11, 4 B.C.

Unfortunately, the date of Jesus' crucifixion is uncertain. Although the majority opinion is that it occurred in A.D. 30, a good argument can be made for A.D. 33 instead. Our knowledge of Roman history allows us to determine that Herod Agrippa and therefore the events of Acts 12 occurred in A.D. 44.

There is no credible reason, then, to question the Bible's historical chronology, even though at times we wish we had more information.

How Can We Know the Bible Includes the Correct Books?

Norman L. Geisler

W hy are there only these 66 books in the Bible? Because God is the ultimate author of the Bible, and He inspired only these 66. All Scripture is breathed out of the mouth of God (2Tm 3:16; Mt 4:4). What the human authors wrote did not originate with them but with God who moved upon them (2Sm 23:2; 1Pt 1:20-21). So God *determined* which books would be in the Bible, and the people of God merely *discovered* which books these were. Believers did not bestow authority on them; God did.

Why did the people of God discover only these 66 books were inspired of God? Because only these had the "fingerprints" of God on them. These fingerprints include characteristics which are the answers to these questions: (1) Was it written by a prophet of God such as Moses (Ex 4:1-9) or Paul (1Co 9:1)? (2) Was it confirmed by acts of God (Heb 1:1; 2:3-4)? Did the human author tell the truth of God known from other revelations and facts (Dt 18:20-22)? (3) Did it have the power of God to edify (2Tm 3:16-17; Heb 4:12)? (4) Was it accepted and collected by the people of God?

The collection of books, known as the canon of Scripture was made gradually as the books were written. When Moses wrote the first five books of the Bible, they were taken immediately and put in the most holy place (Dt 1:24). The book of Joshua was added to the collection upon his death (Jos 24:26). Likewise, the books of Samuel (1Sm 10:25) and the prophets were added after they wrote them (Zch 7:12). Daniel had a collection of Moses' books and the prophetic writings that had been written up to Daniel's time; including a book by his contemporary, Jeremiah (Dn 9:2).

The so-called missing books of the OT, known as the "Apocrypha" (meaning "hidden" or "doubtful") are not missing and do not belong in the OT for many reasons: (1) Unlike the canonical books, the Apocryphal books do not have either an explicit or implicit claim to be inspired by God. In fact, some even disclaim being prophetic (cp. 1 Macc 9:27; 14:41). (2) They were written between 250 B.C. and the first-century A.D., but according to Judaism, the Spirit of prophecy departed from Israel before that time, about 400 B.C. (3) The Jewish historian Josephus gives the names and numbers of the authentic Jewish OT, which correspond exactly with the 39 books of our OT (*Against Apion* 1.8). Judaism, which produced these books, has never accepted them into their Bible (the OT). (4) Neither Jesus nor the apostles ever cited any of the Apocrypha in the NT as inspired. (5) Most of the church fathers of the first four centuries of the Christian church did not accept these books as inspired. (6) Jerome, the great Roman Catholic scholar (c. A.D. 420), who translated the Latin Vulgate Bible, emphatically rejected the apocryphal books. (7) The acceptance of these books in 1546 by the Roman Catholic Church is unjustified, since: (a) they were the wrong group to make this decision (Christians, not Jews); (b) at the wrong time (sixteenth century A.D.) and (c) for the wrong reasons (for example to support their doctrine of prayers for the dead [see 2 Macc 12:45] in response to the Reformation and biblical teaching to the contrary [Heb 9:27]).

The NT books were also written by apostles and prophets of God (Eph 2:20) who were confirmed by acts of God (2Co 12:12; Heb 1:1; 2:3-4), and their books were immediately accepted into the growing canon of Scripture. Luke acknowledged that other narratives were written (Lk 1:1) in his time (possibly Matthew and Mark). In 1 Timothy 5:18, Paul cited the Gospel of Luke (10:7) as "Scripture" alongside the OT. The Apostle Peter referred to Paul's epistles as "Scripture," just like the OT (2Pt 3:16). The first-century church publicly read and circulated the books written by apostles and prophets (Col 4:16; 1Th 5:27). What is more, the early Christian fathers, beginning in the first century, collected every one of the 27 books of the NT and cited almost every verse in over 36,000 quotations! From the second century on, there were collections of these books and translations in languages such as Syriac and Old Latin. All sections of Christendom, including Roman Catholics, Eastern Orthodox, and Protestants, accept all and only the 27 books of the NT as the inspired Word of God, right alongside the 39 books of the OT.

The apocryphal books of the second and third centuries A.D. are universally rejected by the Christian Church. There are many good reasons for this. (1) They were not written by the apostles whose names they bear, since the apostles died in the first century. (2) They contain many heresies and doctrinal errors. (3) They claim to contain childhood miracles of Jesus, but John said Jesus did not perform any miracles until He was an adult (Jn 2:11). (3) They contain highly embellished accounts of Gospel stories, indicating they were later fabrications. (4) They are universally rejected by every section of official Christendom.

In brief, only the 66 books of the common canon claim to be and prove to be the divinely inspired, infallible, and inerrant Word of God. That is, only these books were inspired of God, written by prophets of God, collected by the people of God, and were preserved by the providence of God for the spiritual edification of the people of God (2Tm 3:16-17).

Does the New Testament Misquote the Old Testament?

Paul Copan

Perhaps you've wondered why NT writers appear to take OT verses out of context to make them fit their theology about Jesus' teaching and ministry. Critics cry foul and charge that such "fabricated predictions" refer to something other than a coming Messiah. For example, the context of Hosea 11:1 ("Out of Egypt I called My son") refers to Israel's exodus from Egypt. But Matthew 2:15 says that the "son" was Jesus coming from Egypt. Isaiah 7:14 says "The virgin will conceive, have a son, and name him Immanuel," which directly concerns King Ahaz's time, when a "sign child" was born within Isaiah's lifetime (7:15-16; 8:4). But Matthew 1 says Mary is the virgin fulfilling the Isaiah passage. Rachel's weeping in Jeremiah 31:15 probably refers to the mourning Judah's being taken into exile (Babylon) in 586/7 B.C. But Matthew 2 sees Jeremiah as referring to the weeping mothers after Herod's capricious decree to kill all boys under two in Bethlehem (where Rachel was buried).

Frequently, critics—and Christians too—think *prophecy* means "prediction," and *fulfillment* means "realization of a prediction." From this, critics conclude "fabricated predictions." However, this charge rests on a great mistake, and sometimes Christians become confused by it.

First, if the NT writers "plundered" the OT for proof-texts, why, for instance, doesn't Luke—who mentions the virgin birth—quote Isaiah 7:14 (as Matthew does)? The same could be asked about other such passages. Second, Jewish interpretation of the OT during Jesus' day viewed "fulfillment" more broadly—more varied and nuanced—and the literal approach was only one method among several.

Third—and most importantly—the word *fulfill* (*plēroō*) in the NT is used to portray Jesus as *bringing to full fruition* OT *events/experiences* (the exodus, covenant), *personages* (Jonah, Solomon, David), and *institutions* (temple, priesthood/sacrifices, holy days). *Fulfill* doesn't necessarily or even primarily refer to the mere fulfillment of a prediction. Rather, a theological point is being made: many OT events/institutions—usually related to Israel—foreshadow something greater in Christ and the new community He called together (e.g., Christ's calling twelve disciples, reminiscent of Israel's twelve tribes). Jesus is the true, beloved *Son* that Israel failed to be (Hs 11:1; cp. Mt 2:15; Lk 3:22), the shepherd Israel's leaders weren't (Ezk 34; cp. Jn 10:1-18, the genuine ("true") fruit-bearing vine Israel wasn't (Ps 80:8,14; Is 5:1-7; cp. Jn 15:1-11). In His ministry, Jesus reenacted the history and experiences of Israel—but on a higher plane (e.g., forty days of testing in the wilderness, giving a new "law" from a mountain in Mt 5–7, being in the "belly" of the earth for "three days and three nights," etc.). He takes over Israel's destiny and role, bringing it to fulfillment. The Law of Moses has a handful of messianic predictions, but Jesus' fulfilling the Law (Mt 5:17; Lk 24:44) refers to His bringing it to completion.

Of course, there are predictions regarding the Messiah's birthplace (Mc 5; cp. Mt 2:5), the Messiah's death/atonement (Is 53), and a coming prophet and messenger (Dt 18; Mal 3). But fulfillment of the OT generally refers to the broader idea of perfectly embodying, typifying, epitomizing, reaching a climax. For example, Jesus (citing Is 29:13) said to unbelieving Jews of His day, "Hypocrites! Isaiah prophesied correctly about you when he said: 'These people honor Me with their lips, but their heart is far from Me.'"(Mt 15:7-8). Of course, Isaiah didn't literally predict that Jesus would deal with hostile religious leaders. Rather, Jesus was using the situation from Isaiah's time to epitomize, embody, and typify the same situation in His own day. This was typical of how Jews spoke of "fulfillment"—a "this-is-that" method called *pesher*: "*This* situation is a fulfillment or embodiment of *that* Scripture".

The NT writers weren't immoral or ignorant. They didn't illegitimately rip passages out of their context and deviously reduce them to messianic predictions. And they were well aware that OT writers (such as Hosea) were often commenting on events in Israel's past (such as the exodus in 11:1, "Out of Egypt I called My son") or events in their own day. But NT writers (and Jesus) interpreted the OT in a Christocentric manner: Jesus is the embodiment or completer of foreshadowed OT historical events, images, and personages. While fulfillment includes literal predictions of Christ and the new covenant, it goes far beyond to a richer theological embodiment of what the OT foreshadowed.

Does the Bible Contain Errors?

Paul D. Feinberg

"Why do you believe the Bible? It is an ancient book full of errors and contradictions." We have all heard this many times. However, most conservative evangelical Christians disagree with this claim. They hold to a doctrine called *the inerrancy of Scripture*.

The place to start our discussion is with a definition of inerrancy and error. By *inerrancy* we mean that when all the facts are known, the Bible in its original autographs and properly interpreted, will be shown to be *true* and never false in all that it affirms whether related to doctrine, ethics, the social, or the physical and life sciences. Three matters in this definition are noteworthy. First, there is the recognition that we do not possess all the information to demonstrate the truth of the Bible. Much data is lost due to antiquity. It simply no longer exists. Other data await archaeological excavation. Second, inerrancy is defined in terms of truth which most philosophers today take to be a property of sentences, not words. This means that all the indicative sentences of the Bible are true. Therefore, on this definition, an error in the Bible would require that it made a false statement. Finally, all information in the Bible, whatever the subject, is true. That is, it accurately records events and conversations, including the lies of men and Satan. It teaches truly about God, the human condition, and heaven and hell.

The belief in inerrancy rests on at least four lines of argument: the biblical, the historical, the epistemological and the slippery slope argument.

The *biblical* argument is drawn from what the Bible has to say about itself and is the most important. This argument may be formulated in a circular and non-circular way. It is circular when one claims that the Bible says it is inspired and inerrant, and that this is true because it is found in an inspired and inerrant Scripture. It is not circular when claims are made that are verifiable outside the document. This is possible because the Bible makes historical and geographical statements which are verifiable independently. Inerrancy follows from what the Bible has to say about its inspiration. It is the exhaled breath of God (2Tm 3:16), and is the result of the Holy Spirit's guidance of human authors (2Pt 1:21). It is a divine-human book. Moreover, the accreditation of a prophet in the OT requires nothing less than complete truthfulness (Dt 13:1-5 and 18:20-22). Can God's written communication meet any less a standard? It should be noted that both these oral and written forms of communication involve the human element. This shows that human agency does not necessarily imply the presence of error. The Bible teaches its own authority as well. Matthew 5:17-20 teaches that heaven and earth will pass away before the smallest detail of the law fails to be fulfilled. John 10:34-35 teaches that Scripture cannot be broken. Furthermore, the way Scripture uses Scripture supports its inerrancy. At times arguments in Scripture rest on a single word (Ps 82:6; Jn 10:34-35), the tense of the verb (Mt 22:32) or the number of a noun (Gl 3:16). Finally, the character of God stands behind His word, and He cannot lie (Nm 23:19; 1Sm 15:29; Ti 1:2; Heb 6:18).

A second argument is *historical*. While there have been those who disagree, inerrancy has been the normative Christian view throughout history. Augustine writes, "I have learned to yield this respect and honor only to the canonical books of Scripture: of these alone do I most firmly believe that the authors were completely free from error." Luther says, "But everyone, indeed, knows that at times they [the fathers] have erred as men will; therefore I am ready to trust them only when they prove their opinions from Scripture, which has never erred." John Wesley gave a similar opinion: "Nay, if there be any mistakes in the Bible, there may as well be a thousand. If there be one falsehood in that book, it did not come from the God of truth."

A third argument is *epistemological* (based on what and how we know something). A helpful way to formulate this argument is to recognize that if the Bible is not entirely true, then any of it may be false. This is particularly problematic when some of the most important information communicated is not empirically verifiable. It teaches about an invisible, incorporeal God, angels, and heaven. Yet, there are those who claim that the information that is verifiable has errors. If that is so, why should anyone believe what is unverifiable? Only an inerrant Bible assures us that what we read is true.

The fourth argument is the *slippery slope* (not a fallacy in this case). The argument states that inerrancy is so fundamental that those admitting errors into the Bible will soon surrender other central doctrines like the deity of Christ and/or substitutionary atonement. The denial of inerrancy leads to greater doctrinal error. This does not happen in every case, but it is demonstrable historically as a common trend.

Each of these arguments has been criticized. However, a common and fundamental objection to them contends this doctrine is meaningless since it is true only of non-existent original autographs. But is it meaningless? Not if two conditions are met: we possess a sufficient number of high quality copies of the autographs, and there is a sophisticated discipline of textual criticism. Both of these conditions are met with respect to the Bible.

The fundamental issue is the Bible's teaching of its own inerrancy. And for those who are skeptical, evidence from science, archaeology, and history has supported this claim over and over again.

Is the New Testament Trustworthy?
Darrell I. Bock

Like any ancient book, the NT has a strange feel about it. It reports unusual events as well as strange customs. This naturally raises the question whether we can trust what it tells us. These six statements of fact affirm that the NT can be trusted.

1. The books of the NT were recognized through a careful sifting process. The process stretched from the first to the fourth centuries. The catalysts for the formation were the use of Scripture in worship, the rise of false teaching, which necessitated identifying the authentic works, and persecution which called for the burning of holy books (so one needed to know which those were!). The books included in the NT canon were those regarded as giving evidence of divine authority. So was it associated with an apostle? Was it in line with other authentic works? Was it widely used and received? These were the questions used to identify the trustworthy and authoritative books of the NT.

2. The NT is based on reliable sources carefully used and faithfully transmitted. The Bible is a book both like other books and unlike them. Luke explains that he used sources (1:1-4). Jesus taught that the Spirit would help the apostles recall what Jesus taught them (Jn 14:25-26). To argue that the Bible is a book inspired by God does not dismiss the human elements that make up the book. What are the sources and how were they handled? The texts surrounding Jesus stress the role of eyewitnesses as the root of the tradition (see Lk 1:2). An apostolic association insured the account's credibility. The distance between event and recording is not great—less than a lifetime, a small distance of time by ancient standards. For example, the first century Roman historians Livy and Dionysius of Halicarnassus were centuries removed from many of the events they chronicled. Judaism depended on the ability to pass things on with care from one generation to the next, recounting events with care. This does not exclude some variation, as is obvious by comparing the gospel accounts or parallel accounts in Samuel, Kings, and Chronicles. Judaism, and the Christianity that grew out of it, was a culture of memory, where the basic elements of an account were retained. People memorized long liturgical prayers and more often than not worked from memory rather than from a written page. Anyone who has read a children's book again and again to their child knows that the mind is capable of absorbing vast amounts of wording and retaining it.

Finally, the Biblical text we have today basically reflects the text as it was produced. The NT has far better manuscript evidence than any other ancient document. Where most classical works such as Plato, Herodotus, and Aristophanes have from one to twenty manuscripts, the NT has about 5,400 Greek manuscripts that we can compare to determine the original wording, not to mention over 8,000 ancient Latin manuscripts that translated the original Greek.

3. Assessing trustworthiness means understanding history's complexity. Differences in accounts do not necessarily equal contradiction, nor does subsequent reflection mean a denial of history. Events can be viewed from different angles or perspectives without forfeiting historicity. Thus the differences in the four gospels enrich our appreciation of Jesus by giving us four perspectives on Him—Jesus in four dimensions. Neither is reflection a denial of history. Sometimes the significance of a historical event, like a football play, only becomes clear when successive events are seen. History involves both what happened and its results. Trustworthiness simply affirms that the assessed account is an accurate portrayal of what took place and a credible explanation of what emerged—not that it is the only way the events in question were seen.

4. Trustworthiness demands not exhaustive but adequate knowledge of the topic. Sources are selective, even when they are accurate. The Bible makes this point in John 21:25: "And there are also many other things that Jesus did, which, if they were written one by one, I suppose not even the world itself could contain the books that would be written." When people call Scripture trustworthy, they are arguing that its testimony is not contrary to what happened and is sufficient to give us a meaningful understanding of God and his work for us (2Tm 3:16-17). To speak *accurately* is not the same as speaking *exhaustively*.

5. Archaeology teaches us to respect the content of Scripture. Archaeology seldom can prove that events took place. What it can show is that the details of an account, some of them incidental, fit the time and culture of the text. Archaeology also shows that we should be cautious in pointing out errors in the Bible merely because only the Bible attests to something.

For example, there was once debate about the description in John 5:2 of a pool with five porticoes in Jerusalem called variously Bethesda or Bethsaida. Many questioned its existence despite its wide attestation in ancient tradition. Different spellings of the locale in the NT manuscript tradition added to the tendency by many to reject the claim. In 1871 French architect C. Mauss was restoring an old church and found a cistern 30 meters away. Later excavations in 1957–1962 clarified that it consisted of two pools large enough to hold a sizable amount of water and people. Today virtually no one doubts the existence of John's pool.

6. The Bible's claim for miracles are plausible when one considers the response to resurrection claims. The events of the Gospels were recorded within the lifetime of several of those who claimed to have observed them. Perhaps the greatest evidence for the resurrection is the change and reaction of those who testified to it. The disciples openly admitted that they had no formal training and for a long period were shockingly inept at responding to Jesus. Yet they became courageous leaders. They stood firm in the face of the threat of death and rejection by the Jewish leaders who resisted them. This did not involve one or two people but a whole host of leaders who left their mark on history, notably the former chief persecutor of the church, Paul. Both Peter and he, along with others such as the Lord's brother James, died for their belief in Jesus' resurrection.

Has Historical Criticism Proved the Bible False?

Thomas R. Schreiner

H istorical criticism of the Bible began in earnest in the eighteenth century, flowered in the nineteenth century, and became the dominant approach to the Scriptures in the twentieth century. Historical criticism has at times been rejected by conservatives because it has called into question the accuracy of the Bible. For example, most nineteenth century scholars who researched the life of Jesus provided rationalistic explanations of His miracles, with the result that the supernatural quality of miracles was denied. New Testament scholar F. C. Baur argued that the theologies of Peter and Paul contradicted one another if one read the NT historically. OT scholars, such as Julius Wellhausen, maintained that the Pentateuch was not actually written by Moses. Careful literary and historical study, it was claimed, indicated that the Pentateuch had various sources that were written over the period of hundreds of years, and that the final document was put together by an unknown editor.

Still, it is important to recognize that the rise of historical criticism has also benefited the church. The Christian faith is rooted in history. God has manifested Himself supremely in the person of Jesus Christ. He lived and ministered in a particular time and place—in Palestine in the third decade of the first century. As Christians, then, we believe that our faith is historically rooted. Paul insisted that Christians were foolish to believe in the Christian faith if the resurrection of Jesus did not actually occur (1Co 15:12-19). Hence, we have no fear of historical study but welcome it, for we believe historical research can assist us in understanding the message of the Scriptures.

The benefits of historical study are numerous. The meaning of obscure terms has been elucidated. The discovery of the Dead Sea Scrolls has cast light on the milieu in which the NT was birthed. Study of the ancient Near East and the Greco-Roman world has clarified the extent to which the Scriptures are similar and different from surrounding cultures. Historical criticism has also demonstrated that some traditional views were not credible. It was once thought that the NT was written in a special "Holy Ghost" language, but study of papyri and other sources from the era of the NT demonstrated that the NT was written in the common Greek of the day. The King James Version of the Bible was an outstanding product of the scholarship for its day, but we now have many more manuscripts for both the NT and the OT, and hence our modern English Bibles are even closer to the original today because of recent manuscript discoveries and the careful work of scholars in text criticism.

But historical criticism does suffer from liabilities. Many scholars who practiced historical criticism imbibed the Enlightenment philosophy sweeping Europe in the eighteenth and nineteenth centuries. Their anti-supernatural worldview masqueraded as objective historical criticism. As described above, they rejected the miracles of Jesus and provided rationalistic explanations. But scholars do not reject miracles on historical grounds. They have accepted a naturalistic philosophical standpoint that rules out miracles a priori. Rudolf Bultmann, for instance, virtually defines historical work in such a way that the acceptance of miracles is dogmatically excluded. When we read the NT, we see that credible historical reasons exist to support the resurrection of Christ, but many scholars refuse even to consider the evidence, for they are antecedently convinced that resurrections cannot happen. This fundamental bias, i.e., naturalistic philosophy, is all too often cloaked as "objective history."

Historical criticism hoped that it would succeed where orthodoxy failed. In the sixteenth and seventeenth centuries, orthodox Christians debated the interpretation of the Bible, leading to several different theological systems (Lutheranism, Calvinism, Arminianism). Historical critics believed they were more objective and that by means of a "neutral" scientific approach they could discover what the Bible really taught. But with the arrival of postmodernism this view seems rather naïve to scholars today. And the record of historical criticism reveals that it did not succeed in agreeing upon "the assured results of scholarship." Indeed, a dizzying array of viewpoints and perspectives are present in historical criticism today, and many of them are mutually contradictory.

The work of F.C. Baur and Julius Wellhausen threatened the faith of evangelical believers in the nineteenth century. Yet very few scholars today embrace the conclusions of Baur, and the documentary hypothesis of Wellhausen is severely questioned. The "assured results" of scholarship in one generation are often vigorously challenged by the next. Evangelicals, of course, should be open to correction. Perhaps we have misread some parts of the Bible because of our tradition. On the other hand, we need to be critical and savvy, and reject the temptation of embracing the latest fad in scholarship just because it is current.

Though evangelical scholars have often solved problems raised by historical critics, conservatives have not solved them all. This does not mean the Scriptures are inaccurate in such instances, but that we could resolve such problems if we had enough information. To make such a claim is not a sacrifice of one's intellect. Comprehensive answers are lacking in every historical discipline since the evidence is fragmentary. We can be grateful to historical criticism since it has helped us understand the Scriptures better. But we must also be on our guard. Often historical criticism has veered off into unsubstantiated allegations about the accuracy of the Scriptures, and it has routinely approached the Scriptures with an anti-supernatural worldview. Historical criticism has not demonstrated the Bible to be false. The Bible rightly interpreted has stood the test of time.

What About "Gospels" Not In Our New Testament?

Graham H. Twelftree

The four Gospels in our Bible had all been written by the end of the first century. Apparently no other gospels were written by this time. By the last 20 years of the second century, when Irenaeus the Bishop of Lyon was writing, the four Gospels had been widely and firmly established for some time as the only ones accepted by mainstream Christianity. However, many sections of the Church did not use all of them.

Irenaeus argued against accepting other gospels, such as the Gospel of Truth, alleged to have been written by the Gnostic teacher Valentinus. He said it had only recently been written and "did not agree in any respect with the Gospels of the apostles." This gospel is a homily or meditation and does not resemble our canonical gospels in telling of the activities and teaching of Jesus, including His appearances after Easter. The same is true of the Gospel of Philip, an anthology of sayings from the mid-fourth century, as well as the second-century Greek Gospel of the Egyptians, about which we know little save that it was apparently a collection of sayings. The Gospel of Thomas, which also contains a collection of sayings of Jesus (some of which may be historically authentic) along with minimal narrative material, has been argued to be early. However, because of parallels with literature of this period, many date it late in the second century. More fanciful gospels include the Infancy Gospel of Thomas with its miracles conducted by the child Jesus, ending with the story from Luke of the twelve-year-old Jesus in the temple.

Other gospels approximate those in our canon. For example, the Gospel of Peter came from the middle of the second century. From the fragmentary evidence we have, it told of the trial of Jesus, His crucifixion, and His appearing to a group of His followers. Also, the Gospel of the Ebionites, from Syria in the same period, is a harmony of Matthew, Mark, and Luke. Later in the century Tatian produced a widely used harmony of all four gospels, the *Diatessaron*, which was highly valued particularly in Syria. From papyrus fragments we also have evidence of a handful of other gospels from as early as the second century. A letter of Clement of Alexandria (c. 150–c. 215) discovered in 1958, which tells of a "secret gospel" of Mark, may be a modern forgery.

The Gospel of Hebrews, written before the mid-second century, perhaps in Egypt for Greek-speaking Jewish Christians, was the only gospel apart from the four in our Bible that was ever considered part of the canon by sections of orthodox Christianity. The few remaining quotations of it show it probably began with Jesus' preexistence and included His descent from heaven and subsequent birth. Jesus describes Himself as the son of the Holy Spirit and reports His temptation. There are also examples of His teaching. During the Last Supper, James the brother of Jesus, says he will not eat again until he has seen the risen Jesus. There was probably a story of the burial of Jesus, and those who guarded the tomb may have witnessed the resurrection. As anticipated, there is a story of Jesus appearing to James, reinforcing James's importance to this gospel. Gnostic characteristics, divergence from the biblical gospels, and lack of any connection with an apostle may account for its eventually being excluded from the NT by mainstream Christianity.

Could the Gospel Writers Withstand the Scrutiny of a Lawyer?

John Warwick Montgomery

L awyers distinguish between *making claims* (almost anyone can file a lawsuit) and *proving the case* (which is possible only on the basis of good evidence). Lawyers, therefore, are in the evidence business and will not accept any claim (including religious claims) without good reason to do so. It is highly significant, then, that throughout history so many great lawyers, judges, and legal scholars have come to Christian belief.

This is due in large part to the solidity of the Gospel testimony to Jesus Christ. The Gospel records qualify under the "ancient documents rule" and would be admitted as evidence in any common law court. They assert that they are first-hand, non-hearsay testimony to Jesus Christ (1Jn 1:1, etc.) or are the product of careful research concerning him (Lk 1:1-4). Documents, like defendants, are innocent until proven guilty, and the critics have not been able to impugn the credibility of the Gospels.

The soundness of the four Gospels depends upon their early dating and their authorship by those who knew Jesus personally. Corroboration outside the Gospels comes by way of such early writers as Papias, who was a student of the Apostle John. Papias tells us that the four Gospels were written either by an apostle (Matthew and John) or by an apostle's associate (Mark with Peter, Luke with Paul). The Gospels were in circulation, then, while hostile witnesses of Jesus' ministry were still alive. As F. F. Bruce has argued, these opponents were the functional equivalent of modern cross-examiners: they had the means, the motive, and the opportunity to refute the Gospel accounts of Jesus' miraculous ministry if it had not happened just as the Gospel writers say it did. Since the opposition could not do that, the Gospel narratives stand as powerful evidence that the miraculous picture of Jesus they convey is accurate.

The fact that the first three Gospels were written prior to the fall of Jerusalem in A.D. 70 and the Gospel of John not long thereafter, makes impossible the attempt of liberal Bible critics and secularists to argue that they are the product of a developing oral tradition in which the early church modified Jesus' life and teachings. There was simply insufficient time for doing this. A. N. Sherwin-White has pointed out that the case for accurate reporting is far better in the case of the Jesus of the Gospels than for the best-known contemporary of Christ, Tiberius Caesar, whose career is also known from just four sources.

Harvard professor Simon Greenleaf, the greatest common-law authority on the law of evidence in the nineteenth century, wrote, "All that Christianity asks of men on this subject is [that the testimony of the Gospels] be sifted as it were given in a court of justice. . . . The probability of the veracity of the witnesses and of the reality of the occurrences which they relate will increase, until it acquires, for all practical purposes, the value and force of demonstration."

Aren't the Gospels the Product of Greek Thinking?

Ronald Nash

For more than a century, liberal critics of the Christian faith have been claiming that early Christianity was heavily influenced by Platonism, Stoicism, the pagan mystery religions, or other movements in the Hellenistic world. A series of scholarly books and articles had refuted most of these claims by the 1940s. But new generations of liberal scholars have revived many of these older discredited positions.

The favorite target among the four Gospels has been the Gospel of John. Critics say John 1:1-18 was influenced by a Jewish thinker named Philo who lived in Alexandria, Egypt. Rudolf Bultman made a career of claiming that parts of John's Gospel were influenced by Gnosticism and/or various mystery religions. Such influences allegedly extended to the Apostle Paul as well.

Thinking people should ask the following questions of all claims about any alleged dependence of early Christianity upon pagan sources: (1) What is the evidence for such claims? (2) What are the dates for the evidence? An embarrassingly high amount of the alleged evidence turns out to be dated long after the writing of the NT. (3) Is the language used to describe the supposed evidence faithful to the original source material, or does it include interpretive material such as Christian language, themes, or imagery? (4) Are the alleged parallels really similar, or are the likenesses a result of exaggeration, over simplification, inattention to detail, or the use of Christian language in the description? (5) Is the alleged parallel between the NT and a supposed pagan source the sort of thing that could have arisen independently in several different movements? (6) Is the claim of influence or dependence consistent with the historical information we have about the first-century church?

Origins of the Gospel: Human Ideas or Divine Revelation?

Jeremy Royal Howard

I s the NT merely a reflection of the religious ideas of the men who wrote it, or is it actually God's revelation? This question has circulated among scholars of religion for over a century, and many of them have answered that the NT is a reflection of religious *idea* rather than divine revelation. Two factors lead them to this conclusion: First, they presuppose that God either does not exist or does not speak if He does exist. Second, they believe similarities between the NT and religious and philosophical ideas from the Greek world make it appear that authors of the NT were inspired more by Greek philosophers than by God.

The Christian will immediately reject the first of these two factors, for we believe in God and are not predisposed to doubt that He communicates through Scripture. It is the second factor that seems more threatening. Are there vital similarities between the NT and the musings of the Greek world, and if so, does this indicate that the NT is a manmade idea rather than divine revelation?

The world of ideas is like a vast web stretching across time and culture. Each idea is connected to and influenced by a multitude of other ideas. Original ideas are hard to come by; genuinely independent ideas are essentially nonexistent. Even ideas that change the world are little more than the rearrangement and reapplication of previously existing ideas. For example, in 1769 Nicolas Cugnot invented the automobile. Powered by steam, Cugnot's three-wheeled machine carried four passengers at a speed of two miles per hour. Cugnot's idea was revolutionary, but it was nevertheless dependent on his prior knowledge of wheels, carriages and mechanized motion. The similarity of the automobile to such things as the horse carriage indicates that Cugnot simply adapted and advanced previously existing ideas, and illustrates the fact that even the most innovative of ideas does not require a supernatural explanation. All one need do to explain an idea's origin is examine the relevant historical and cultural contexts and discover what things led to its formulation.

Is the NT merely an innovative religious idea? That the NT and the Greeks used similar terminology and conceptions for such things as the soul, wisdom, and reason is taken by some scholars as an indication that the NT borrowed ideas that were common to the age and simply reshaped them. This means that the gospel marked a new, manmade religious idea rather than a revelation from God.

What are we to say to this? To begin with, by its own testimony the Bible is a revelation of God and not merely the religious speculations of creative men. Recall the "This is the Lord's declaration . . ." formula found throughout the OT, and Christ's commissioning of the apostles to speak His gospel in the infallible power of the Spirit in the NT. But what about the fact that the NT evinces some similarity with Greek thought? Does this indicate that the Bible is human rather than divine in authorship? No, it does not. We understand that divine revelation must make use of ideas that are common to mankind, else God's communication to us would be entirely mysterious and incomprehensible. Imagine God telling us about Himself without making use of ideas with which we are familiar! If He tells us He is a loving Father, we understand what He means because we already understand the ideas of love and fatherhood. What makes revelation unique from idea, therefore, is not that revelation does not utilize idea, but that revelation is of God rather than man, and that in revelation previously existing ideas are adopted or modified by God and thereby used as tools to make His communication of new information comprehensible. That the NT contains concepts that are similar to Greek thought is not altogether surprising to us, for it indicates that God has deigned to reveal Himself using words and concepts that could be understood in the Greek-dominated NT era. Therefore, we are justified to say the NT is God's revelation and not man's religious invention so long as the common ground between the NT and Greek thought is not highly pronounced. It is on this point that many non-Christian scholars attempt to make their case. They claim that the NT bears striking resemblance to other religious ideas of the Greek era.

Is the New Testament Greek? Allegations that the NT is dependent on Greek ideas are more than a century old. It is said that the NT borrowed certain of its elements from Greek philosophy, Greek mystery religion, or Greek Gnosticism. These theories has been roundly refuted and are no longer considered legitimate by the majority of scholars. Nevertheless, these and similar allegations still find audience among those who wish to portray Christianity as human idea rather than divine revelation. We will examine these allegations and explain why they are without merit.

Presupposing that God either does not exist or does not communicate with man, several scholars claimed in the early twentieth century that the NT had taken some of its most significant ideas from Greek philosophy. For instance, it was said that the apostle Paul's desire to be rescued from his "body of death" indicated that he taught Platonic dualism, wherein all material things are held to be evil, and the good, immaterial human soul is imprisoned by the evil, material human body. But as Christian philosopher Ronald H. Nash says in The Gospel and the Greeks, a responsible reading of Paul reveals no such teaching. For Paul the body is a wonderful creation of Holy God that we humans have tainted with our sins. His wishing to be set free from his body is an expression of his desire to be away from sin and at home with the Lord who restores purity to both soul and body.

What about the role Greek mystery religion supposedly played in shaping Christianity? Some have said that NT's teachings about Christ's divinity, resurrection, and believer's baptism were borrowed from several such religions, for these commonly emphasized secret ceremonies and the heroic actions of mythic mediators. For instance, in the cult of Mithra—the most important of the mystery religions—the universe is portrayed as the battleground between good and evil gods. It was said that our souls have fallen from celestial glory and are now imprisoned in our bodies, and that our only hope for restoration is to fight alongside Mithra, the god who seeks to overcome evil and save mankind. But are there any real parallels with the NT here? Mithra was never purported to be anything other than a myth by even his most devout followers, and his myth did not include any such thing as his dying for humanity's sins. Additionally, the NT teaches neither materialistic dualism nor polytheism. Besides these major points, all evidence indicates that Mithraism did not even exist until well after the NT was written. If similarities exist between the two religions, it is Mithraism that borrowed from Christianity, not vice versa. These and other problems also apply to the contention that other varieties of mystery religion influenced Christianity.

Finally, what of the allegation that Greek Gnosticism shaped NT teachings? Taking its name from the Greek word for "knowledge" (*gnosis*), Gnosticism taught that a mythic redeemer was sent to earth from heaven to offer us salvation by sharing with us the secret knowledge of our former and forgotten state—namely that our pure souls once preexisted in heaven and are now trapped in evil bodies. You see by now that body-spirit dualism runs throughout Greek thought. Scholars who claim that the NT is dependent on Gnosticism fail to recognize the fact that NT doctrine is radically opposed to such dualism. There is but one God according to Christianity, and He made all things to be good, whether they be material or immaterial. There is also the problem of chronology again—Gnosticism did not come to mature expression until after the writing of the NT.

In each allegation cited above, superficial similarities between Christianity and Greek sources are inflated many times over and are thereafter portrayed as evidence against Christian revelation, while obvious dissimilarities are glossed over or completely ignored. What few similarities that do exist are minimal, and these count only as evidence that God has graciously communicated truth in terms that were understandable in the NT era.

Isn't that Just *Your* Interpretation?

Paul Copan

F ew things are more frustrating than carefully presenting reasons for the meaning of a text—biblical or otherwise—only to be casually dismissed with "That's just *your* interpretation!" Whether Scripture, history, literature, or politics are under scrutiny, we witness people reducing meaning to personal interpretation or perspective. They follow Nietzsche by saying, "There are no facts—only interpretations"?

But isn't *that* statement presented as a fact—not just an interpretation? Many claim that conclusions about abortion are just matters of "interpretation" or "perspective," but they give the impression that if you disagree with them, you're wrong. To deny objectivity is to assume something's objectively true for all people: "Everything is a matter of interpretation whether or not you agree with my statement." We have only two alternatives: triviality ("It's all perspective including mine"—so why believe it?) or incoherence ("Everything's a matter of perspective except mine"—making a person an exception to his own rule).

Most people appeal to "interpretation" because they don't like another alternative. "Interpretation" is often a smokescreen for pursuing one's own agenda or autonomy. To better discern whether this is so, we can ask: "Do you mean that you *don't like* my interpretation or that you have *good reasons* for disagreeing?" Other questions worth asking are: "Can a perspective *ever* be correct? Are some things *not* a matter of perspective (such as a flat earth versus a round earth)? How can you know that your interpretation and my interpretation are actually different?"

Even if we don't always get things right, we can discern that some perspectives better approximate the truth than others. We generally tend to trust the *Wall Street Journal* over tabloids—even though good newspapers may be wrong at points. The fact that we can recognize some interpretations as more plausible than others (and thus more likely true) indicates that not everything is a matter of interpretation. Therefore, we must be willing to give non-arbitrary reasons for the most plausible position. After all, if everything is perspective, how can we distinguish between reasonable and wacky ideas?

Despite our limitations, we still cannot escape objectivity. To deny its possibility is to affirm its actuality. Even the "perspectivist" believes those disagreeing with him are objectively wrong.

Numbers in the Bible

Kirk E. Lowery

The modern reader of the Bible—especially of the OT—often finds its use of numbers strange. The ancient world did not use numbers for every aspect of life. Their technology did not require many places past the decimal point of precision, or even a decimal point at all. The Bible has been closely read and interpreted by many cultures through more than four millennia. So the modern reader reads these ancient texts through the lens of all this history of interpretation. How others in the past have interpreted the numbers of the Bible influences a reader's understanding. How ought the numbers found in the Bible to be understood? They are to be understood in the same way that any other part of the text is understood: by how they are used and by keeping in mind both the textual context in which numbers occur and also the cultural context of how numbers were used by those ancient societies with which Israel lived and interacted.

Assyria, Egypt, Greece, and Rome used the decimal system for numbers. That is, numbers were expressed in base 10. ("Number" refers to the mathematical entity of quantity. "Numeral" refers to the symbol used to represent a number.) Sumerians and ancient Babylonians used the sexagesimal system, base 60, which is not unfamiliar to us since we use it every day—our system of timekeeping and navigation uses the sexagesimal system: 60 seconds to one minute, 60 minutes to one hour; 360 degrees to a circle subdivided into 60 minutes/degree and 60 seconds/minute. The ancient Israelites used the decimal system, as did their immediate neighbors in Canaan. For the most part, the major inscriptions of early Israel write out the numbers by words—"ten" rather than "10"—as is also true of the OT itself. There is no instance of symbols being used, but all numbers are written out as words. The earliest (c. 140 B.C.) use of the Hebrew alphabet for numerals is to be found on Maccabean coins.

How did the biblical writers use numbers? They used them to count things and people. They used them for weights, measures, and time. They were familiar with arithmetic: addition (Gn 5:3-31; Nm 1:20-46), subtraction (Gn 18:26ff), and multiplication (Lv 25:8; Nm 3:46ff). Arithmetic processes are not mentioned in the NT. The frequent use of fractions shows a basic understanding of division: half (Ex 24:6); one fourth (Neh 9:3; Rv 6:8); one fifth (Gn 47:24); a tenth (Nm 18:26). Numbers are important in Daniel, Ezekiel, and Revelation. In summary, the biblical writers used numbers literally, rhetorically, and symbolically. They are never used mystically. Each use is addressed in turn below.

When the Bible uses numbers in the ordinary way, do they mean what they apparently mean? Some interpreters suppose that since the biblical writers were "prescientific," the numbers are not to betaken seriously. This supposition is flawed, however, for many non-scientific cultures record numbers that can be taken perfectly seriously (such as the astronomical observations of the Babylonians or the administrative records of the ancient Egyptians). The use of numbers is very culture-specific: Some languages have only the numbers "one, two, many," because they do not need greater precision than that. Modern society is permeated with numbers for every conceivable aspect of life. The ancient world was not that way. The ancients did not give a unique number to their citizens, did not number their roads, etc. But regardless of the level of technological development, every society has to deal with numbers in a real way to function. For some, the system may be simple, for others, very complex. Ancient Israel was no exception; tolls and taxes were recorded, and censuses were taken.

The biblical writers often used round numbers, a fact that should be noted in questions of reliability and trustworthiness of the biblical record. For example, we find "a hundred" (and "100") used as a round number (Gn 26:12; Lv 26:8; 2Sm 24:3; Ec 8:12; Mt 19:29), as well as "a thousand" (Dt 1:11; 7:9). The word "about" often precedes rounded numbers: "about 3,000 men" (Ex 32:28). On the other hand, numbers which could be interpreted as rounded numbers are often intended as actual amounts: "1,000 pieces of silver" (Gn 20:16). In general, one should assume a number is not rounded unless there is reason to believe otherwise. Smaller numbers are less likely to be rounded than larger ones. Much ink has been spilled debating the meaning of large numbers in the Bible. There are the large, indefinite numbers, and these do not present an interpretive problem. The highest recorded numbers are one million (2Ch 14:9), ten thousand times ten thousand (Dn 7:10), thousands of thousands (Rv 5:11), and 200 million (Rv 9:16), the highest number recorded.

The long life spans of the pre-flood patriarchs have been compared to the Sumerian king list, whose life spans are recorded in the tens of thousands of years. The Sumerian kings' life spans have been called "mythical," so why not the biblical patriarchs' ages? After all, everyone knows humans rarely live beyond 100 years, never mind 500 or 1,000. The actual fact is that we don't know. The Sumerian king list records life spans on an order of magnitude greater than the biblical names. If both reflect a tradition about antediluvian times, what they may both be saying is that those ancient people lived an extraordinarily long time. Some have suggested that environmental conditions could explain it; others suggest mankind's closer proximity to its original sinless estate explains it. We just don't know how to explain the apparently impossible life spans. What we have is a witness (the Bible) that has proved trustworthy too often to dismiss.

The Bible records the number of men capable of bearing arms at the time of the exodus to be 603,550 (Nm 1:46). From this, it has been calculated that the entire population leaving Egypt would be about two million. Could such a number survive in the wilderness? The answer is no. Neither could a hundredth of that many survive on their own. It required God's provision because that part of the world would have been simply unable to support large numbers of nomads, especially without modern farming methods and technology. It required God to actively intervene in Israel's physical history in order for them to leave Egypt and subsequently survive. That is the point of the Exodus narrative.

There have been various attempts to reduce the real numbers of the exodus by understanding the Hebrew term for "thousand" (*eleph*) as "captain" or "family, clan." There is evidence for this use of the term in Nm 1:16; Jdg 6:15; 1Sm 10:19; and Mc 5:2. But in the census lists of the book of Numbers, the numbers of the tribes is calculated in terms of thousands, hundreds, and fifties. Gad, for example, numbered 45,650 (Nm 1:25). And the total given to Israel's army (Nm 1:46) can only be arrived at if we calculate using *eleph* as meaning "thousand." Difficult to explain or not, the text is clear as to its intended meaning.

Numbers are also used in the Bible for rhetorical effect. They are used for contrast in poetic parallelism: "As they celebrated, the women sang: Saul has killed his thousands, but David his tens of thousands" (1Sm 18:7). Perhaps the most common is to use the formula $x \ldots x + 1$ to express progression, intensification, completion, or some sort of climax: "The LORD says: I will not relent from punishing Israel for three crimes, even four . . ." (Am 2:6). Amos used the phrase in a string of condemnations of the sins of the surrounding lands. By using the same phrase for Israel and Judah, he was saying "you are no better than they," and so had a stronger impact upon his audience. The $x \ldots x + 1$ formula is also used in the NT (e.g., Mt 18:20). Perhaps the most popular interpretation of numbers in the Bible is their symbolic meaning. The numbers 1, 3, 5, 7, 10, 12, and 40 among others have been assigned various meanings such as "unity," "perfection," "completion," and "generation." Where do these interpretations come from? The surprising fact is that only one number in the entire Bible is explicitly said to be symbolic: "Here is wisdom: The one who has understanding must calculate the number of the beast, because it is the number of a man. His number is 666" (Rv 13:18). Nowhere else are we told that numbers are used symbolically in any way. Any other symbolism for a number must be inferred from the biblical text itself by demonstrating a frequent association of a particular number with a particular concept. The only candidate for such an association is the number 7. And its usage is so diverse (seven days of creation; Jacob's seven years of service for Rachel; seven-fold curse of Cain; praising God seven times a day as in Ps 119:164) that it is hard to pin down a consistent meaning, but "completeness" or "perfection" appear to be the intended symbolism most of the time.

Where does all the other traditionally associated meanings and instances of symbolism come from? Modern lists of symbolic meanings of the biblical use of numbers most closely follow the system of meanings proposed by the sixth century B.C. Greek mathematician and philosopher, Pythagoras. Famous for his "Pythagorean Theorem," he also founded a religious cult with the belief that the "real" world was the realm of numbers and that those numbers explain why the physical world is the way it is. He speculated on the mystic and symbolic properties of numbers, which are the early origins of number theory. The Gnostics picked up his ideas in the apostolic and post-apostolic eras. Even the early church fathers were influenced by this approach to biblical interpretation, although not universally. Irenaeus (c. A.D. 140–200) classified it with other heresies: "Nor should they seek to prosecute inquiries respecting God by means of numbers, syllables, and letters. . . . For system does not spring out of numbers, but numbers from a system; nor does God derive His being from things made, but things made from God. For all things originate from one and the same God" (*Against Heresies,* Bk II:25:1). This is a direct refutation of Pythagorean metaphysics.

It is a small step from looking for symbolic meaning in numbers to seeking *hidden* meaning in numbers. After Alexander the Great conquered Palestine, Greek philosophies influenced Jewish thinking. From Pythagorean influence sprang Jewish *Gematria*, the system of interpretation that says there is hidden, intended meaning in the numeric values of a word. Since the Greeks had no separate writing system to express numerals, the ancients used Greek letters instead. Words could be broken up into letters, and mathematical operations could be done on the numeric values of those letters. Those numeric values were given mystical meanings loosely based upon Pythagorean numeric metaphysics described above. The Jews applied these procedures to the words of the Hebrew Bible using the letters of the Hebrew alphabet for numbers and claimed to discover hidden meaning and messages from God intended for the faithful. The church fathers were attracted to this form of interpretation of the Bible because of its apparent value in proving the inspiration and truth of the Scriptures. In this way, *Gematria* passed into Christian circles and is still practiced today by many.

There is no historical or archaeological evidence of any culture using letters for numerals before the Greeks. The human authors of the OT would have had no cultural model or literary form to suggest to them that they write a message in code. There is no hint in the Bible that there is any message encoded in the letters of the text. There is no procedure or mathematical operation common to the time of the writers of the Bible that the writers could conceivably expect a reader to know to use to discover the encoded meaning. We must conclude that the only way intelligible results can be obtained this way is by starting with the message one wishes to find! Then, using mathematical deduction, one proceeds to create the steps needed to get to that message from the numeric values of the biblical text, just like one would attempt to prove a theorem in number theory.

God's message of salvation for mankind was intended to be intelligible to everyone, of all ages and from all cultures. Certainly numbers in the Bible are sometimes difficult to understand, and there are "mysteries" about the future that are deliberately couched in ambiguous or symbolic wording. But at no time—with the one exception in Revelation noted above—is the reader exhorted to resort to mathematics. God does not speak to us in "code."

The Chronology of the Kings of Israel and Judah

Kirk E. Lowery

Whether it is a simple story or a complex history, a key element is all types of writing is time. It establishes cause and effect, act and consequence. The book of Kings is not exempt from the need to relate one event to another in time. The author traces the action of kings and rulers throughout time by recording the beginning, end, and duration of one reign after another. Modern readers naturally want to relate the chronology of Kings to the dating systems we use today so that we can relate the events narrated there to each other and to contemporaneous events in the lands surrounding ancient Israel and Judah, to recover the original context of those events.

Kings synchronizes the reigns of the northern and southern kingdoms of the Divided Monarchy as well as proving the number of years a king reigned. But there is a significant problem. These numbers and the synchronomies appear to be in constant contradiction with one another. It appears difficult if not impossible to create a chronology that accounts for all these numbers and agrees with established chronologies of the ancient near east. These conflicts have led many to conclude that the book of Kings cannot be a faithful witness to the history of Israel. If the writer got the numbers wrong, what else did he get wrong?

Here is an example of a problem: often the synchronomy given for the beginning of a reign does not correlate with the total number of years given for that reign. First Kings 15:25 says the reign of Nadab of Israel begins in the second year of Asa of Judah. First Kings 15:28 says Nadab died in the third year of Asa, that is, he reigned for one year. But 1 Kings 15:25 says he reigned for two years. This is one category of conflict. A second category of conflict is concerning the year a king is supposed to have begun his reign. Second Kings 3:1 says Joram began to reign in Israel in the eighteenth year of Jehoshaphat of

Judah. But 2 Kings 1:17 says he began to reign in the second year of Jehoram the son of Jehoshaphat. The sum of regnal years for Israel and Judah is a third source of discrepancy. The total number of years for the kings of Israel from Jehu through Pekahiah is 114 years and seven months. For the same period of time in Judah (from Athaliah through Azariah) the total comes to 128 years, a 14 year discrepancy. When we compare the sum of the regnal years for Israel as compared to the same period for Assyria, we find Israel's kings reigned 12 years longer than the Assyrian kings. And Judah's kings reigned longer by 25 years! Since the numbers do not match up, we must conclude that either someone made an error or the numbers mean something different than we suppose.

In 1951 Edwin Thiele published *The Mysterious Numbers of the Hebrew Kings* in which he presented solutions to the problems outlined above. His discoveries and principles used to harmonize the regnal years of Israel and Judah with an absolute chronology are summarized here.

In the northern kingdom, Israel, the regnal year was calculated from the month of Nisan in the spring, but in Judah, the regnal year began in the month of Tishri in the autumn. Both of these systems overlap the January new year of modern calendars. It must also be kept in mind that both calendar systems are lunar rather than the solar calendar used today, that is, each month consisted of exactly 30 days following the phases of the moon. An important consequence of all this is that a regnal year in Israel begins in the spring and will overlap parts of two regnal years in Judah which begin in the autumn. If a king of Judah came to the throne just before January, his accession year would synchronize with, for example, the third regnal year of a king in Israel. However, if the Judean King came to the throne six months later in the following summer, his accession year would synchronize with the fourth year of the Israelite king.

A second principle used to resolve numeric conflicts is to understand that the method of calculating the regnal years was different in the two kingdoms. Is the first year of a king to include a partial year up to the next new year, or is the first year of a king's reign to be calculated from the following new year's beginning? In the ancient near east, some countries followed the former method and others the latter. The former method is called "accession year" dating, and the partial year is not counted; it could be called "Year Zero." The latter method is called "non-accession year" dating, and counts any partial year as "Year 1." This means that nations using the non-accession year dating system are always one year ahead of those that use accession year dating. And for every new king, the years increase by one in absolute time. For non-accession year dating, one must subtract one year for every king, in order to keep in sync with absolute chronology.

Judah used the accession-year system for Rehoboam through Jehoshaphat; then the non-accession-year system was employed from Jehoram to Joash. Beginning with the next ruler, Amaziah, Judah returned to the accession-year system until the destruction of Jerusalem. In Israel, only the non-accession-year system was used throughout its history, that is from Jeroboam to Jehoahaz. For example, the total number of official years of reign for the Judean kings of Rehoboam through Jehoshaphat are 79, the total number of regnal years for the same period in Israel (Jeroboam through Ahaziah) is 86. But when we subtract one year for each of the seven kings of Israel because of Israel's use of the non-accession-year system, the final sum is 79 years, which agrees with the Judean record.

A further source of confusion is how the regnal years are reported. Since each nation had its own method of reporting (accession-year or non-accession-year), it reported the numbers of the other kingdom according to its own method. Thus, Rehoboam had a 17-year reign according to Judah's accession-year recording system, but Israel's non-accession-year system reckoned 18 years for Rehoboam. First Kings 15:25 says Nadab's rule over Israel began in the second year of Asa of Judah. Since Israel used a non-accession-year system, the second year of Asa would be the first year according to Judean accession-year dating. Depending upon which source the author was using, *The Book of the Chronicles of Israel* (1Kg 14:19) or *The Book of the Chronicles of Judah* (1Kg 14:29), the calculation of the regnal years and the synchronization between two kings must take these differences into account.

A fourth principle used to resolve regnal year numeric conflicts is to recognize that some reigns overlap (especially in Israel) and some kings were coregents (especially in Judah). Sometimes these overlappings and coregencies are mentioned explicitly in the text (e.g., 1Kg 16:21-23) in a form called "dual dating." More often, the overlapping reigns must be deduced and reconstructed. In all, nine overlapping reigns have been identified, six for Judah and three for Israel.

How is the relative chronology of the Hebrew kings correlated with contemporary historical events? Assyrian king-lists record an eclipse which astronomical calculations determine to have occurred on June 15, 763 B.C. This allows us to fix the absolute date of most of the Assyrian kings and hence the various events of their reigns from their court records. In the sixth year of Shalmaneser III, the Assyrians fought a coalition of Aramean kings (now modern Syria) called "the Battle of Qarqar" in 853 B.C., and among the names of the kings listed is Ahab of Israel. (This event is not recorded in the Bible.) In the eighteenth year of Shalmaneser III, in 841 B.C., Assyrian records show that Shalmaneser received tribute from Jehu, king of Israel. There are twelve years between the Battle of Qarqar and the receipt of Jehu's tribute and also twelve years between the death of Ahab and the ascension of Jehu (1Kg 22:51). Thus, Ahab died in 853 B.C. and Jehu ascended the throne in 841 B.C. This allows for further calculations of absolute dates for many other kings of Israel and Judah. Another synchronization from Assyrian records is the year 701 B.C. when Sennacherib of Assyria besieged Jerusalem during the fourteenth year of Hezekiah's reign (2Kg 18:13). From the Battle of Qarqar in 853 B.C. to Sennacherib's campaign against Hezekiah in 701 B.C. is a span of 152 years, according to Assyrian chronology. According to the properly calculated years of Israelite and Judean kings from the death of Ahab to the fourteenth year of Hezekiah is also 152 years, proving the synchronization and method of reckoning regnal years is correct.

The history of biblical studies in the twentieth century has shown again and again that major "problems" of the biblical record have been the result of modern ignorance of the ancient world. The resolution of the apparent conflicts of the chronology of the book of Kings shows the reliability and trustworthiness of the biblical record to the history of the ancient Near East.

Are the Biblical Genealogies Reliable?

Kenneth A. Mathews

Biblical genealogies must be understood in the context of how genealogies functioned in the ancient Near East. Typically, genealogies expressed more than family descent. They reflected political and socio-religious realities among people groups. For example, "Salma fathered Bethlehem" (1Ch 2:51) describes the founder of the village Bethlehem. Therefore, the genealogies were fluid, showing differences due to changing political and social realities.

The adoption of Joseph's sons Ephraim and Manasseh by Jacob created a new way of interpreting the twelve-tribe configuration (Gn 48:5). "Joseph" appears in the blessing of Jacob (Gn 49:22-26), but the blessing of Moses counts twelve tribes by deleting Simeon and dividing the house of Joseph into Ephraim and Manasseh (Dt 33:17). Thus, as we see from this example, the contents of genealogies were selective, not intended to be exhaustive and precise.

Shortening genealogies by omitting names was also commonplace. Matthew's genealogy of Jesus exhibits a schema in which three sets of fourteen generations are achieved (Mt 1:17). The number "fourteen" was desirable because of the importance attributed to the symbolic meaning of seven ("complete, perfect"). Thus, "Joram fathered Uzziah" (Mt 1:8) omits three generations (2Ch 21:4–26:33) so as to accomplish the desired number (cp. also Ezr 7:1-5 with 1Ch 6). From this example, we discover another unexpected feature in biblical genealogies. Genetic terms, such as "son of" and "father," were flexible in meaning, sometimes indicating a "descendant" and "grandfather or forefather." The word "daughter," for example, could mean a subordinate village affiliated with a nearby city, and thus can be translated "surrounding settlements" in Judges 1:27 (NIV). With these features in mind, when we study biblical genealogies we find that they are reliable.

One technique in the ancient world for legitimizing a new ruling king was through the concoction of a fictional ancestry. Moreover, scholars often assume that persons named in genealogies are metaphors for tribes and actually have no familial connection. The charge of fiction has been leveled against the genealogies of the twelve tribes of Israel as descended from the one person Jacob (e.g., Gn 46:8-27; Nm 1:20-43; 1Ch 2:1-2). The argument that the "sons of Jacob" reflect only an evolving social reality and not a reliable domestic one is an unnecessary assumption that contradicts the plain meaning of the biblical witness. The biblical account of the patriarchs reveals a family story primarily and a national one secondarily. Also, since genealogies impacted domestic, legal, and religious matters of importance, reliable genealogical records and censuses were fastidiously maintained (Nm 1:45; Ru 4:10; 1Ch 4:33; 9:1; Neh 7:5; cp. Nm 27:1-11; Ezr 2:62).

A special problem is the long life spans in Genesis 5:1-32 (e.g., Adam, 930 years). The Sumerian king list presents a list of the reigns of kings and includes a reference to a great flood. The king list claims fantastic numbers, the longest reign at 72,000 years. After the flood the regal years diminish. Despite its fantastic numbers, however, the king list includes historical individuals, not just legendary ones.

Both Genesis and the Sumerian king list remember a time in the hoary past when people lived long periods. The spans before Noah's flood are longer and afterward they gradually decrease. The long lives of the patriarchs, such as Adam and Noah, shrink to moderate figures when compared to the Sumerian king list. A significant difference is Adam's genealogy is not for political or antiquarian purposes, but shows that the descending ages of humanity are due to a moral factor when God judged a corrupt humanity (Gn 6:1-8).

Although the ages are reliable, this genealogy cannot be used to reconstruct the age of the earth. Genesis does not present genealogies for establishing absolute chronology (cp. 1Kg 6:1). Also, Genesis 5 does not possess a complete list. Genesis 5 and 11 exhibit ten-name genealogies that consist of stereotypical patterns. The two genealogies are also *linear*, meaning they include only one descendant per generation (*segmented* genealogies have more, Gn 10:1-32). Since genealogies may telescope generations (see above) and Genesis 5 is highly stylized, it is likely an "open" (selective) genealogy that spans many generations.

Did Those Places Really Exist?

E. Ray Clendenen

The ancient Egyptian equivalent of a "voodoo doll" was to write one's enemy's name on a clay statue or pottery vessel and then smash the pot to pieces while pronouncing a curse. Archaeologists have uncovered hundreds of inscribed pottery pieces dating to about the time of Joseph (nineteenth–eighteenth century B.C., Egyptian twelfth dynasty). These contain the names of many towns in Palestine and their rulers considered at the time to be enemies of the Egyptian state. Many of these are towns mentioned in the Bible, which underlines the authenticity of the biblical account. They also verify that cities were ruled at the time by "kings."

Some of the towns identified are Acco (Jdg 1:31), Aphek (Jos 12:18), Achshaph (Jos 11:1), Ashkelon (Jos 13:3), Beth-shean (Jos 17:11,16), Beth-shemesh (Jos 15:10), Bozrah (Gn 36:33), Damascus (Gn 14:15; 15:2), Ekron (Jos 13:3), Laish (Jdg 18:29), Midian (Ex 2:15-16), Migdol (Ex 14:2; Nm 33:7), Rehob (Nm 13:21; Jos 19:28,30), Shechem (Gn 12:6; 33:18; 37:12-14), Byblos, and Jerusalem (Jos 10:1).

Although not referring to the Patriarch of Israel, the name *Aburahana* as an Egyptian transcription of a Semitic name is also found in these texts (*m* and *n* often interchange in such transcriptions). The Hebrew word *chanikim*, rendered "trained," found in the Bible only in Genesis 14:14, is also found in the execration texts, supporting the credibility of the Genesis 14 account.

Is the Old Testament Trustworthy?

Walter C. Kaiser Jr.

W hat is a modern reader of the OT to do with a book that teaches animal sacrifice, male circumcision, strange dietary codes and festivals based on an agricultural cycle? Its contents appear to be so ancient and so removed from our day that some easily dismiss it as a "primitive religion!" Contrary to such a premature judgment, seven affirmations show that the OT is relevant and altogether trustworthy.

1. **In every part of the OT the writers claim the divine origin of their writings.** One instance of such inspired utterances comes from the core of the OT: the Ten Commandments. Here we learn that the stone tablets on which the commandments were written were "inscribed by the finger of God" (Ex 31:18; cp. Dt 5:22). More regularly, however, God spoke through people. "The Spirit of the LORD spoke through me, His word was on my tongue" (2Sm 23:2). Indeed, Nathan the prophet knew that he had spoken his own words, which were not the same as the words from divine revelation. When he spoke God's message, he prefaced it, as did the OT prophets repeatedly, with, "This is what the LORD says" (2Sm 7:5). Even in the wisdom books of the OT, Agur introduced himself as deficient and ignorant. He complained: "I am more stupid than any other man, and I lack man's ability to understand. I have not gained wisdom, and I have no knowledge of the Holy One" (Pr 30:2-3). So how, then, would he know how or what to write about God? He asked the same questions in verse 4. But by verses 5-6 he had the answer: "Every word of God is pure . . . Don't add to His words,

or He will rebuke you, and you will be proved a liar." The first part of verse 5 is a quote from David's Psalm (18:30), while verse 6 is a quote from Deuteronomy 4:2.

2. **The 39 books of the OT were immediately received as authoritative and canonical.** One of the most popular misconceptions is that a group of scholars held a rabbinical council in Jamnia in A.D. 90 to decide which books they would regard as authoritative for composing the OT. But this is incorrect, for (1) the council's decisions had no binding authority; (2) the discussions at that council were merely about the correct interpretations of Ecclesiastes and Song of Solomon; and (3) the list of books they regarded as canonical were already treated as these same thirty-nine books in our current OT. Instead, the books of the OT were *progressively recognized* by those closest to the writers of the OT that what they wrote was indeed a revelation from God. Daniel, writing about 75 years after the prophet Jeremiah, regarded Jeremiah's prophecy about the seventy-year captivity (Jer 25:11-12) as "the word of the LORD" (Dn 9:2). In fact, he places Jeremiah among "the books," i.e., he placed Jeremiah's recent book in the group of books called the "Scriptures."

3. **The text of the OT books was uniquely preserved when compared with other ancient writings.** Prior to the discovery of the Dead Sea Scrolls in A.D. 1947, we were limited to the Greek text of the Septuagint, the Samaritan Pentateuch, and the Hebrew text of the Nash Papyrus dating from around A.D. 1000 for checking on the accuracy of the preservation of the OT text. That has all changed now. In the 800 exemplars of OT biblical texts in the Dead Sea Scrolls, we now possess texts from 250 B.C. to A.D. 50. Moreover, the earliest example of an OT text is Numbers 6:24-26 from the mid-seventh century B.C. in the Ketef Hinnom Plaques. So carefully preserved are these texts that when we studied the Dead Sea Scroll of Isaiah, only three minor spelling changes (comparable to the difference between spelling "Saviour" and "Savior") were found in a text that covers about 100 pages in many English translations. That is an outstanding record of preserving the text of the Bible, which represents over a 1000 years of copying the text.

4. **The historical chronology found in the histories of the kings of Israel and Judah is completely verified and trustworthy.** If chronology is the backbone of history, then it was necessary for someone to untangle the dates and systems of correlations between the kings of northern Israel and Judah if any confidence, much less sense, was to come out of these scores of numbers in Kings and Chronicles. But that is what Edwin Thiele did as his doctoral dissertation for the University of Chicago. He first established as an absolute date (on our

Julian calendar) June 15, 763 B.C. from the astronomical citations on the Assyrian Eponym, or Man of the Year, lists. These annual lists also made allusions to several of the Hebrew kings, thereby providing excellent synchronisms. From there he was able to show how some 500 numbers (all except one, which was later solved) were easily reconciled and totally trustworthy in every detail.

5. **Archaeology has helped to show that the culture, persons, and events of the OT are trustworthy.** Archaeology has done much to further the cause of showing the reliability of the OT. Where there were alleged missing persons mentioned in the OT, but not known from external sources, such as King Sargon in Isaiah 20, or a Governor Sanballat of Samaria (Neh 2:10), or Kings David, Ahab, Jehu, Hezekiah, Menahem, and even a prophet Balaam, in each case spectacular finds have vindicated the claims of the OT. In like manner, where the OT claimed there were peoples such as the Hittites or the Horites, later finds vindicated the presence of these as well as other alleged missing peoples. A similar list of alleged missing places could be gathered, such as the land of Ophir, or the sites along the trans-Jordanian route of the wilderness wanderings. But once again archaeology has given great help here as well. This is not to say that all of those alleged by critics to have been created by the OT have been fully identified. We still cannot find the external validation for "Darius the Mede" (Dn 5:31). But the success of archaeology in the twentieth century alone is startling in its extent and in the depth of its influence.

6. **The present literary form of the books comes to us from the times they purport to represent.** No section of the OT has received more critical dissecting than the first five books of Moses, the Pentateuch. It was alleged that the books did not come by divine inspiration to Moses around 1400 B.C., but rather came from the hands of at least four main compilers (called J, E, D, and P) ranging from the eighth century to 400 B.C. when final editing was supposedly done! At the heart of this theory was the book of Deuteronomy, which critical scholars claimed was first written in 621 B.C. when King Josiah found the Book of the Law. But Deuteronomy exhibits the same literary format that is unique to the middle of the second Millennium B.C. Hittite Suzerainty Treaties (c. 1200–1400 B.C.) with the same six sections to these treaties that are found in the book of Deuteronomy. Had Deuteronomy been compiled, as the critics claim, in the first millennium (621 B.C.), the same Assyrian treaties had by that time deleted two of the six sections. Thus, according to the literary forms and criteria of the critics themselves, the key book in the disputed first five books must be placed in the days when Moses lived (i.e., around 1400 B.C.).

7. **The writers of the OT were aware that they were writing not only for their generation, but also for those who would come later.** The most convenient way to demonstrate this is to go to 1 Peter 1:10-12, where Peter stated, "It was revealed to them [the prophets of the OT] that they were not serving themselves but you [people of Peter's generation and us]."

How Has Archaeology Corroborated the Bible?

Walter C. Kaiser Jr.

The past century or so has witnessed some of the most remarkable archaeological discoveries of the Christian era. No single discipline has contributed as much as archaeology to the interpretation and delight of reading the Bible.

However, the discipline has had its embarrassing moments as well. For example, in 1929 Sir Leonard Wooley declared while excavating in Mesopotamia, "I have found the flood!" Unfortunately for him and for the discipline of archaeology, there were embarrassed faces when other layers of flood sediment turned up at various strata throughout the area. Others have claimed to have found the location of the Garden of Eden, the Ark of the Covenant and the like, but such claims must not be confused with real and legitimate discoveries throughout the ancient Near East.

The real role of archaeology is not to "prove" the Bible, for that kind of "proof" is available only in certain deductive sciences such as mathematics and logic. On the contrary, the role of archaeology is: (1) to supply cultural, epigraphic, and artifactual materials that provide the background for accurately interpreting the Bible, (2) to anchor the events of the biblical text in the history and geography of the times, and (3) to build confidence in the revelation of God where the truths of Scripture impinge on historical events.

Over the last century or so archaeology has strengthened the case for biblical reliability. Missing individuals, peoples, places, and obscure customs, historical and political settings have been helpfully identified.

Missing Individuals. It had been fashionable in some circles for many years to ridicule Isaiah 20:1 for its allusion to "Sargon king of Assyria." Excavations of Nineveh had seemingly revealed all the kings of Assyria, but there was no Sargon. The Bible must have gotten it wrong. However, in 1843, Paul Emile Botta found a virgin site northeast of Nineveh, later excavated by the University of Chicago and published in the 1930s. Sargon had built there his own capital in 717 B.C. His son, however, moved the capital back to Nineveh, so the site was lost as was Sargon's name. Now Sargon is one of the best known Assyrian monarchs.

Likewise, the Bible contended that King Belshazzar was the final ruler of Babylon (Dn 5:1,30), but until A.D. 1929 the extra-biblical evidence pointed to Nabonidus as king at the Fall of Babylon in 539 B.C. This apparent conflict was solved when documents were discovered revealing that Nabonidus spent his time in Arabia, leaving the affairs of the kingdom to his eldest son Belshazzar, who reigned as co-regent for a decade or so.

Discoveries of other biblical names have confirmed biblical reliability, including King Jehoiachin's presence in Babylon, Sanballat as governor of Samaria along with some of Nehemiah's adversaries such as Tobiah the Ammonite, and Geshem the Arab (Neh 2:19). Other discoveries confirm the well-known biblical individuals Balaam, David, Ahab, Jehu, Hezekiah, Menahem, and others.

Missing Peoples. Until Hugo Winckler discovered the Hittite empire in 1906, many unbelievers doubted the Bible's insistence that the Hittites were part of the land of Canaan (Gn 10:15; Jos 1:4). Now they are so well documented that a score of volumes has been necessary to build a Hittite dictionary based on the tablets left in their civilization.

Another mystery group were the Horites, descendants of Esau from Edom (Gn 36:20; Dt 2:12,22). But in 1995 Giorgio Buccellati discovered the Horite capital city beneath the modern Syrian city of Tell Mozan.

Missing Places. First Kings 9:28 claimed King Solomon brought back sixteen tons of gold from Ophir. But where was Ophir and did it really exist? In 1956 at Tell Qasile in Israel, broken pottery was found with an inscription referring to a shipment of "gold of Ophir for Beth-Horon, thirty shekels." Thus, Ophir was confirmed as known in the world of commerce with its trade in gold. Ophir is identified today as a port some sixty miles north of Bombay.

Another example is the disputed list of sites along the route of the exodus in Numbers 33. But Charles Krahmalkov noted three ancient Egyptian maps of the road from Arabah to the Plains of Moab, with the earliest of the three maps inscribed on the walls of Karnak in the reign of Thutmosis III (c.1504–1450 B.C.). According to this list, the route from south to north follows precisely the way the Israelites listed in Numbers 33 with four stations especially noted: Iyyim, Dibon, Abel, and Jordan.

Other Sensational Finds. Discovered by Grenfeld in Egypt in 1920, the "John Rylands Papyrus" yielded the oldest known fragment of a NT manuscript. This small scrap from John's Gospel (Jn 18:31-33,37-38) was dated by papyrologists to 125 A.D., but since it was so far south into Egypt, it successfully put an end to the then-popular attempt to late-date John's Gospel to the second century rather than to the traditional first century date of A.D. 85–90.

The Dead Sea Scrolls, found in 1948 in caves at Qumran, near the northwest end of the Dead Sea, gave us some 800 manuscripts of every book (in part or the whole) of the OT except for Esther. Prior to that, the earliest Hebrew texts dated to around A.D. 1000, but the Scrolls at Qumran are generally more than one thousand years older! These Hebrew texts illustrate that 1000 years of copying had provided us with an amazingly pure text, with one of the best examples being the book of Isaiah where only three words had slight modifications.

In 1990 a bone chest was discovered accidentally during work in Jerusalem's Peace Forest. This "Caiaphas Ossuary" belonged to the High Priest from A.D. 18–36 (see his cynical words in Jn 11:49-53). The inscription, found in two places, read: "Caiaphas" and "Joseph, son of Caiaphas." First-century Jewish historian Josephus provided the full name, "Joseph, who is called Caiaphas of the high priesthood."

Space precludes discussion of the many more archaeological corroborations, such as the Pontius Pilate Inscription; the Pool of Siloam, excavated in 2004; and the amazing Ketef Hinnom Amulets discovered in 1979 (with inscriptions of Nm 6:24-26 and Dt 7:9 perfectly matching the biblical Hebrew text—amazing since these seventh to sixth century B.C. amulets contain OT texts skeptics argued could not have been written until the 400s B.C.).

Archaeology, then, has illuminated and corroborated the Bible in numerous ways. The interpreter finds in archaeology a good friend for understanding and substantiating Scripture.

Did the Apostles Report Jesus' Words Accurately?

Jeremy Royal Howard

A great many people base their lives and eternity on Jesus and His teachings, and yet Jesus Himself left us no writings. Obviously, not a single scrap of audio or video recorded His teachings. So how can we know what He taught? The NT claims to convey Jesus' teachings accurately, but how can we be sure that the apostles got it right? There are at least four reasons for trusting that the NT reports Jesus' words accurately.

Master Teacher—Rather than broadcasting His teachings randomly in hopes that someone would by chance remember what He said, Jesus chose a group of 12 men to be His full-time students. For three years they listened closely as Jesus taught the crowds. They also received private instruction on the side (Mt 24:3; Mk 13:3). Jesus used proven teaching tools such as parables, repetition, and visual aids to make learning easier. Jesus also taught the disciples *how* to spread His message (Mk 6:7-11), and commanded them to give their lives to this task (Mt 28:18-20).

Fresh Memories—The disciples did not divorce themselves from Jesus' storyline once He ascended to heaven (Ac 1:9). Instead, they returned to Jerusalem and became the focal point of ongoing controversy. In the weeks, months, and years after Jesus' ascension, the disciples repeatedly defended their beliefs and explained Jesus' teachings to anyone who would listen. Thus their memories were rehearsed daily as they gave unbroken attention to spreading Jesus' teachings. In later years, as speaking and traveling grew more difficult due to old age, these men set their memories down in the Gospels.

Powerful Memories—Living in the age before notepads and computers made data storage a cinch, Jewish students of religion had to achieve herculean feats of memorization. It was said that advanced students were like a basket full of books; they kept *everything* in their heads. Though Jesus' disciples lacked formal education, it is certain that from the moment Jesus called them to be His students they knew they were expected to comprehend and remember His teachings. Possibly they even took detailed notes during Jesus' ministry, as was sometimes done by students of leading rabbis. These notes would have been available to support the memory in years to come.

The Counselor—Jesus' strategic teaching efforts and the prowess of well-honed memories put the disciples in a good position to remember Jesus' teachings, but there was another factor that helped them preach and write with accuracy: Jesus sent the Holy Spirit to help His disciples comprehend and remember His teachings (Jn 14:26). The NT shows that the disciples became aware of the Spirit's role in their writings. Paul quoted the words of Jesus as recorded in Luke 10:7 and called it Scripture (1Tm 5:18). Paul was convinced that Luke had accurately reported Jesus' teachings, plus he believed God had inspired Luke's Gospel. Similarly, Peter affirmed that Paul's writings are Scripture (2Pt 3:15-16). Clearly, the men whom Jesus appointed to spread His teachings believed they were enabled by God to report Jesus' teachings correctly.

SECTION 4

Jesus Christ

Christ: The Fulfillment of Prophecy

D. James Kennedy

S ome time ago I had the opportunity to speak to a man who had no belief whatsoever in the Scriptures as any sort of divine revelation from God. He was a writer who was articulate and well-educated. While he was well-read, he was completely ignorant of any evidences for the truthfulness of the Christian faith and the Scriptures which reveal it. He said the Bible was simply a book written by men, just like any other book. I said, "That's very interesting. I would like to read some statements to you about someone and have you tell me, assuredly, without question, about whom I am reading." He agreed and I began to read:

- "Those who hate me without cause are more numerous than the hairs of my head" (Ps 69:4).
- "Why do the nations rebel and the peoples plot in vain?" (Ps 2:1).
- "The kings of the earth take their stand, and the rulers conspire together against the LORD, and His Anointed One" (Ps 2:2).
- "Even my friend in whom I trusted, one who ate my bread, has raised his heel against me" (Ps 41:9).
- "I will strike the shepherd, and the sheep will be scattered" (Zch 13:7).
- "Then I said to them, 'If it seems right to you, give me my wages; but if not, keep them.' So they weighed my wages, 30 pieces of silver. 'Throw it to the potter,' the LORD said to me—this magnificent price I was valued by them. So I took the 30 pieces of silver and threw it into the house of the LORD, to the potter" (Zch 11:12-13).
- "They are striking the judge of Israel on the cheek with a rod" (Mc 5:1).
- "I gave My back to those who beat Me, and My cheeks to those who tore out My beard. I did not hide My face from scorn and spitting" (Is 50:6).
- "They pierced my hands and my feet" (Ps 22:16).
- "My God, my God, why have You forsaken me?" (Ps 22:1).

- "Everyone who sees me mocks me; they sneer and shake their heads: 'He relies on the LORD; let Him rescue him; let the LORD deliver him, since He takes pleasure in him'" (Ps 22:7-8).
- "They gave me gall for my food, and for my thirst they gave me vinegar to drink" (Ps 69:21).
- "I am poured out like water, and all my bones are disjointed" (Ps 22:14).
- "Yet He Himself bore our sicknesses, and He carried our pains" (Is 53:4).
- "Like a lamb led to the slaughter and like a sheep silent before her shearers, He did not open His mouth" (Is 53:7).
- "They divided my garments among themselves, and they cast lots for my clothing" (Ps 22:18).
- "He submitted Himself to death, and was counted among the rebels; yet He bore the sin of many and interceded for the rebels" (Is 53:12).
- "You may not break any of its bones" (Ex 12:46).
- "He protects all his bones; not one of them will be broken" (Ps 34:20).
- "They will look at Me whom they pierced" (Zch 12:10).
- "They made His grave with the wicked and with a rich man at His death" (Is 53:9).
- "For You will not abandon me to Sheol; You will not allow Your Faithful One to see decay" (Ps 16:10).
- "You ascended to the heights, taking away captives; You received gifts from people" (Ps 68:18).
- "This is the declaration of the LORD; 'Sit at My right hand until I make Your enemies Your footstool'" (Ps 110:1).

Having read all of this, I said to him, "About whom did I read?"

He replied, "Well, you obviously read of the life and ministry and suffering and death and resurrection of Jesus of Nazareth."

I said, "Is there any question in your mind about that?"

He answered, "No, that could refer to no one else."

I replied, "Well then, I would want you to understand that all of the Scriptures I just read to you are taken from the OT, which was completed some 400 years before Jesus was born. No critic, no atheist, no agnostic has ever once claimed that any one of those writings was written after His birth. In fact, they were translated from Hebrew into Greek in Alexandria some 150 years before He was born. If this is merely a book written by men, would you please explain to me how these words were written?"

He said, "I haven't the faintest idea." He was completely nonplussed. He had never heard those things before in his life. Indeed they cannot be explained by any purely humanistic presuppositions.

It is noteworthy that in no other religious writings in the world do we find any specific predictive prophecies like we find in the Scripture. You will find no predictive prophecies whatsoever in the writings of Buddha, Confucius, Mohammed, Lao-Tse, or Hinduism. Yet in the Bible there are well over 2000 prophecies, most of which have already been fulfilled.

They are so specific in nature that they burn all the bridges behind them. If they are not fulfilled, it leaves no room for excuse. How can these be explained? Of all the attacks that have ever been made upon the Bible, there has never been one book written by a skeptic to disprove the prophecies of the Scripture. The Bible prophecies are altogether unexpected! I know of no one ever prophesying that any other human being would rise from the dead and ascend into Heaven. That is exceedingly improbable. The chance of it happening by coincidence is incalculable. No, the Bible is not merely a book written by men; it is a book written by God through men, and the heart of its prophetic message is Jesus Christ.

What Does It Mean To Say, "Jesus Is Messiah"?

Walter Russell

The Bible is more focused upon proving that Jesus is the Messiah than proving that Jesus is God. While some NT passages clearly declare Jesus preexisted as deity, dozens demonstrate Jesus of Nazareth is the long-awaited Davidic Messiah-king of Israel. In other words, Jesus is the only one anointed with the Holy Spirit by God the Father and thereby uniquely authorized and empowered to bring about God's kingdom on earth. He is the Anointed One (Hebrew = "Messiah"; Greek = "Christ"). While His messianic identity includes His divine preexistence, this isn't the primary emphasis of the NT. That's why all four Gospels speak of Jesus' anointing (baptism) with the Holy Spirit as the beginning of His ministry as the Christ (Mt 3:13-17; Mk 1:9-11; Lk 3:21-22; Jn 1:32-34). For this reason, Christ is a title or office, not a part of Jesus' name. Whenever "Jesus Christ" or "Christ Jesus" or "Lord Jesus Christ" is used, the NT is saying, "Jesus the Messiah" or "Messiah Jesus" or "Lord Jesus the Messiah."

To understand the full significance of saying, "Jesus is Messiah," we must think primarily historically and secondarily theologically. For example, in Luke 4:16-30, Jesus' inaugural address in the Nazareth synagogue, we must think historically to understand what Jesus is claiming about Himself. He quotes from Isaiah 61:1-2, a favorite messianic passage of the Jews in Jesus' day and one of a cluster of OT passages speaking of the Spirit of the Lord anointing the Servant of the Lord to preach good news to needy people. In Luke 4:21, Jesus claims that the Spirit-anointing that Isaiah prophesied had been fulfilled in His anointing (baptism) in John the Baptist's presence a short time before (Lk 3:21-22). In other words, Jesus claims to be the Anointed One, the Messiah of Israel. Moreover, Jesus makes the very unpopular point that His present messianic ministry would be gracious to Gentiles, not wreaking vengeance upon them or overthrowing Rome (Lk 4:23-30)! Jesus' claims can only be understood when we see them primarily as claims to be the Messiah who is the unique representative of the Father.

Even in passages clearly emphasizing Jesus' deity (e.g., Jn 1:1-18), such a theological emphasis is secondary to the historical emphasis that the Word who preexisted as God has become flesh and dwelt among us as Messiah. The double mention of John the Baptist, Messiah's forerunner, reveals the messianic framework is primary (Jn 1:6-8,15).

Even Jesus' miracles aren't to prove His deity, but His Spirit-anointed identity (e.g., Jn 6:1-15). Also, the confession Jesus spent three years soliciting from His disciples was not that "You are God" (which He is), but that "You are the Christ" (Mt 16:16; Mk 8:29; Lk 9:20). Moreover, rejection of Jesus' works is not a rejection of His deity per se, but rather is a blasphemy against the Holy Spirit Who has empowered these works by the Anointed One (Mt 12:22-32; Mk 3:20-30). Lastly, Jesus' resurrection is the occasion of His coronation or official installation as the messianic ruler (Ps 2, esp. vv. 7-12; Mt 28:16-20; Ac 13:30-33; Rm 1:1-5; Heb 1:1-14).

In defending Jesus' identity, we should confidently set forth, as the NT does, that "Jesus is Messiah!"

What Does the Hebrew Bible Say About the Coming Messiah?

Michael Rydelnik

How can someone be convinced that Jesus truly is who He claimed to be—the Messiah of Israel and the world? One of the ways Jesus Himself proved this was by citing the Hebrew Bible's prophecies of the Messiah and noted how He fulfilled them. For example, Jesus said, "These are My words that I spoke while I was still with you—that everything written about Me in the Law of Moses, the Prophets, and the Psalms must be fulfilled" (Lk 24:44).

To what prophecies was He referring? Probably not merely individual, messianic texts, but to the whole Hebrew Bible. Even so, there are numerous specific predictions about the coming of the Messiah that Jesus fulfilled. In fact, the entire life of the Messiah can be found in the Hebrew Scriptures, demonstrating that Jesus is actually the Promised One.

Messiah's Birth. The Hebrew Bible contains several predictions of the Messiah's birth. Micah foretold that Messiah would be born in Bethlehem, when he wrote, "Bethlehem Ephrathah, you are small among the clans of Judah; One will come from you to be ruler over Israel for Me" (Mc 5:2).

Also, Genesis 49:10 predicted that the Messiah would come in the first century A.D. It says, "The scepter will not depart from Judah or the staff from between his feet until He whose right it is comes and the obedience of the peoples belongs to Him." Besides plainly stating that the messianic King would come from the line of Judah, additionally it says that He would come before the "scepter" and "staff" depart from Judah. The word "scepter" in Hebrew, as used here, refers to tribal identity. The word "staff" means a "judge's staff" and refers to judicial authority. The prediction is that Messiah would come before Judah lost its tribal identity (lost in A.D. 70 with the destruction of the Temple) and judicial authority (lost in A.D. 6 or 7 when the Romans replaced Herod Archeleus with a Roman governor). Based on these two elements, the Messiah needed to come by the first century.

Additionally, Isaiah predicted that the Messiah would be born of a virgin. King Ahaz and Judah were under threat from two northern kingdoms that wanted to remove the Davidic king and thereby jeopardize the Messianic promise. Isaiah brought both his son Shear Jashub and a message of hope to King Ahaz, an offer that Ahaz rejected. At this point, Isaiah gave two predictions. The first, a far prophecy (7:13-15), assured the enduring nature of the Davidic house until the coming of the Messiah. Isaiah wrote, "Therefore, the Lord Himself will give you a sign: The virgin will conceive, have a son, and name Him Immanuel" (v. 14). The sign of hope would be the Messiah's supernatural birth by a virgin in the distant future. The second prediction (7:16-17), related to the near situation, and predicted that by the time "the boy" Shear Jashub reached an age to know right from wrong, the imminent threat of the two northern kings would be removed. So, the Hebrew Bible predicted that the Messiah would be virgin born in Bethlehem by the time of the first century.

Messiah's Nature. Although some thought that Messiah would just be a glorious king, the Scriptures foretold that Messiah would have a unique nature. For example, in the same prophecy (Mc 5:2) that predicted that the Messiah would come from Bethlehem, it is also said that His origin would really be "from antiquity, from eternity" indicating His eternal nature.

Isaiah also foresaw that the Messiah would have a divine nature. In a birth announcement, Isaiah gave the royal names of the future messianic king: ". . . . Wonderful Counselor, Mighty God, Eternal Father, Prince of Peace" (Is 9:6). These glorious titles of deity indicate that the Messiah would be God Himself.

Messiah's Life. Isaiah foretold the characteristics of the Messiah's life. In the messianic age, "the eyes of the blind will be opened, and the ears of the deaf unstopped. Then the lame will leap like a deer, and the tongue of the mute will sing for joy" (Is 35:5-6). So, when the Messiah would make His appearance, He was to be a miracle worker. Isaiah also predicted that Messiah's teaching would "bring good news to the poor . . . [and] heal the brokenhearted" (Is 61:1). Despite these many signs, Isaiah foretold that Messiah would also be "despised and rejected by men" and that His own people would confess that "we didn't value Him" (Is 53:3).

Messiah's Death. Daniel 9:26-27 predicted the time of the Messiah's death. He would be "cut off" before A.D. 70, when the Romans would "destroy the city (Jerusalem) and the sanctuary (the Temple)."

King David foretold that Messiah would die by crucifixion, saying "they pierced my hands and my feet" (Ps 22:16). So David predicted Messiah's crucifixion more than 300 years before that manner of execution was known.

More significant than the time or manner of His death, Isaiah predicted that the Messiah's death would be as a substitution for humanity's sin. The Servant of the Lord, would die a disfiguring death (Is 52:14); He would be "pierced because of our transgressions, crushed because of our iniquities" (53:5); The Lord would punish Him "for the iniquity of us all" (v. 6). The Servant would have "submitted Himself to death" and as a result "He bore the sin of many" (v. 12).

Messiah's Resurrection. The prophets not only foretold the Messiah's death-they anticipated His resurrection as well. In Isaiah 52:13-53:12, after describing Messiah's substitutionary death, Isaiah promised that the Lord would "prolong His days" (Is 53:10) and that Messiah would see "the light" of life (v. 11fn). David also expressed his own confidence that God would "not abandon him to Sheol" because the Messiah, God's "Faithful One" would not "see decay" (Ps 16:10).

Messiah's Return. The Hebrew Scriptures present the Messiah in two ways: as a Suffering Servant and as a victorious and righteous King. Although this has confused many, the difficulty is resolved by recognizing that the prophets anticipated two appearances of the Messiah. First, He would come as an atoning sacrifice for sin. Second, He would come to establish His righteous kingdom. One of the passages that links the two comings is Zechariah 12:10. It speaks of Messiah coming to deliver Israel at the last battle and then "they will look at Me whom they pierced." These verses depict Messiah's second coming as the victorious king but also recognize His first appearance as the Pierced One. Then, when He comes, He will fulfill Isaiah's prediction that "He will reign on the throne of David and over his kingdom, to establish and sustain it with justice and righteousness from now on and forever" (Is 9:7).

Mathematician Peter W. Stoner calculated the probability of one person fulfilling not all the messianic predictions of the Bible, or even the ones mentioned in this article, but just eight messianic predictions. He found that the probability would be 1 in 10^{17} or 1 in 100,000,000,000,000,000. The likelihood of this occurring is comparable to covering Texas with 10^{17} silver dollars, marking only one of them, stirring the mass of dollars, and then having a blindfolded man randomly pick up the marked silver dollar. This is the likelihood of Jesus of Nazareth randomly fulfilling only eight of the Messianic predictions of the Hebrew Bible.

Are Jesus' Claims Unique Among the Religions of the World?

Gary R. Habermas

H ave all major religious teachers proclaimed approximately the same message? For example, do we assume that many of them taught that they were God? Actually, Jesus made a number of crucial claims that are unlike those made by the founders of any other major religion. These cannot be accounted for merely as minor differences, either.

It may surprise many that we have no reliable historical data that *any* of the founders of the world's major religions ever claimed to be God. No early writings attest such a claim on behalf of these persons. For example, Chinese teachers Confucius and Lao-Tzu exerted moral, social, and cultural influences on their students, but were not theologians. Many of their aphorisms are reminiscent of the Hebrew Proverbs. Strangely, Buddha may have been an atheist!

The Qur'an definitely does not elevate Muhammad to the place of Allah. While we are told that Muhammad is Allah's chief prophet, there is no attempt to make him deity. To the contrary, Allah has no partners (Surahs 4:171; 5:72, 116).

The OT places no leader or prophet on God's level. Rather, we are told that God will not share His glory with anyone else (Is 48:11). So Abraham, David, and Isaiah are not candidates for deification.

Perhaps Krishna comes closest to being understood as God by his followers. While he is referred to in the lofty terms of deity in the Bhagavad-Gita (for example, 4:13; 9:18-20,23), scholars are not sure if Krishna ever lived, and, if he did, what century it was. Moreover, these writings do not claim to be historical treatises of any actual teachings and are thought to have been written perhaps many hundreds of years after the general time Krishna may have lived. Thus, tracking any possibility of original claims is fruitless.

Further, to be God in the usual Hindu sense would be quite distinct from the Judeo-Christian tradition. In the latter, God is by nature totally apart from His creation; humans do not reach deified status. In the Bhagavad-Gita, however, the process of enlightenment can be attained by those who return to the Godhead and achieve their own divinity (especially 18:46-68). In a certain sense, all persons have divine natures.

Contrary to other religious teachers, Jesus claimed dual titles of divinity. Particularly, He said He was both the Son of God (Mt 11:27) and the Son of Man (Mk 2:10-11). He spoke of His Father in very familiar ways (Mk 13:36) and even claimed to forgive sins, for which He was charged with blasphemy (Mk 2:5-7).

In perhaps the clearest indication of His self-claims, when the High Priest asked Him if He was the Christ, the Son of God, Jesus plainly declared that He was. Then He asserted, further, that He was also the Son of Man who would co-reign on God's throne and come on the clouds in judgment. The High Priest pronounced that these claims constituted blasphemy (Mk 14:61-64).

These saying of Jesus were recorded in documents that were written just decades after the events, and there are strong reasons to hold that each was composed by authors who were close to the occurrences. Moreover, many of the individual passages exhibit critical earmarks that argue for their historicity. Lastly, very early creedal texts like Acts 2:36 and Romans 1:3-4; 10:9 also apply lofty titles of Deity to Jesus Christ.

Many religious teachers have claimed to present God's way. But Jesus declared not only that He was initiating God's path of salvation (Mk 1:15-20), but that what His hearers did specifically with *Him* determined their eternal destiny (Mt 10:37-40; 19:23-30). Further, of these religious founders, only Jesus taught that His death would serve as a payment for human sin, achieving what we could not (Mk 10:45; 14:22-25).

Additionally, only Jesus has miracles reported of Him by early sources. Further, according to the Gospels, Jesus taught that His resurrection from the dead would be the sign that evidenced the truth of His message (Mk 14:28; Mt 12:38-42; 16:1-4). For NT writers, Jesus' resurrection evidenced His claims, showing them to be true (Rm 1:3-4; 1Pt 1:3-6). After all, dead men do not do much! So if Jesus was raised, God must have performed the event in order to approve Jesus' message (Ac 2:22-24; 17:30-31).

Can Naturalistic Theories Account for the Resurrection?

Gary R. Habermas

One of our first thoughts when we hear someone claim to have witnessed a miracle is that there must be some sort of natural explanation. After all, even if miracles occur, they are not the norm in nature.

In the Gospels we are told there was a similar response. Pilate was surprised to hear that Jesus had died so quickly. He called the centurion to make sure (Mk 15:44-45). When the Jewish priests were told the report of the empty tomb, they spread the tale that Jesus' disciples had stolen His body (Mt 28:12-15).

Even believers reacted this way. When Mary Magdalene initially saw Jesus, she made a natural assumption, supposing that He was the gardener (Jn

20:10-15). When the disciples heard the report of the women who had gone to Jesus' tomb, they thought the women were spreading rumors or false tales (Lk 24:11). Later, when they saw the risen Jesus, these same followers thought they were seeing a ghost or perhaps even an hallucination (Lk 24:36-43).

Throughout history, many have made similar responses regarding Jesus' resurrection. These attempts were far more common in the nineteenth century than they are today. Even if we were to ignore the majority of the information in the Gospels, appealing only to those historical facts that are acknowledged by virtually every critical scholar who studies this subject, both conservative and liberal, we still have many major responses to each of the natural theories. Not surprisingly, comparatively few scholars today think that any of these alternative hypotheses really works.

For example, very few critics have proposed that perhaps Jesus never died on the cross, but "swooned." Dozens of medical studies have shown how death by crucifixion kills and how this would be recognized by those present. Most of these reports argue that the chief cause of death is asphyxiation. It is even quite easy to ascertain when the victim is dead—he remains hanging in the down position without pushing up to breathe. Additionally, a death blow frequently insured their demise. The prevailing medical explanation of Jesus' chest wound is that the presence of blood and water indicate He was stabbed through the heart, thereby insuring His death.

Many scholars think that another serious problem dooms the swoon theory by itself. If Jesus had not died on the cross, He would have been in exceptionally bad shape when His followers saw Him. Limping, bleeding profusely from His many wounds and probably even leaving a bloody trail, stoop-shouldered and pale, He hardly would have been able to convince His disciples that He was their risen Lord, Conqueror of death, and in a transformed body at that! Many historical reasons and the near-unanimity of scholarly opinion indicate that Jesus' disciples at least truly believed they had seen Him resurrected. On such grounds, the swoon thesis is actually self-refuting. It presents a Jesus who actually would have contradicted the disciples' belief in His resurrection simply by appearing in the horrible physical shape that is demanded by this view!

But could the disciples have stolen His dead body? This approach has been almost ignored for more than 200 years because it would not explain the disciples' sincere belief that they had seen the risen Jesus, for which they were clearly willing to die. Their transformations need an adequate explanation. Neither would it explain the conversions from skepticism by James, the brother of Jesus, or by Paul, occasioned by their own beliefs they had also seen the risen Jesus, facts noted by critical scholars.

Would someone else have stolen Jesus' body? But this approach basically addresses nothing but the empty tomb. It provides no explanation for Jesus' appearances, which are the best evidence for the resurrection. Further, it also fails to account for the conversions of either James or Paul. Besides, many candidates, such as the Jews or Romans, would have no motivation for taking the body. This alternative simply accounts for far too little of the known data. It is no wonder that critics virtually never opt for it.

There are myriad problems with hallucination theories, too. We will mention just a few. Hallucinations are private experiences, whereas our earliest accounts report that Jesus also appeared to groups. Further, the dissimilar personalities witnessing the appearances clearly militate against everyone inventing a mental image, and often at the same time, as well. So do the reactions of those disciples who responded by doubting, further arguing against hallucinations. The conversions of James and Paul are extremely problematic for this view, since unbelieving skeptics would hardly want to hallucinate a vision of the risen Jesus! In no way were they expecting or wanting Jesus to rise from the dead. And if hallucinations are the best explanation, the tomb should not have been empty!

Could the resurrection accounts have developed later, mere stories that grew over time? Here again, that the disciples truly believed they had seen the risen Jesus is highly problematic for this view, too, since it indicates that the original accounts are derived from the eyewitnesses themselves, not from some later stories. Further, that these appearances were reported extremely early, within just a few years of the crucifixion, attests that at least the core message was intact from the outset. Moreover, the empty tomb would be a constant physical reminder that this was not just some ungrounded tale. Both James and Paul again provide even more insurmountable problems for this view, for these skeptics were convinced that they had also seen the risen Jesus; tales developing years later fail to account for their conversions.

For reasons such as these, most critical scholars today reject the naturalistic theories as adequate accounts of Jesus' resurrection. They simply do not explain the known historical data. In fact, many scholars even critique the alternatives that are periodically suggested!

Here we have a strong witness to the historical nature of Jesus' resurrection. Naturalistic theories have failed. Further, there are many historical evidences that favor the resurrection. Together we have a powerful indicator that this event actually occurred in history. After all, the more thoroughly alternative theses fail, the more we are left with the evidences themselves, and they are powerful indicators that Jesus rose from the dead.

The Disciples' Conviction and the Historicity of the Resurrection

Gary R. Habermas

Virtually all scholars today who study these matters, whether conservative, moderate, or liberal, acknowledge that Jesus' earliest followers were *convinced* not only that Jesus was raised from the dead, but that He had appeared alive to many of them on several occasions. Further, it is also almost unanimously recognized that two former skeptics, James the brother of Jesus and Saul of Tarsus (Paul), also became believers after they, too, were *convinced* that they had seen the risen Jesus.

Multiple grounds support this early Christian conviction. Even today's very critical scholars agree that Paul, the author of undisputed genuine epistles, provides eyewitness testimony to his own experience of the resurrected Jesus. Further, Paul included a crucial report concerning other appearances of Jesus in the exceptionally early creed in 1 Corinthians 15, which is usually dated to the A.D. 30s. Paul carefully checked out this material with the other key apostles in Jerusalem on at least two occasions (Gl 1:18-2:10). Paul also knew that the other apostles were preaching the same message regarding the risen Jesus (1Co 15:10-15). Paul's eyewitness testimony at each of these points is crucial.

Moreover, the conversion of James from skepticism, the willingness of the earliest disciples to suffer persecution and even martyrdom, the empty tomb, and the presence of other early reports of Jesus' resurrection especially in Acts are further indications of the apostolic conviction that Jesus had been raised. In brief, the earliest Christian message was that Jesus had appeared to His followers after His death.

Of the many evidences for the resurrection, the most significant is that the earliest disciples were utterly convinced they had seen the risen Jesus. The reason is straightforward. Virtually every contemporary scholar recognizes the strong data showing that Jesus died by crucifixion. So if a number of persons actually saw Him afterwards, both individuals and groups alike, this would constitute the clearest indication that He had been raised. No other evidence provides such a direct indication of this event. This is clearly what the witnesses proclaimed.

Some critics may counter that we know the early disciples truly *thought* that Jesus had been raised. But perhaps a natural hypothesis explains their beliefs.

However, now the questioner has a major dilemma. Natural theories have been proposed for centuries and each fails by a large margin to explain the recognized historical data. Incredibly, most contemporary scholars even recognize this failure. Very few critics even propose alternative hypotheses!

The earliest disciples clearly taught that they saw the risen Jesus, for which there is plenty of supporting details. What happens when these facts are not naturally explained, as even the majority of contemporary critical scholars admit? The resurrection of Jesus becomes the best explanation of the known data.

All the evidence favors the view that the disciples actually experienced the risen Jesus. There is no viable evidence to the contrary. So we are left with a succinct conclusion. When the many reasons supporting the conviction that Jesus actually appeared to the early Christians are juxtaposed with the recognized failure of natural alternative theses, we are justified in concluding that Jesus was actually raised from the dead.

Did Jesus Really Rise from the Dead?

William Lane Craig

To answer our question from a historical standpoint we must determine, first, what facts concerning the fate of Jesus of Nazareth can be credibly established on the basis of the evidence and, second, what the best explanation of those facts is. With respect to that first question, there are at least four facts about the fate of the historical Jesus which are widely accepted by NT historians today.

Fact 1: After His crucifixion Jesus was buried by Joseph of Arimathea in a tomb. This is highly significant because it means that the location of Jesus' tomb was known in Jerusalem to Jews and Christians alike. New Testament scholars have established the fact of Jesus' entombment on the basis of evidence such as the following: (1) Jesus' burial is attested in the very old information (from before A.D. 36) which was handed on by Paul in 1 Corinthians 15:3-5; (2) The burial story is independently attested in the very old source material used by Mark in writing his Gospel; (3) Given the understandable hostility in the early Christian movement toward the Jewish leaders, Joseph of Arimathea, as a member of the Jewish high court that condemned Jesus, is unlikely to be a Christian invention; (4) The burial story is simple and lacks any signs of legendary development; (5) No competing burial story exists. For these and other reasons, the majority of NT critics concur Jesus was in fact buried by Joseph of Arimathea in a tomb.

Fact 2: On the Sunday after the crucifixion, Jesus' tomb was found empty by a group of His women followers. Among the reasons that have led most scholars to this conclusion are the following: (1) In stating that Jesus "was buried, that He was raised on the third day," the old information transmitted by Paul in 1 Corinthians 15:3-5 implies the empty tomb; (2) The empty tomb story also has multiple and independent attestation in Mark, Matthew, and John's source material, some of which is very early; (3) The empty tomb story as related in Mark, our earliest account, is simple and lacks signs of legendary embellishment; (4) Given that in Jewish patriarchal culture the testimony of women was regarded as unreliable, the fact that it is women, rather than men, who are the chief witnesses to the empty tomb is best explained by the narrative being true; (5) The earliest known Jewish response to the proclamation of Jesus' resurrection, namely, the "disciples came during the night and stole Him while we were sleeping" (Mt 28:12-15), was itself an attempt to explain why the body was missing and thus presupposes the empty tomb. For these and other reasons a majority of scholars hold firmly to the reliability of the biblical testimony to Jesus' empty tomb.

Fact 3: On multiple occasions and under various circumstances different individuals and groups of people experienced appearances of Jesus alive from the dead. This fact is virtually universally acknowledged among NT scholars, for the following reasons: (1) Given its early date as well as Paul's personal acquaintance with the people involved, the list of eyewitnesses to Jesus' resurrection appearances which is quoted by Paul in 1 Corinthians 15:5-8 guarantees that such appearances occurred; (2) The appearance narratives in the gospels provide multiple, independent attestation of the appearances. Even the most skeptical critics therefore acknowledge that the disciples had experiences of seeing Jesus alive after His death.

Finally, fact 4: The original disciples suddenly and sincerely came to believe Jesus was risen from the dead despite having every predisposition to the contrary. Consider the situation the disciples faced following Jesus' crucifixion: (1) Their leader was dead, and Jewish Messianic expectations included no idea of a Messiah who, instead of triumphing over Israel's enemies, would be shamefully executed by them as a criminal; (2) According to OT law, Jesus' execution exposed Him as a heretic, a man literally accursed by God; (3) Jewish beliefs about the afterlife precluded anyone's rising from the dead to glory and immortality before the general resurrection of the dead at the end of the world. Nevertheless, the original disciples suddenly came to believe so strongly that God had raised Jesus from the dead that they were willing to die for the truth of that belief.

We come now to our second concern: What is the best explanation of these four facts? In his book *Justifying Historical Descriptions,* historian C. B. McCullagh lists six tests historians use to determine the best explanation for a given body of historical facts. The hypothesis given by the eyewitnesses, "God raised Jesus from the dead," passes all these tests. (1) It has great explanatory scope: it explains why the tomb was found empty, why the disciples saw post-mortem appearances of Jesus, and why the Christian faith came into being; (2) It has great explanatory power: it explains why the body of Jesus was gone, why people repeatedly saw Jesus alive despite His earlier public execution, and so forth; (3) It is plausible: given the historical context of Jesus' own unparalleled life and claims, the resurrection makes sense as the divine confirmation of those radical claims; (4) It is not ad hoc or contrived: it requires only one additional hypothesis: that God exists; (5) It is in accord with accepted beliefs. The hypothesis, "God raised Jesus from the dead," does not in any way conflict with the accepted belief that people do not rise naturally from the dead. The Christian accepts that belief as wholeheartedly as he accepts the hypothesis that God raised Jesus from the dead; (6) It far outstrips any of its rival theories in meeting conditions (1 through 5).

Down through history various alternative explanations of the facts have been offered, for example, the conspiracy theory, the apparent death theory, the hallucination theory, and so forth. Such hypotheses have been almost universally rejected by contemporary scholarship. No naturalistic hypothesis has, in fact, attracted a great number of scholars. Therefore, the best explanation of the established facts seems to be that God raised Jesus from the dead.

Thus, we have firm historical grounds for answering our question in the affirmative. The historical route is not, however, the only avenue to a knowledge of Jesus' resurrection. The majority of Christians, who have had neither the resources, training, nor leisure to conduct a historical inquiry into this event, have notwithstanding come to a knowledge of Jesus' resurrection through a personal existential encounter with the living Lord himself (Rm 8:9-17).

How Can Jesus' Death Bring Forgiveness?

Chad Owen Brand

O ccasionally stories are told about someone being sentenced for a crime when suddenly another person steps up and says, "I will take the punishment for him." Most such stories are not based in fact. But the NT teaches that in Jesus' death, He has taken the penalty for our sin upon Himself.

Scripture teaches all humanity is tainted and corrupted by sin, both because of the sin of our father, Adam (Rm 5:12-21), and because we ourselves are all sinners (Eph 2:1-3). God, as the righteous judge, cannot and will not simply overlook sin, since sin violates His nature and brings destruction to the perfect world He created. God would be unjust simply to say, "Oh well, boys will be boys." Instead, sin must be punished, and since all of us have broken God's law, we rightly deserve full punishment. Yet amazingly, Jesus came to take our punishment upon Himself.

The NT speaks of Jesus' death providing forgiveness in at least three ways. First, Jesus' death was a sacrifice for our sins. Christ fulfills the OT sacrificial system in being both high priest and sacrifice (Heb 5-10). On the Day of Atonement animals were killed before the altar and their blood was sprinkled on the mercy seat in the Holy of Holies. Under that seat was God's law written on tablets of stone. Looking down from heaven God could see the law, but when the sacrificial blood was sprinkled, the law—as reminder of the peoples' sin—was covered. Without the shedding of blood, there is no forgiveness of sin (Heb 9:22).

Second, the NT speaks of Christ's death as a "propitiation" for our sin (Rm 3:21-26). This word, *hilasmos*, carries the meaning of "an offering satisfying God's wrath toward sin," yet remarkably, God Himself provides this offering. When Jesus died on the cross He cried out, "My God, My God, why have You forsaken Me?" (Mt 27:46). The Father was pouring out His wrath because "He made the One who did not know sin to be sin for us, so that we might become the righteousness of God in Him" (2Co 5:21).

Third, and related to both points already made, the Bible speaks of Christ's death as a substitution. Jesus did not come to be served but to serve and "to give His life—a ransom for many" (Mk 10:45). Jesus "gave Himself for our sins to rescue us from this present evil age" (Gl 1:4). Isaiah's predictions of a coming Suffering Servant are fulfilled in the death of Jesus, who "was pierced because of our transgressions, crushed because of our iniquities . . . and the Lord has punished Him for the iniquity of us all" (Is 53:5-6). He died in our place.

By faith, and faith alone, we receive the forgiveness Christ provides through His humiliating and painful death, with the result: eternal life (Eph 2:3-10).

The Incarnation: Could God Become Man Without Ceasing to Be God?

James A. Parker III

The answer to this question is yes. Not only is it possible, but it happened in time and space. Neo-orthodox theologians have said that the question is logically unanswerable because faith is an illogical paradox and can only be seen through the eyes of faith. In recent years liberal theologians have denied the reality of the incarnation on the grounds that the incarnation is a myth and not true in any objective sense. In the 19th century advocates of the kenotic Christology argued that in the incarnation the divine Logos suspended the characteristics of deity because they were in principle incompatible with human attributes—thus making nonsense of the claim that Jesus Christ was fully God and fully man (as both the Bible and historic Christian confessions have claimed.)

Historic theism has argued that God is omniscient, omnipotent, sinless, and incorporeal, that these attributes are essential and necessary to deity. Characteristically human beings do not exhibit these attributes. So how can Jesus be simultaneously fully divine and fully human? Thus people have attacked the doctrine of the Incarnation, claiming that it is illogical and contradictory at the heart of its fundamental claims that Jesus Christ is fully God and fully human.

This alleged logical contradiction is based on a fundamental misunderstanding of how human nature is defined, according to Thomas V. Morris in his book *The Logic of God Incarnate*. Morris has argued that the way out of this apparent impasse is to have a clearer understanding of three important concepts: (1) essential vs. non-essential properties, (2) essential vs. common properties, and (3) the difference between being fully and merely human.

On the first issue Morris argues that an essential property is a property that if removed, fundamentally changes the thing in question. If God's attributes of omnipotence, omniscience, etc. were removed then He would no longer be deity. So these are essential attributes. While it is a common attribute for a human being to have two hands, this is not an essential property to humanness. The heart of the attack on the Incarnation comes from the critics on the basis that lack of omniscience, omnipotence, etc. is essential to humanness, since human beings do not have these qualities.

This brings us to Morris's second distinction: essential vs. common properties. It is a common property that everyone on the planet earth was born on planet earth, but this is simply a common property, not essential to their humanness. You could be born on the moon and still be human. Morris then asks the question on what basis one knows that the absence of the attributes of omniscience, etc. are essential human properties, and not just common properties.

Lastly, Morris argues "an individual is fully human (in any case where) that individual has all essential human properties, all the properties composing basic human nature. An individual is merely human if he or she has all those properties plus some additional limiting properties as well, properties such as that of lacking omnipotence, that of lacking omniscience, and so on." So, orthodox Christians, in affirming the Incarnation, are claiming "Jesus was fully human without being merely human."

Ronald Nash summarizes the implications of the argument as follows: "This means two things: Jesus possesses all the properties that are essential to being a human being, and Jesus possesses all the properties that are essential to deity. The historic understanding of the Incarnation expresses the beliefs that Jesus Christ is fully God—that is, He possesses all the essential properties of God: Jesus Christ is also fully human—that is, He possesses all the essential properties of a human being, none of which turn out to be limiting properties: and Jesus Christ was not merely human—that is, He did not possess any of the limiting properties that are complements of the divine attributes. In the face of these distinctions, the alleged contradiction in the Incarnation disappears."

SECTION 5

Theology

Does the Bible Affirm Open Theism?

John M. Frame

A group of thinkers known as "open theists," such as Clark Pinnock, John Sanders, Gregory Boyd, and William Hasker, seek to do justice to the give-and-take in Scripture between God and human beings. For example, in Exodus 32:7-10, God tells Moses He will destroy Israel for worshipping the golden calf and raise up a new nation from Moses himself. Moses intercedes, however, and in 32:14 God "relented concerning the disaster." God also seems to "change his mind" in Isaiah 38:1-5, where Isaiah prophecies that King Hezekiah will die, but in response to Hezekiah's repentance adds 15 years to his life. And in Jonah 3–4, God retracts an announcement of judgment in response to Nineveh's repentance.

From these and other such passages, open theists infer that God is a temporal being (not "above time" as in much traditional theology), that He changes His mind, that His plans are influenced by creatures, that He sometimes regrets actions He has performed (as Gn 6:6), and that He does not have exhaustive knowledge of the future. On their view, God's regretting and relenting come about because human free decisions are utterly undetermined and unpredictable. So God must adjust His plans to the free choices of human beings.

We should not ignore these "relenting" passages. On the other hand, we should not forget the pervasive biblical emphasis on God's sovereign control of the world and His exhaustive knowledge of past, present, and future. God brings about natural events (Ps 65:9-11; 135:5-7), even apparently random ones (Pr 16:33). He controls the smallest details of nature (Mt 10:29-30). He governs human history (Ac 17:26; Is 10:5-12; 14:24-27). If someone dies accidentally, it is because "God caused it to happen" (Ex 21:12-13). Contrary to open theism, God brings about human free decisions, even sinful ones (Gn 45:5-8; Jdg 14:4; 2Sm 24; Is 44:28; Lk 22:22; Ac 2:23-24; Rv 17:17). He hardened Pharaoh's heart (Ex 4:21; 7:3), and others as well (Dt 2:30; Jos 11:18-20; 1Sm 2:25; 2Ch 25:20), for His own purposes (Rm 9:17). He is also the source of human faith (Jn 6:37,44,65; Ac 13:48; 16:14-15; 18:27;

Eph 2:4-10; 2Tm 1:9) and repentance (Zch 12:10; Ac 5:31; 11:18). So human freedom is not indeterminate as open theists maintain. We are free in that we do what we want to do; but behind our plans and desires are those of God (Jms 4:13-16).

In general, God "works out everything in agreement with the decision of His will" (Eph 1:11; cp. Lm 3:37-38; Rm 8:28; 11:33-36). And God cannot fail at anything He seeks to do (Ps 33:11; 115:3; 135:6; Pr 21:30; Is 14:27; 43:13; 46:10; 55:11; Dn 4:35; Rv 3:7).

Since God controls everything, He knows everything, including the future. Knowing the future is a test of a true prophet (Dt 18:22) and indeed of a true God (Is 41:21-23; 42:9; 43:9-12; 44:7; 48:3-7). Through His prophets, God often predicts the future centuries in advance (as Gn 9:26-27). Contrary to the open theists, who think God cannot anticipate human free decisions, He often predicts human behavior in detail (1Sm 10:1-7; Jr 37:6-10; Mt 26:34). He predicts the behavior and character of human beings in the distant future (1Kg 13:1-4; Is 44:28–45:13).

How then should we understand God's "relenting?" For one thing, God states as a general policy in Jeremiah 18:5-10 that if He announces judgment and people repent, He will relent; similarly if He pronounces blessing and people do evil. In other words, relenting is part of God's unchanging plan, not a change forced on Him by His ignorance. Further, God is not only transcendent, but also immanent (involved in our experience). He has dwelled on earth in the tabernacle and temple, in Christ, and in His general omnipresence (Ps 139:7-12). When God interacts with people in time, He does one thing, then another. He curses, then blesses. His actions are in temporal sequence and therefore, in one sense, changing. But these changes are the outworking of God's eternal plan, which does not change.

It is important, then, to see God as working from both above and below, in eternity and time, not only in time as open theists propose.

Why Does God Hide Himself?

Kenneth T. Magnuson

The question, "Why does God hide Himself?" is asked at times not only by the atheist or agnostic seeking to cast doubt on God's existence, but also by believers seeking a personal experience of God. It is therefore related to further questions. The doubter or skeptic may ask, "Is there a God?" Or, "If God exists, how can we know He exists, and why doesn't He reveal Himself more clearly?" The anxious seeker may ask, "Is God in control of the universe?" And, "Is God concerned about my life and problems?" In times of trouble, many wonder if God is there and if He cares. And finally, the doubter, seeker, and follower alike may ask, "How can I know God?"

A biblical perspective on God's hiddenness encourages us not to become overly anxious. God does, in fact, reveal Himself, but perhaps not in the way some demand or expect. In one sense, God is indeed hidden because He is Spirit, and cannot be seen physically (Jn 4:24). The demand for certain types of physical evidence of God will leave us wanting, and may be misplaced, as it diminishes the need for faith. Further, God may deliberately hide Himself in order to expose people's hearts, drawing closer those who believe, while turning away from those who turn from Him (Dt 31:17; Is 59:2).

Yet the Bible encourages us with the promise that if we seek God faithfully, we will find Him (Jr 29:13). While God is hidden in some sense, He is knowable, so we may ask God to show Himself to us (Pr 8:17; Jr 29:13; Mt 7:7-8). We may also look for and acknowledge the ways that God has already chosen to reveal Himself. First, God has revealed Himself to us in His Word (Ex 3:14; Heb 1:1; cp. Lk 24:27); Second, God has revealed Himself decisively in His Son, Jesus Christ (Jn 1:1,14; 14:8-9; Col 2:9; Heb 1:1-3); Third, God has revealed Himself and His power through creation (Ps 19:1-2; Rm 1:20); Fourth, God reveals Himself through the power and the indwelling of His Spirit (Jn 14:16-17; 1Jn 5:6-12). Finally, God reveals Himself through the witness of believers (Ac 1:8; 2:1-4; 1Jn 1:1-4).

How Can God Have All Power and Be Loving and Yet There Be Evil?

Gregory E. Ganssle

What philosophers call "the problem of evil" is a family of arguments from the existence or nature of evil to the conclusion that God does not or probably does not exist. The most popular form of the argument used to be an argument that the mere existence of evil is logically incompatible with God's existence. If God exists, it was thought, evil could not and if evil exists, God could not. I call this argument *the charge of contradiction.* The claim is that there is a *logical contradiction* in asserting that God is all powerful, God is all loving, and that evil exists. Wouldn't this kind of God eliminate all evil? The existence of God, on this view, is on par with a square circle. Given the existence of evil, it is impossible for God to exist. The challenge is to show that theism is logically consistent.

Few people today think this argument succeeds. If God might have a good reason to allow evil, then it is possible that both God and evil exist. We need not know what God's actual reasons are, but if it is possible He has them, then the argument is defeated. Most think that it is possible that God has good reasons to allow evil and that, therefore, there is no contradiction between God's existence and the existence of evil. Even atheist philosophers rarely support this kind of argument any more.

Today, the most important form of the argument against the existence of God from evil is called *the evidential argument from evil.* The one who presses this argument admits that the existence of God and the reality of evil are not logically *incompatible.* Rather, the argument is that the amount and the kinds of evil we find in the world are strong *evidence* against the existence of God.

Even though it is *possible* that God has a reason to allow the evils we find in the world, it does not seem likely that there actually are good reasons to allow some of the evils we see. We cannot prove that there is none, but if we have lots of cases in which it *seems* as though there is no good reason, we will conclude that there probably is no good reason to allow these evils. If it is true that probably there is no good reason to allow these cases of evil, then it is probable that God does not exist. This argument is called the evidential argument because we cannot prove that there is no good reason to allow the particular evils we are thinking about. These evils do, then, look like good evidence that God does not exist.

In order to begin to answer this argument, we must think about the claim that it is probable that no good reason exists to allow the evil in question. Why should we believe this is true? The one who puts this argument forward will appeal to cases of evil in which it is difficult to find a reason that might fit. Does this mean we ought to conclude that it is probable that there is no reason? No.

The reasoning here goes as follows: It seems like there is no reason to allow this evil therefore, probably there is no reason to allow it. Sometimes this kind of reasoning is strong and other times it is weak. Let me illustrate. The argument is of the form: It seems like there is no x, therefore, probably there is no x. The Bible has numerous cases where one could mount this argument. Let's take the case of Lazarus's death in John 11. Lazarus was likely in the prime of his life. He's a good man and a close friend of Jesus. Lazarus becomes ill and dies. The citizens of his village, Bethany, could see such an evil and after three days of mourning come to the conclusion that there is no reason for this. Therefore, God doesn't exist. Then Jesus comes to Bethany. Lazarus's sisters, Mary and Martha, chastise Jesus for not getting there sooner. As we read John's account, we see that unbeknownst to Mary and Martha, Jesus had reasons for delaying. Moreover, there were reasons Lazarus was permitted to die in the prime of his life. When Jesus arrived at Lazarus's tomb, He prayed and then called Lazarus to come out of the tomb four days after his death. The reason for Lazarus's sickness, death, Jesus' delay, and Lazarus's resuscitation was that God's glory might be seen.

Some of the citizens might have thought they had a strong case against the existence of God the three days after Lazarus died. But subsequent events place the evil of Lazarus's death in a much different context. In light of this context, Lazarus's death is seen to be part of a much greater good than anyone in Bethany could imagine.

The pattern that we see in this and numerous other biblical cases shows that there are times when we can't say, "If God had a reason to allow this particular case of evil, we would probably know what it is."

There are two reasons we can't always make this claim. First, we can figure out reasons that God might have for many (perhaps most) of the evils in the world. For example, both human freedom and a stable, cause-effect universe are necessary for any meaningful action. Meaningful action, then, may be a reason that God allows various kinds of evil. Second, it is reasonable to think that God will have reasons that we cannot grasp for allowing evils in our lives. In fact, to think that we should be able to figure out God's reasons for allowing every case of evil implies that we think God is not much smarter than we are. If God is the almighty creator of the universe, there will be evil the reason for which we cannot discern. This is exactly what we should expect if there is a God. It cannot be counted as evidence against God.

So even though it might seem, at first glance, that there are no good reasons to allow certain evils we see, this does not provide strong evidence that these evils are really unjustified. The argument that the kinds of evil we see make it unlikely that God exists has been seen to be pretty weak.

The philosophical problem of evil has to do with what is reasonable to believe. To what degree is it reasonable to believe in God in light of what we seem to know about evil? We have seen that evil does not contradict God's existence. Nor is it strong evidence against the existence of God. The evil in the world, then, does not make it unreasonable to believe in an all-powerful and all-loving God.

How Can the Bible Affirm Both Divine Sovereignty and Human Freedom?

Bruce A. Ware

God is the sovereign ruler over the universe and all human affairs, and human beings are responsible before God for the moral choices and actions they make. Yes, the Bible teaches both, and both are true.

What does the Bible teach about God's sovereign rulership?

Consider Daniel 4:35, where we are instructed that God "does what He wants with the army of heaven and the inhabitants of earth. There is no one who can hold back His hand or say to Him, 'What have You done?'" In light of this verse, three observations are needed. First, God's rulership is the exercise of "His will." That is, He decides in advance what He wants to happen so that "His will" precedes and directs all that occurs. Second, He exercises His will universally—over those in heaven and all the inhabitants of earth. There is no place where His will does not pertain or is not exercised. And third, no creature of God can thwart the fulfillment of God's will or charge God with wrongdoing. In short, God's rulership by His will is absolute, universal, and effectual.

Consider further the kinds of reality over which God reigns. The Bible contains a number of "spectrum texts" which display God's ultimate control of both good and evil, light and darkness, life and death. In Isaiah 45:6-7, God announces "I am Yahweh, and there is no other. I form light and create darkness, I make success and create disaster; I, Yahweh, do all these things" (see Ex 4:11; Dt 32:39; 1Sm 2:6-7; Ec 7:13-14; Lm 3:37-38). And, while we gladly affirm that God is good (only!) and that God neither approves evil in itself, nor does any evil reside in Him (Ps 5:4), yet we must affirm with the large and sweeping testimony of Scripture that He reigns over all of life, both its good and evil, and that in all that occurs "the decision of His will" (Eph 1:11) is fulfilled.

What does Scripture teach about human moral responsibility?

From page 1 of the Bible, we are put on notice that God holds us accountable for the moral choices and actions we make. The law of God—whether the simple law not to eat of one tree in the garden (Gn 2:16-17), or the Law given on Sinai (Ex 20), or the law of Christ (1Co 9:21; Gl 6:2)—establishes the moral framework within which our lives are lived. God will "repay each one according to his works" (Rm 2:6), and this judgment will be based on whether we persevere in doing good (Rm 2:7) or whether we do not obey the truth, but obey unrighteousness (Rm 2:8). There is no denying the fact that God considers humans as being responsible for the choices and actions they make, and the final judgment day will bear testimony to how we have chosen to live our lives.

So, God is the sovereign ruler over all, and human beings are responsible before Him, but just how can both be true?

We cannot understand fully how both are true together, but that they must work together is demanded by Scripture's clear teaching. Consider one illustration from Scripture where both are seen—namely, a lesson from Joseph's story (Gn 37–45). Joseph's brothers were deeply jealous of him and grew to despise him. When the opportunity presented itself, they sold him into Egypt (37:25-36) where Joseph was misunderstood and mistreated. Despite this, God's hand was on Joseph and he was elevated to second in command in Egypt (Gn 41). During a famine, his brothers traveled to Egypt to purchase grain, and there Joseph made himself known to his brothers. What Joseph tells them is as incredible as it is instructive: "Therefore it was not you who sent me here, but God" (Gn 45:8).

"Wait!" we might protest. "Surely they *did* send Joseph to Egypt!"

So they did, and so Joseph previously acknowledged (45:4). But, to get at the full reason Joseph was sent to Egypt requires looking not just to the brothers but also, more importantly, to God! So it is clear: *both* God and the brothers are responsible for sending Joseph to Egypt. *Both* God's sovereign rulership and the brother's moral actions are active. As Joseph puts it later in speaking with his brothers, "you planned evil against me; God planned it for good" (Gn 50:20). The brothers acted for evil, and God acted in the same events for good.

Not every question is here answered, but we see that we must affirm both the sovereign rulership of God and the genuineness of our moral responsibility. Both are joined together in Scripture, and what Scripture has joined together, let no man separate.

How Can the Bible Affirm Both Divine Sovereignty and Human Freedom?

William Lane Craig

The biblical worldview involves a very strong conception of divine sovereignty over the world and human affairs, even as it presupposes human freedom and responsibility (cp. the accounts of Saul's death in 1Sm 31:1-6 and 1Ch 10:8-12). An adequate doctrine of divine providence requires reconciling these two streams of biblical teaching without compromising either. Yet this has proven extraordinarily difficult. On the one hand, the Augustinian-Calvinist perspective interprets divine providence in terms of predetermination, God choosing in advance what will happen. It is hard to see how this interpretation can preserve human freedom or avoid making God the author of sin, since (for example) it would then be He who moved Judas to betray Christ. On the other hand, advocates of revisionist views (*e.g.*, open theism) freely admit that as a consequence of their denial of God's knowledge of future contingent events a strong doctrine of providence becomes impossible. Ironically, in order to account for biblical prophecies of future events revisionists are often reduced to appealing to the same deterministic explanations that Augustinian-Calvinists offer.

Molinism offers an attractive solution. Luis Molina (1535–1600) defined providence as God's ordering of things to their ends, either directly or indirectly through secondary causes. In explaining how God can order things through secondary causes which are themselves free agents, Molina appeals to his doctrine of divine middle knowledge.

Molina analyzes God's knowledge in terms of three logical stages. Although whatever God knows, He knows eternally, so that there is no temporal succession in God's knowledge, nonetheless there does exist a sort of logical order in God's knowledge in the sense that His knowledge of certain truths is conditionally or explanatorily prior to His knowledge of certain other truths.

In the first stage God knows all possibilities, not only all the creatures He could possibly create, but also all the orders of creatures which are possible. By means of this so-called natural knowledge, God has knowledge of every contingent state of affairs which could possibly be actual and of what any free creature could freely choose to do in any such state of affairs.

In the second stage, God possesses knowledge of all true counterfactual propositions (statements of the form "If *x* were the case, then *y* would be the case"), including counterfactuals about what creatures would freely do in various circumstances. Whereas by His natural knowledge God knew what any free creature *could* do in any set of circumstances, now in this second stage God knows what any free creature *would* freely do in any set of circumstances. This so-called "middle" knowledge is like natural knowledge in that such knowledge does not depend on any decision of the divine will; God does not determine which counterfactuals are true or false. By knowing how free creatures would freely act in any set of circumstances He might place them in, God thereby knows that if He were to actualize certain states of affairs, then certain other contingent states of affairs would be actual as a result. For example, He knew that if Pontius Pilate were the Roman procurator of Judea in A.D. 30, he would freely condemn Jesus to the cross.

Intervening between the second and third stages of divine knowledge stands God's free decree to actualize a world known by Him to be realizable on the basis of His middle knowledge. By His natural knowledge, God knows what is the entire range of logically possible worlds; by His middle knowledge He knows, in effect, what is the proper subset of those worlds which it is feasible for Him to actualize. By a free decision, God decrees to actualize one of those worlds known to Him through His middle knowledge. In so doing He also decrees how He Himself would freely act in any set of circumstances.

Given God's free decision to actualize a world, in the third and final stage God possesses so-called free knowledge of all remaining propositions that are in fact true in the actual world, including future-tense propositions about how creatures will freely behave.

Molina's scheme effects a dramatic reconciliation of divine sovereignty and human freedom. In Molina's view God directly causes certain circumstances to come into being and brings about others indirectly through either causally determined secondary causes or free secondary causes. He allows free creatures to act as He knew they freely would when placed in specific circumstances, and He concurs with their decisions in producing the effects they desire. Some of these effects God desired unconditionally and so wills positively that they occur. Others He does not unconditionally desire, but He nevertheless permits due to His overriding desire to allow creaturely freedom, knowing that even these sinful acts will fit into the overall scheme of things, so that God's ultimate ends in human history will be accomplished. God thus providentially arranges for everything that happens by either willing or permitting it, and He causes everything that does happen, yet in such a way as to preserve freedom and contingency.

Is God a Male?

Chad Owen Brand

W hen Scripture speaks about God, it invariably uses masculine imagery. God is King, not queen. God is Father, not Mother. When Scripture uses pronouns in reference to God, it always uses male pronouns—*He, Him, His.* God is never "she" or "it." Even though the NT term for the Spirit, *pneuma,* is a neuter noun, the writers of the NT always use masculine pronouns to refer to the Spirit. It is "the Spirit, He," not "It" (e.g., Jn 15:26). In addition, the church is represented as the wife or bride of Christ, who is Husband (Eph 5:22-33). This is similar to OT imagery in which Israel was the wife of Yahweh (Hs 1–3; Ezk 16).

It is also important to recognize that this is not merely functional terminology. That is, it is not just language that is designed for us in our relationship to God. God the Father is Father of God the Son (Jn 17:1-5). Even in the internal relationships within God's being, it is the relationship of a father to a son. Furthermore, we are not intended to use the human standard of a father or husband to interpret God's fatherliness or Christ's husband character, but rather, we are to see God as the epitome of what those ought to be, and then to measure our experience by the standard of the Father and Christ.

Is this patriarchal? Yes, quite clearly it is. But as Christians we are bound to take our theology from Scripture, not from the cultural standards around us. Most of the cultures surrounding ancient Israel had goddess figures, as did the Roman culture of NT times. But the writers of Scripture always treated this as among the most heinous kinds of idolatry. If we are to be faithful to our Christian heritage, we must stick to Scripture.

Does this patriarchalism mean the Bible holds women to be inferior? Not at all. God is often depicted as treating His people in the way a caregiver would treat a child. Jesus said, "I wanted to gather your children together, as a hen gathers her chicks under her wings, but you were not willing!" (Lk 13:34-35). The Bible elevates women in ways contrary to the pagan cultures of the day. They are equal partners of the grace of God given in Christ (Gl 3:28).

But Scripture still speaks of God in a masculine manner. God is Father, and we ought to be eternally grateful for the fact that He is the ultimate model of what a father ought to be. Christ is Husband, and as such He reveals what the true husband does for his wife. Both women and men in our time ought to be grateful for the fact that God is the perfect example of what these relationships entail. This enables both men and women to know the Father and Christ in ways that are life-transforming.

The Trinity: Is it Possible that God Is both One and Three?

Douglas K. Blount

L ike Jews and Muslims, Christians are monotheists. In other words, they believe in the existence of precisely one God. Unlike other monotheists, however, Christians also believe that, while there exists just one God, He is three persons—Father, Son, and Holy Spirit. The belief that the one and only God exists eternally as three persons is known as the doctrine of the Trinity. And this doctrine plays an important role in Christian faith. In fact, the doctrine of the Incarnation—which says Jesus is God the Son become a man and is thus both fully divine and fully human—assumes it. This latter doctrine lies at the very heart of Christian faith.

On its face, however, the doctrine of the Trinity might look like a contradiction. It might seem impossible that God be both one and three. Indeed, the apparent absurdity of this doctrine has led to at least two major errors, each of which elevates one of the doctrine's claims at the other's expense. On one hand, some stress the "oneness" of God at the expense of His "three-ness," claiming that there is only one divine person. Those who describe God in this way usually say that the one divine person appears in different guises or masks, sometimes as Father, other times as Son, and still other times as Spirit. Since this view says the one divine person changes His mode of appearance, it is called *modalism*. On the other hand, some stress God's "three-ness" at the expense of His "oneness," claiming each of the three divine persons is a distinct god. This view, which says there are three gods, is called *tritheism*.

But modalism and tritheism are at odds with the Bible, which presents God as both one and three. There is just one God (Dt 6:4); yet this God is three persons—Father, Son, and Spirit (Mt 3:16-17; Mk 1:9-11; Lk 3:21-22). No doubt it is difficult (or perhaps even impossible) for us to understand how God is both one and three. But something's being difficult (or even impossible) for humans to understand doesn't make it a contradiction.

A contradiction involves saying something is both true and false at the same time and in the same way. So, for instance, one who says both that Napoleon lost the Battle of Waterloo and that Napoleon did not lose the Battle of Waterloo contradicts himself. It is logically impossible that Napoleon both lost that battle and did not lose it. His claim is contradictory.

Now if Christians said both that (1a) there exists precisely one God, and that (1b) it is not the case that there exists precisely one God, they would contradict themselves. So also if they said both that (2a) there exist three divine persons and that (2b) it is not the case that there are three divine persons, they also would contradict themselves. But Christians do not affirm both 1a and

1b. Neither do they affirm both 2a and 2b. Rather, they affirm 1a and 2a. And this would be contradictory only if either 1a entails 2b or 2a entails 1b.

To put the point differently, when Christians say that God is both one and three, they do not say that He is one in the same way in which He is three. So, for instance, they do not say both that (1a) there exists precisely one God, and that (1c) there exist three gods. Nor do they say both that (2a) there exist three divine persons, and that (2c) there exists only one divine person.

Since 1c entails 1b, affirming both it and 1a would be contradictory. And since 2c entails 2b, affirming both it and 2a also would be contradictory. But, as a matter of fact, Christians deny both 1c and 2c. In affirming 1a and 2a, then, Christians affirm that in one way God is one and in another way He is three. And in so doing they do not contradict themselves.

So, then, those who think the doctrine of the Trinity is contradictory seem to misunderstand either the nature of a contradiction or the doctrine itself. Perhaps they confuse contradiction with mere paradox, taking our inability to understand *how* the doctrine is true to entail it is false. But our inability to understand *how* God is both one and three tells us far more about ourselves than it does about God. The Bible presents God as both one and three; that suffices for us to know that He is so, regardless of whether we understand the *how* of it.

Can God Create a Stone Too Heavy for Him to Lift?

Charles Taliaferro

The question should immediately strike one as a word game. Many puzzles exist in the same category such as, "Can God eat oatmeal that no one can eat?" Such puzzles are intended to reveal a logical problem with the divine attribute of omnipotence. If God can create a stone too heavy for even Him to lift, there is one task God cannot do, namely lift any conceivable stone. But if God can lift any stone then again there appears to be one task God cannot do, namely God cannot create a stone too heavy for God to lift. The argument concludes there cannot be an omnipotent God.

The most plausible and common philosophical response to this puzzle is to challenge the coherence of the task demanded. In order for someone to conclude that there is some state of affairs God cannot bring about, the objector must establish that the state of affairs is a genuine, bona fide possibility. It is no imperfection of anyone to be unable to make the concept of justice dance with the number two. The concepts of justice and the number two are not the sorts of things that can dance.

Does the above reply make "logic" something greater than God? No, "logic" is not the name of some concrete or abstract thing which can carry out tasks. When you cannot do something contradictory (such as make a square circle) it is not as though there is a force called logic restraining you. "Logic," in this context, may be formulated in terms of two laws: the law of identity (A is A) and non-contradiction (A is not not-A). These are not "laws," however, like the laws of nature (e.g., the laws of motion). They are, rather, necessary conditions of there being anything at all and for there being thought or language about anything at all. God the Son is identified in the NT as the Logos. Some philosophers and theologians have understood this to imply that logic and reason are attributes of God's excellent nature.

The stone paradox may be resolved in terms of strict logic, but does it not generate a more general problem? Can the God of Christian theism commit suicide? Tell lies? Do evil for its own sake?

Two replies should be considered. One is to claim God can bring about any of these states of affairs, but because of God's essential goodness, God does not do so. On this view, God is still omnipotent in the sense of being able to bring about any state of affairs. A second reply is to question an assumption behind the objection. Why think of divine omnipotence exclusively in terms of the bare scope of power? An important classical Christian tradition (Augustine, Anselm, Aquinas) holds God's power is also supremely good. Is the "power" to do evil for its own sake a worthy, good power? Arguably, God's excellent power is the power to do good, not evil. A further exploration of this concept of divine power leads us away from the apparent word game of the stone paradox, and focuses the mind on the nature of God's excellence, the object worthy of worship.

How Does the Holy Spirit Relate to Evidence for Christianity?

Gary R. Habermas

It is often assumed that the Holy Spirit's witness to a believer is not very helpful in a study of apologetics. After all, this testimony is only given to Christians, and it is not verified or falsified by evidences. So does it follow that this witness is no more than a subjective conviction?

In the few NT passages that address this subject, we are told that, at a minimum, the witness of the Holy Spirit is a personal word to the believer that they are children of God (Rm 8:15-17). The Holy Spirit testifies to believers as family members (Gl 4:6-7). So the believer will experience the presence of the Holy Spirit (Jn 14:16-17). This is one way to know that we are truly believers (1Jn 3:24; 4:13).

Some commentators think this inner witness does more than just testify to the reality of one's salvation. Even if this is so, it seems clear that this aspect is the most directly involved in each of these texts. Stated briefly, the

Holy Spirit's presence is the clearest indication that a particular individual is saved.

Since the unbeliever cannot understand things pertaining to salvation (Jn 14:17; 1Co 2:14), one might question the value of the Holy Spirit's witness in an apologetic context, since it is less useful when interacting with non-Christians. But this seems to assume that dealing with unbelievers is the only purpose for defending the faith.

Apologetics may have even more value in strengthening the faith of believers through a variety of avenues. Since the chief purpose of the Holy Spirit's witness is to provide personal assurance of the believer's salvation, the resulting confidence can play a very valuable role in convincing believers of their own relationship with the Lord. This might provide assistance, for example, in dealing with religious doubt.

Moreover, the witness of the Holy Spirit provides indirect confirmation of the truth of the Christian Gospel. After all, if we are the children of God and joint-heirs with Jesus Christ as we suffer and are glorified with Him (Rm 8:17), then it would follow that God's Gospel path, the very basis of this assurance, is likewise true.

The witness of the Holy Spirit rests on the truth of the Christian message. The truth of Christianity is confirmed by a variety of strong evidences. So the witness rests on a highly evidenced foundation. Accordingly, believers are justified in holding that the Holy Spirit has provided just such a personal witness to them, indicating they are God's children. While there is no external proof of such a claim, especially with unbelievers, neither is it disproven by science or reason. Some additional degree of confirmation might be gained by the community of believers, who share this testimony.

So when someone becomes a Christian and experiences the Holy Spirit's presence, it ought not surprise them, since this is precisely what Scripture teaches! It should be normal fare for the believer. Briefly stated, the study of apologetics indicates that Christianity is true; the witness of the Holy Spirit performs the related function of identifying those who are members of the faith.

SECTION 6

Science and Faith

Scripture and the Prescientific Worldview
Jeremy Royal Howard

To the claim that science and Scripture are often contradictory, one Christian viewpoint responds with the following observations: (1) When conflict arises, it arises not between science and infallible Scripture, but between *interpreters* of science and *interpreters* of infallible Scripture; (2) Interpreters of science and Scripture are capable of ignorance, misinterpretation, misapplication, and bias. These observations highlight the need for proper interpretation and application in both fields of study.

Context is Key. The context in which divine revelation was given is key to proper interpretation and application of Scripture. Two questions in particular help set the context for the relationship between science and Scripture.

First, were the Scriptures originally given to people who were scientifically informed and conversant with technically accurate descriptions of the structure and operations of nature, or were the Scriptures instead given to prescientific people whose descriptions of nature were based on casual observation and untested presupposition rather than scientific scrutiny? The answer is clear. The Scriptures originated among prescientific Hebrews who could not have guessed at many of the scientific truths that are commonplace knowledge today. In fact the Hebrews would have strongly objected to many science claims we know to be true. This is no mark against their intelligence, but rather a mark of their position in history. They were not afforded the chance to learn many of the counter-intuitive, expectation-defying truths about nature that have been unfolded since the scientific revolution.

Second, what message did God seek to communicate through Scripture? Arguably He did not aim to reveal scientific truths. Other things—more important things—were at stake. For instance, the earliest books of the Bible were written by Moses between 1440 and 1400 B.C. The audience was the Hebrew people, who for the previous 400 years had been captive as a slave force in Egypt. The Hebrews did not have the Scriptures to guide them during those years in Egypt, for no Scriptures had been written by that early date. When it comes to the things of God, many of them were perhaps as ignorant as their Egyptian neighbors. They had Egyptian habits and Egyptian beliefs, as demonstrated in the fiasco with the golden calf (Ex 32). In this context of spiritual ignorance, God chose Moses as His spokesman to the Hebrews. Moses' tasks included teaching the Hebrews basic truths about God, His will, and the human condition. Was the overturning of prescientific misconceptions even on the agenda?

Having seen that the Scriptures came to a prescientific people whose most critical need was spiritual enlightenment, we next examine two topics in Scripture to see whether our expectation that the Bible will reflect prescientific understandings is confirmed.

The Stars. The Bible portrays stars as small objects nearby over our heads, lodged in a dome-like firmament. This was a widespread view among the ancients, who had no concept of the interstellar distances modern science has revealed. Recall Icarus, the Greek mythical figure who by flying high in our sky came so close to the sun that his waxen wings melted, sending him plummeting to his death. That Icarus could get appreciably closer to the sun by climbing several hundred feet into the sky demonstrates the prescientific belief that the sun hangs low over our heads. The biblical adoption of this common prescientific view is seen in numerous texts, perhaps most vividly in one of Daniel's visions (Dn 8). Daniel watched as "a little horn" grew up into the heavenly host and knocked them to Earth, where the stars proved small enough to be trampled underfoot. Though this was a vision, it fits with four common prescientific beliefs among the ancients about the literal structure of the heavens: (1) stars are a short distance over our heads rather than millions of light years away; (2) stars are small enough to be jostled by a narrow object rising from Earth; (3) stars are packed so close together that a swipe across the night sky could swat many of them out of position; (4) stars can fall to the surface of Earth.

The Bible elsewhere depicts a star as visibly moving through our atmosphere, leading the Wise Men to end their brief stay in Jerusalem and walk a few miles before the star stopped to hover over Bethlehem (Mt 2:9). Whatever light source God used here, it was not a literal star. We can say this because we know what no ancient could have guessed: stars are supergiant spheres of raging nuclear plasma that dwarf Earth by many magnitudes and indwell the far faraway reaches of outer space. Stars cannot fall to Earth anymore than you can fall to the moon from your backyard, nor can they descend into our atmosphere to act as navigators. Any attempt to argue that the Star of Bethlehem can be identified with stars, planets, comets, or supernovae robs the event of its supernatural element, plus it is ill-fitting with Matthew's language, especially where he says the star "stopped above the place where the child was" (v. 9). This describes a small body moving not through space but rather through the lower reaches of our sky. That it stopped and hovered over a small village, pinpointing it, confirms this conclusion beyond all doubt. Whatever motion literal stars and comets appear to exhibit from our vantage point as they wheel around in our night skies, none of them could be described as moving in such a way as to distinguish Bethlehem from any other point on the map.

The Sun. The Bible portrays the sun as orbiting around Earth. For example, King David says of the sun: "It rises from one end of the heavens and circles to the other end" (Ps 19:6). Solomon wrote: "The sun rises and the sun sets; panting, it returns to its place where it rises" (Ec 1:5). Granted, these are poetic descriptions, and even today people who know better speak of the sun rising and setting. But the trouble is the ancients did *not* know better. For them, rising and setting were accurate descriptions of a sun in motion. Rather than countering this prescientific view, biblical descriptions of the sun orbiting the Earth reflect the universal view among the ancients that Earth is literally stationary and that the sun orbits it. Even up to the dawn of the scientific revolution, learned people found it impossible to accept that Earth orbits the sun. Besides appealing to Scripture to support geocentrism (as Martin Luther vociferously did, going so far as to call Copernicus a "fool" and an "upstart astrologer"), they assumed they would feel Earth's motion under their feet and that they would be buffeted constantly by high winds if Earth really rode a circuit around the sun. We might be tempted to laugh at their stance, but the more appropriate response is to recognize how context and presupposition can limit our openness to learning surprising science facts.

Is the Bible Errant? Do these and other scientifically inaccurate descriptions indicate that Scripture is errant? Critics have said so, and many believers have feared so. But biblical errancy is an unnecessary conclusion. In view of the prescientific vantage point of the original recipients of Scripture, it was necessary for God to speak to them in ways that accommodated their prescientific views of nature if successful communication was to occur. They simply did not have the conceptual grid for receiving technically accurate descriptions of nature's structure and operation. In the first place, the biblical authors themselves would have been unable to comprehend or accept scientifically accurate descriptions. Unless one wishes to argue for the discredited dictation view of biblical inspiration, which says God took control of the author's consciousness, with the result that they wrote as mindless robots conveying the dictates of God, the inability of prescientific human authors to comprehend modern science truths is a serious obstacle to the idea that Scripture could serve as a vehicle for disclosing science insights thousands of years before their time. Second, as much difficulty as authors such as Moses had in serving as spokesmen for God to the Hebrews (they were commonly mocked, disobeyed, ignored), imagine how the difficulties would have multiplied if God had asked them to reveal not only controversial religious truths, but also mind-blowing science truths that could not be verified in an age before telescopes and microscopes. It seems likely that the Hebrews would have gone from calling men like Moses nuisances to outright madmen. Further, their writings would have been rejected as discredited ravings, never revered as Scripture.

Concluding Statements. (1) It is fitting that the Bible, given originally to a prescientific people, would reflect prescientific views of nature's structure and operations; Scripture would have been incoherent to its original audience (and to the biblical human authors themselves) if it used scientifically accurate descriptions; (2) Accommodation to prescientific descriptions of nature is a mark of God's grace, not biblical error or divine ignorance; God knows nature infallibly well, but He chose to speak to the Hebrews in a manner they could understand given their time and place in history; (3) To properly interpret Scripture, the reader must bear in mind the issue of divine accommodation to prescientific views; many believers throughout history, not having the benefit of scientific learning or a grasp of divine accommodation in texts that touch on domains into which science can speak, have mistakenly thought the Bible was seeking to make technically accurate claims about the structure and function of nature, and thus have wrongly resisted scientific advancement in the name of being true to Scripture; (4) The fact that the Hebrews did not originate science fits with the argument that their God-given Scriptures accommodated rather than overturned prescientific views; if God really meant to speak with scientific precision on all matters addressed in Scripture, revealing science facts otherwise unknown to the ancients, it is conspicuous that science was not birthed among fervently religious Hebrews; (5) The Bible has too often been presented as an obstacle to scientific progress; this fact stems in part from the tendency of Bible readers to misinterpret the Bible's intentions, taking its statements about nature to be attempts at scientific description when in fact they were merely casual descriptions suitable to the pre-science or non-science vantage points; (6) Scientists who claim that science proves God does not exist are speaking as non-scientists, for science is the study of material reality and causation and has no application to questions of the existence of an eternal Spirit Being; (7) Scientists must bear in mind that science is not the only source of knowledge; any claim that science is the sole source of knowledge is self-defeating, for science itself cannot demonstrate the truth of the claim that science is the sole source of knowledge; (8) Bible believers must weigh carefully all claims made by scientists; science is self-correcting over time, but the journey through bias and error can be lengthy; (9) Bible believers should enthusiastically embrace the scientific endeavor as a quest to discover truths about God's creation, many of which cannot be known apart from science, and some of which may run counter to our customary ways of reading Scripture; (10) The model expressed in this essay does not undermine biblical authority, but instead emphasizes the context and intentions of biblical revelation; if the Bible reflects prescientific viewpoints, and does so for the sake of successfully communicating to a prescientific people, we do not compromise biblical authority by choosing a non-literal reading of Bible passages that touch on the structure and functions of nature.

What Is the Relationship Between Science and the Bible?

J.P. Moreland

C hristians are committed to the reality of knowable truths from the Bible and science. Further, Christians seek to integrate claims from both sources into an integrated worldview. How is this done? What is the relationship between the Bible and science?

Some claim that the history of Bible-science interaction is largely a war with theology constantly losing. But for two reasons, this claim is false. First, the relationship between the Bible and science is much richer than what can be captured by a warfare metaphor (see below). Second, many times the teachings of the Bible and science confirm each other, but when there have been differences, it is not always the Bible that has been re-examined. Sometimes, scientific claims have been re-interpreted. For example, shortly after Darwinism arose, creationists predicted that there would be gaps in the fossil record with no clear transition forms, and evolutionists predicted that thousands of transitional forms would be discovered. Evolutionists were wrong.

In general, the warfare metaphor is not adequate. At least five different models have been offered to capture the integration of science and the Bible. Each position is not exhaustive and one can subscribe to all five on a case-by-case basis. Thus, these views provide tools for Christians in the task of integrating science and the Bible.

1 Distinct Realms: Claims from the Bible and science may involve two distinct, non-overlapping areas of investigation. For example, debates about angels or the extent of the atonement have little if anything to do with organic chemistry. Similarly, it is of little interest to theology whether a methane molecule has three or four hydrogen atoms in it.

2. Complementary Descriptions of the Same Realm: Claims from the Bible and science may involve two different, complementary, non-interacting approaches to the same reality. Sociological aspects of church growth and certain psychological aspects of conversion may involve scientific descriptions of certain phenomena that are complementary to a theological description of church growth or conversion. Claims in chemistry that water comes from combining hydrogen and oxygen are complementary to theological claims that God providentially creates water.

In general, we may describe God's activity in terms of primary causes (when God acts in an unusual way, and directly, miraculously produces an effect) or secondary causes (when God acts in ordinary ways by sustaining and using natural processes to accomplish a result). The complementary approach is most effective when God acts by way of secondary causes.

3. Direct Interaction: Claims from the Bible and science may directly interact such that either one area of study offers rational support for the other or one area of study raises rational difficulties for the other. For example, certain theological teachings about the existence of the soul raise rational problems for scientific claims that deny the existence of the soul. The general theory of evolution raises various difficulties for certain ways of understanding the book of Genesis. Some have argued that the second law of thermodynamics supports the theological proposition that the universe had a beginning. Special creationism—for example, young-earth and progressive creationism—are applications of this approach to the question of the origin and development of life.

4. Presuppositional Interaction: Biblical teaching can be used to support the presuppositions of science. Some have argued that many of the presuppositions of science (e.g. the existence of truth; the rational, orderly nature of reality; the adequacy of our sensory and cognitive faculties as tools suited for knowing the external world) make sense and are easy to justify through Christian theism but are without justification in a worldview that does not include God.

5 Practical Application: Biblical teaching can help one practically apply principles discovered in science and vice versa. For example, theology teaches that fathers should not provoke their children to anger and psychology can add important details about what this means by offering information about family systems, the nature and causes of anger, etc. Psychology can devise various tests for assessing whether one is or is not a mature person, given a normative definition (a definition of what ought to be the case and not just a description of what actually is the case) from the Bible as to what a mature person ought to be like.

It is the direct interaction approach that opens up the possibility that scientific and biblical claims may provide mutual intellectual support or be in conflict with one another.

Three things should be kept in mind in approaching areas of apparent conflict.

First, the vast majority of biblical teaching and scientific claims have little to do with one another directly, and it is wrong to give the impression that most of the issues from these two sources support or conflict with each other. Areas of potential conflict are quite small compared to the vastness of ideas from the Bible and science.

Second, there are several areas where scientific discoveries have lent support to biblical assertions: evidence that the universe had a beginning; evidence that the universe is fine-tuned and delicately designed so that life could appear; evidence that strongly suggests that there is no naturalistic explanation for the origin of life and, moreover, that life is characterized by information which always comes from a mind; evidence that some components of living things are irreducibly complex such that all their parts need each other to function and, thus, could not have evolved gradually; numerous examples of archeological confirmation of biblical claims; psychological discoveries of the importance of a unified spiritual, moral free agent to explain human functioning and maturity.

Third, we should face areas of conflict honestly but confidently in light of points one and two. Christians ought to make sure they have understood scriptural and scientific data correctly, and seek solutions that are both biblically and scientifically adequate. Given that Christianity provides a reasonable worldview for justifying science, that most areas of science and the Bible do not directly interact, and that many scientific discoveries have added confirmation to biblical teaching, there is no reason why Christians cannot be rational in admitting that there are currently areas of apparent conflict for which they do not have adequate solutions. No worldview is without some problems and unresolved questions. Still, contrary to popular opinion, the difficulties that scientific claims raise for biblical teaching are far from overwhelming, and they are fewer in number than one would expect by listening to propagandists from secular culture.

Are the Days of Genesis to Be Interpreted Literally?

Ted Cabal

This question has stoked controversy among conservative Christians in recent times, but proven of little interest to theistic evolutionists and those rejecting Genesis as God's inerrant Word. The debate has been primarily between young- and old-earth creationists who believe God literally created the various kinds of living things (contra the common descent of Darwinism). Both sides hold that humans have not descended from other species, and reject the atheism and macroevolutionary theory of neo-Darwinism.

The two creationist camps, however, differ in interpreting the creation days of Genesis. Both sides understand these days to be important in the relationship of the Bible to science. If the days were consecutive 24-hour periods, and the earth was created on the first day, then calculations based on biblical genealogies reveal the earth was created only thousands of years ago. If the days are either of indeterminate length or non-consecutive, then the Bible does not reveal when the earth was created. Interestingly, both sides agree the genealogies reveal Adam and Eve were specially created only thousands of years ago.

Young earth creationists (YCs) interpret the days as 24-hour, consecutive periods for reasons such as these: (1) The days in Genesis 1 are consecutively numbered and comprised of an "evening and morning;" (2) Exodus 20:8-11 commands a literal week of six days work and one day rest based on God's original creation/rest week: the two weeks are then of equal duration. (3) According to Romans 5:12, "sin entered the world through one man, and death through sin," but old-earth creationism would have animal death entering the world before the sin of Adam and Eve.

Old earth creationists (OCs) argue against 24-hour creation days for reasons such as these: (1) The Hebrew word for "day" (*yom*) is used in different ways in the creation account. For instance, Genesis 1:5 refers *yom* only to daytime (daylight), not nighttime. Also, Genesis 2:4, literally translated, speaks of "the *yom* that the LORD God made the earth and the heavens." (2) God's rest on the seventh "day" has no evening and morning (Gn 2:2-3), and Hebrews 4:3-11 portrays this same Sabbath as continuing to the present time.(3) Adam could not have named all the birds and animals in 24 hours according to Genesis 2.

Both sides believe they have strong arguments favoring their interpretation and rebutting the other side. And historically, debate regarding biblical interpretation has often led historically to a clearer understanding of God's Word. But it is also highly debatable whether this issue merits the rancor and division too often attending it. Some YCs accuse OCs of compromising the Bible with "evolutionary" science. Some OCs charge YCs with undermining biblical credibility by generating a false conflict between science and the Scriptures.

Happily, one thing is not debatable among those who believe the Bible: even if the correct interpretation of the creation days is not readily apparent in the present generation, the Bible can be trusted in every way. Debates about biblical interpretations should not be interpreted as the failure of Holy Scripture.

Does the Bible Provide Guidance Regarding Genetic Engineering?

Scott B. Rae

Since human beings weren't able to manipulate the genetic code when the Bible was written, it doesn't directly address genetic engineering. However, it *does* give general principles that have application to genetic technologies. God charged Adam and Eve to exercise dominion over His creation (Gn 1:27-28). Their mandate? To subdue and kindly master the earth, unlocking its resources to benefit themselves and their successors—in a sense continuing the spirit of creation by being subordinate "creators" with God in unlocking the secrets of the creation to benefit humankind.

The command to subdue the earth takes on added complexity after the entrance of sin into the world in Genesis 3. Exercising dominion over creation after the Fall now involved dealing with sin's effects in the world. Dominion now involved working toward improving the creation, or reversing the effects of the entrance of sin. The most important of sin's effects was the new reality of death (Genesis 3:2-3), which was universal in its scope (Romans 5:12). That is, after the Fall, death, decay, and deterioration faced every person. Thus, dominion over the creation largely involved dealing with death and disease—the cause of death in most cases—so that mankind could alleviate the harshness of life after the Fall, even genetic disease. In order to exercise dominion, God (through general revelation) provided human beings with resources necessary for accomplishing that task. That ingenuity and wisdom come from God as His "common grace" gifts to humans (Is 28:23-9).

The knowledge and skill necessary to develop the kinds of technologies that enable mankind to subdue the creation are part of God's general revelation. Humans didn't acquire the ingenuity and skill to develop sophisticated technology on their own apart from God. It's not an accident that these technologies came to be so useful in our exercise of dominion over creation. They are gifts from God. Thus, technologies that generally improve the lot of humanity and specifically help reverse the effects of sin's entrance into the world are part of God's common grace. The skill and expertise needed to bring about these creation-subduing technologies come ultimately from God, being His good gifts to humans in harnessing creation.

This is particularly the case when it comes to medical technology. Since death is one of the primary consequences of the entrance of sin into the world, and disease is the primary cause of death and physical deterioration, medical technologies bringing cures to diseases and other afflictions are among God's most gracious gifts to the human race.

Medical technology can be part of God's common grace to assist humans in fulfilling their role in exercising loving dominion. The more controversial technology of genetic engineering should be used only for *therapeutic* reasons (repairing damage)—in keeping with the creation mandate—not for *eugenic* reasons (creating a kind of super race, as Hitler hoped to do with the Aryan race under Nazi rule, considering other races inferior). C.S. Lewis warned: "[if] the dreams of some scientific planners are realized" by using their power to make their descendants into what they please, then their "conquest of Nature . . . means the rule of a few hundreds of men over billions upon billions of men."

Are Miracles Believable?

Ronald H. Nash

M iracles are essential to the historic Christian faith. If Jesus Christ was not God incarnate, and if Jesus did not rise bodily from the grave, then the Christian faith as we know it from history and from the Scriptures would not—could not—be true (see Rm 10:9-10). It is easy to see then why enemies of the Christian faith direct many of their attacks against these two miracles in particular and against the possibility of miracles in general.

What one believes about the possibility of miracles comes from that person's worldview. On the question of miracles, the critical worldview distinction is between naturalism and supernaturalism. For a naturalist, the universe is analogous to a closed box. Everything that happens inside the box is caused by or is explicable in terms of other things that exist within the box. *Nothing* (including God) exists outside the box; therefore, nothing outside the box we call the universe or nature can have any causal effect within the box. To quote the famous naturalist, Carl Sagan, the cosmos is all that is or ever has been or ever will be. The major reason, then, why naturalists do not believe in miracles is because their worldview prevents them from believing.

If a naturalist suddenly begins to consider the possibility that miracles are really possible, he or she has begun to move away from naturalism towards a different worldview. Any person under the control of naturalistic presuppositions could not consistently believe in miracles. No arguments on behalf of the miraculous can possibly succeed with such a person. The proper way to address the unbelief of such a person is to begin by challenging his or her naturalism.

The worldview of Christian theism affirms the existence of a personal God who transcends nature, who exists "outside the box." Christian supernaturalism denies the eternity of nature. God created the world freely and *ex nihilo* (out of nothing). The universe is contingent in the sense that it would not have begun to exist without God's creative act and it could not continue to exist without God's sustaining activity. The very laws of the cosmos that naturalists believe make miracles impossible were created by this God. Indeed one of naturalism's major problems is explaining how mindless forces could give rise to minds, knowledge, and sound reasoning.

How Can Modern Medicine Relate to the Old Testament?

John A. Bloom

M any laws in the Pentateuch (Genesis–Deuteronomy) relate to diet and hygiene for the Hebrew people. Theologians for centuries thought that these merely served a ceremonial function or formed a cultural barrier to separate Israel from the surrounding pagan cultures. However, with the rise of modern medicine and the germ theory of disease in the nineteenth century, it was recognized that obeying these laws also confers important health benefits. These commands are unique compared with the health practices of neighboring cultures in OT times, suggesting that God inspired Moses in giving these laws. Moreover, they show that God's rules are not arbitrary and that He has our best interests at heart.

Laws instructing people to wash after touching the dead or sick (Lv 13–15; Nm 19), to properly dispose of excrement and blood (Lv 17:13; Dt 23:12-13), and to isolate (quarantine) diseased individuals and anything they touch (Lv 13) are extremely effective at limiting the spread of disease. Modern medicine has also shown that circumcision confers a health benefit—the wives of circumcised men have a much lower risk of contracting cervical cancer because the lack of a foreskin reduces the male's ability to harbor and transmit the human papillomavirus. Interestingly, the study of blood clotting factor levels in newborns has also shown that circumcision on the eighth day—the age prescribed to Abraham (Gn 17:12)—is the safest time in a man's life to have this surgery.

As our understanding of germs and parasites improves, the OT prohibitions against eating unclean animals, or even associating with them, receive increasing medical verification. For example, people commonly argue that we no longer need to treat pigs as unclean because we now know how to cook pork well. However, modern research on the flu virus shows that most new deadly strains of influenza arise under conditions where people are in close contact with pigs and birds. Pigs function as a bridge between the bird and human forms of influenza; thus new deadly flu outbreaks usually originate in China, Hong Kong, and other areas where people live in close proximity to pigs.

The medical benefits of many other commandments are well known, even if modern culture is not inclined to obey them. For example, avoiding adultery and fornication is the best way to protect oneself against sexually transmitted diseases (Ex 20:14; Pr 5); avoiding addictions will spare one from alcohol, drug, and tobacco-related diseases (Pr 20:1; 23:19-21,29-35); and prayer, mediation, and treating others fairly minimize the damaging effects of stress (Lv 19:13-18; Ps 23; 27:1-3; 91:3-7). Modern medicine shows that "living by the Book" brings many practical blessings, just as God promised (Ex 15:26), which makes it all the more reasonable to trust God regarding promised spiritual blessings for those who follow in faith.

Is Psychology Biblical?

John Coe

The answer is yes and no, depending upon four different ways we can interpret this controversial question. But before we get to those four ways, let's consider definitions of the term *psychology*.

Definitions: (1) As a *task,* psychology has to do with observing and reflecting on persons and their complex situations with the goal to understand human nature and its components, growth, dysfunction, and wisdom for living. (2) As a *product*, psychology is the more or less systematic body of information resulting from a mind engaged in understanding human nature, change, etc. (e.g., Freud's psychology). (3) As an *intervention*, psychology or psychotherapy is a relationship between therapist and persons that consists of empathic listening, understanding, loving care, and when appropriate, verbal interpretations of dysfunction in order to facilitate healthy relationships, awareness, wisdom, and growth.

(1) Is there a psychology contained in the Bible? Understanding the question in this sense, the answer is clearly yes. Theologians for centuries have talked about OT anthropology or psychology, NT psychology, Pauline psychology, etc. The biblical authors, under inspiration of the Holy Spirit, provided numerous observations and reflections on the nature of the human soul (Gn 2:7; Lv 24:17), spirit (Is 29:24), body (Is 31:3), mind (Php 2:3), heart (Ps 90:12), dysfunction (Jms 1:8), flourishing (Eph 3:16-19), process of change (Rm 12:1-2), and wisdom for living (Pr). Clearly God, as Creator of mankind, has an exhaustive and systematic psychology of persons and has communicated many of these crucial insights through the reflections of the inspired biblical authors.

(2) Are psychologies formed apart from the Bible? Obviously the psychological reflections of Sigmund Freud and Carl Rogers are unbiblical in the sense that their musings are not included in the Bible. However, whether their views are biblical in the sense of being consistent with or reflected in the Bible is more complex. For example, we can find correlation between Freud's view of the "unconscious" and "repression" and the biblical understanding of the "hidden heart" that insists there is always more going on deep with a person than on the surface (Pr 14:13), often due to the heart's deceptive nature (Jr 17:9, Rm 1:18). Though Freud has some true and wise things to say about the nature of the hidden motives of the heart, his worldly view of the "unconscious" and his causally deterministic explanation of mental functioning are clearly unbiblical. Thus psychologies based on observations and reflections from outside the Bible are a mixed bag that must be critiqued idea-by-idea.

The benefit of investigating these extrabiblical psychologies is twofold: (1) They may provide concrete examples that exemplify biblical truths. (2) They may further elucidate elements that the biblical writers only touch upon (e.g., addictions and anger).

(3) Is it biblical to engage in the task of psychology that involves not only the Bible but also extrabiblical observation and reflection? Contemporary Christians disagree on this point. Some adherents of the biblical counseling position deny any biblical warrant for this, while some integrationists maintain that there is biblical precedent for this task of doing psychology.

The writers of Proverbs were OT wise men who had the unique role of instructing Israel to live well in all areas of life under God on the basis of their wisdom and experience (Pr 1:1-6,8-9; 4:1; 6:20). The essence of this wisdom involves having a right relationship with God (Pr 1:7), who is the ultimate source of all wisdom (Pr 2:6) and revelation, which is central to the mental health of a people (Pr 29:18). However, the wise men also insisted that there is an important extrabiblical source of wisdom for living, discernible by observing and reflecting upon the natural world (Pr 6:6; 30:24-28) and especially persons and their complex situations (Pr 24:30-34). God created the world by wisdom (Pr 3:19-20) such that His wisdom is imprinted onto creation as the natural order of things (Pr 8:22-31). By observing these wisdom laws in nature and human life, we can discover a set of wise principles of sowing and reaping to avoid folly and live a good life under God in accordance with the created way of human nature (Pr 8:32-36).

Consequently, the OT wise men provide biblical precedent and justification for the science of psychology. In the case of the biblical proverbs, God worked through the wise men's experience to produce inspired observations and principles for living. While the wisdom collected in Scripture has a divine sanction and authority, the church's ongoing work in psychology is subject to scrutiny from the Scriptures, reason, and observation. Though unbelievers can discover wisdom for living through psychology, only the believer can know and live out these principles as one ought in relation to God.

(4) Is psychotherapy biblical? Certainly the intervention of psychotherapy is biblical in the sense that Scripture encourages empathy, truthful understanding, and caring relationships between persons. This is evident in the admonition regarding "speaking the truth in love" (Eph 4:15), in the "one another" injunctions (Col 3:12-14, 1Th 5:11,14), in the gifts of the church (Rm 12:4-8), and in the reflections and counsel for wise living found in Proverbs (Pr 4:1-5). However, the content of what psychotherapy passes on as wisdom is to be judged by Scripture (Pr 21:30), truth (8:7), and its appropriateness to the situation (25:11).

Didn't the Church Oppose Galileo?

Mark A. Kalthoff

S imply questions do not always have simple answers. "Didn't the church oppose Galileo?" is certainly one such question. Everyone "knows" the church opposed Galileo, but what does this mean?

Despite the complexity of Galileo's engagement with the church, there are several relevant facts that can be simply stated.

For one thing, every significant player in the Galileo affair was a committed Christian. This was no tale of a secular scientific community pitted against a backward antiscientific church. The Roman Catholic Church provided greater patronage to astronomical study than did all other contemporary institutions combined.

That being said, straightforward readings of certain Bible passages (Gn 1; Jos 10:12; Ps 19:4-6; 93:1; 104:5,19; Ec 1:4-5) suggest an earth-centered cosmology with the sun revolving about a stationary earth. By the early seventeenth century, in the wake of the Protestant Reformation and the Roman Catholic Council of Trent, such a plain interpretation of these passages was normative throughout Christendom. Moreover, both common sense and the weight of contemporary scientific opinion opposed the idea of the earth's motion.

Hence, any public defender of the Copernican (sun-centered) cosmology would have to overcome two difficult challenges. He would have to supply conclusive scientific evidence for the earth's motion and the sun's fixity—something that was not then available, even to Galileo. In addition, he would have to provide expert theological guidance to explain how properly to interpret those biblical texts that seemingly contradicted the Copernican hypothesis. Galileo was not a theologian. He was a mathematician and natural philosopher.

Although Galileo believed that he possessed proof of the Copernican hypothesis (in his theory of the tides), he was mistaken. His theory was seriously flawed. Overconfidence in the strength of his case lead Galileo to tread out of his area of expertise and into the territory of biblical interpretation. As a layman, he overstepped his bounds by presuming to give guidance on reading the Bible.

What did the Roman Catholic Church do? It acted prudently and conservatively by upholding the received biblical and scientific opinion of the day. In 1616 the Theological Consultors of the Holy Office (advisors to the Pope) declared the Copernican theory heretical and foolish. Protestant leaders, such as Martin Luther and John Calvin, had expressed similar disapproval of Copernicanism.

In 1633, Galileo was judged to be "vehemently suspected of heresy" and sentenced to house arrest for defending the Copernican hypothesis. Of greater significance is the fact that the church never formally condemned the Copernican theory *ex cathedra*. That is, it never formally made opposition to Copernicanism an article of faith. Neither had any Protestant denomination done so. The Pope, his advisors, and other Christian leaders, may have erred in their personal opinions on the matter, but all stopped short of asserting that anti-Copernicanism should be an official doctrine of Christianity. Galileo was punished as a Christian layman, for overstepping his bounds in a theological matter (biblical interpretation) that touched on a scientific question. In the end, this was a religious dispute about biblical interpretation between Christians within the Roman Catholic Church.

Did the Church oppose Galileo? Yes it did. But that opposition was grounded in a careful attempt to preserve both Christian and scientific integrity in a time of tumultuous change. The remarkable fact is that, despite the inclinations of its leaders, both Protestant and Catholic, the Christian churches never made opposition to Copernicanism an official article of faith.

Does Science Support the Bible?
Walter L. Bradley

Two major areas of scientific inquiry can in principle either support or undermine the Bible, namely, what science tells us about the nature of our universe and planet and what it can tell us about the history of our universe and planet. Biblical theism describes a God who is immediately responsible for all physical reality, with the laws of nature seen as descriptions of God's customary way of caring for his creatures (as in Col 1:17). Biblical theism also affirms that God sometimes works in extraordinary (or supernatural) ways to shape and care for His creation (Gn 1:1). The challenge is, can the biblical and scientific pictures of our universe and planet be harmonized?

Our Remarkable Home. One of the most surprising scientific developments of the twentieth century has been the discovery of the many remarkable features of our universe and planet that are essential to make it such an ideal habitat for life. First, we need sufficient elemental diversity, combined with a relative abundance of critical elements, to make possible the production of complex "molecular machines" capable of processing energy, storing information, and replicating molecules like RNA, DNA, and protein. Second, at least one element in this complexity of life must be capable of serving as a ready connector, reacting with essentially all elements to form bonds that are stable, but not too stable to be broken during "reuse"; carbon is such an element. Third, we must have an individual element or compound that is liquid at certain temperatures on planet earth and very abundant that can serve as a universal solvent. This liquid must be capable of dissolving most elements and/or compounds essential to the chemistry of life; that describes water. Fourth, we need long term sources of energy that fit with the chemical energy in the carbon bonds so that this energy can fuel the chemical reactions we find in the carbon-based, chain molecules that are essential to life.

At least 50 such requirements have been identified, all necessary for life to exist in our universe.

God's Remarkable Design. God has satisfied these many necessary requirements for life in three remarkable ways: the elegant mathematical form that is encoded in nature that we call "the laws of nature"; the fine tuning of the 19 universal constants (e.g., the speed of light, gravity force constant, mass of the electron, the unit charge), and the unbelievably demanding initial conditions which God had to set. For example, the ratio of the strong force constant to the electromagnetic force constant must fall within a window of 5 percent of the actual ratio if we are to have elemental diversity and a star like our sun that gives a long-term, stable source of energy. To match the energy of the light from the sun to the chemical bonding energy in organic compounds, six of the universal constants have to be carefully tailored to each other. The speed of light (c), the mass of the electron (m_e), the mass of the proton (m_p), Planck's constant (h), the gravity force constant, and the unit charge must have carefully matched magnitudes that satisfy the following algebraic equation: $m_p^2 \cdot G/[h\ c] > \sim [e^2/\{hc\}]^{12}[m_e/m_p]^4$.

Remarkably, these six constants do indeed have exactly the right relative values for the energy from the sun to be matched precisely to that needed to facilitate critical chemical reactions in organic molecules.

Many scientists have remarked with admiration about this amazing characteristic of our universe. For example, the famous English astronomer Sir Fred Hoyle, comments: "A common sense interpretation of the facts suggests that a super intellect has 'monkeyed' with the physics as well as the chemistry and biology, and there are no blind forces worth speaking about in nature."

Possibly the most impressive scientific achievement of the twentieth century is the discovery of DNA, upon which is encoded the information of life. That such a remarkable information storage system would exist and that the DNA molecules would somehow come to be encoded with the very precise information needed for life is the amazing climax to an amazing testimony from science of God's providential care for us in His creation. For example, the accidental origin of the cytochrome-C molecule to have the required sequencing of the various amino acids has a probability of only 1 in 10^{60}.

These findings from recent science give an even more profound significance to Paul's testimony in Romans 1:20 that God's divinity can be seen in the invisible elements of His universe.

Can We Harmonize Genesis 1 and Science? While the scientific discoveries of the twentieth and twenty-first century have strengthened belief in a Designer/Creator, highly publicized conflicts between science and the Bible such as the Scopes "Monkey Trial" have eroded confidence in the biblical inferences about natural history found in Genesis 1–2. This conflict is the result of unsubstantiated scientific claims and unnecessarily limited interpretations of Genesis 1–2 (whether they be of the liberal or conservative variety).

The unsupported claim from science is that the origin of life and its progression from simple to complex forms are achieved by molecular selection and mutation/natural selection respectively. While this synthesis of mutation/natural selection adequately explains how organisms become more adapted to their environment and how incremental improvement in existing characteristics might occur, it seems incapable of explaining the ultimate origin of multi-component systems, such as the human eye. New multicomponent systems would have no advantage from natural selection until the individual parts had already evolved to an advanced stage of development. Yet without natural selection to guide this development, it is almost impossible to imagine how complex, multicomponent systems can originate. Biochemist Michael Behe has dubbed this process "Darwin's Black Box"—a whimsical term for a device that does something but whose inner workings cannot be seen and sometimes are not comprehensible.

How Should a Christian Understand the Age of the Earth Controversy?

Ted Cabal

Only three major Bible-Science controversies have confronted the church: (1) the Copernican controversy; (2) the Darwinian controversy, and (3) the age-of-the-earth controversy. The question about the age of the earth did not become significantly heated until the latter third of the twentieth century. The primary disputants today are young- and old-earth creationists (YCs and OCs); theistic evolutionists and those not holding to biblical inerrancy have little interest. The debate does not pertain to dating Adam's creation since both sides believe this occurred only thousands, not millions of years ago. Nor is the controversy about the age of the universe because some YCs believe in an old universe. And both creationist camps oppose Darwinian common descent. What is needed is a clearer understanding of both sides and a discussion of how significant an issue this is for biblical faith.

Some OCs contribute to the controversy by contending YCs undercut biblical credibility with an artificial clash between science and Scripture. The biggest source of the controversy, however, is the contention of some YCs that only belief in a young earth is doctrinally acceptable. Some YC's believe this doctrine is so clear that its rejection compromises biblical authority. While OCs agree biblical genealogies teach the recent creation of Adam, they disagree that Scripture teaches the creation days were consecutive 24-hour periods.

Some YCs argue that old-earth views, by placing animal death before the fall, conflict with Romans 5:12. OCs respond that Romans 5:12 says nothing about animal death. The Apostle Paul's context treats only of sin and death's entrance into the human race.

Some YCs worry that old-earth interpretations make the Bible subservient to science. It is true that old-earth interpretations arose due to the (pre-Darwinian) discovery of enormous numbers of extinct animals such as dinosaurs. But this same data also led YCs to interpret Scripture in light of science (such as interpreting the book of Job to describe dinosaurs). Indeed, some YCs have suggested plate tectonics as the possible interpretation for

Genesis 10:25, and some offer a young-earth "big bang" interpretation of the first four creation days. Moreover, virtually all creationists now believe biblical descriptions of a stationary earth and revolving sun are from a human observational standpoint, and are not intended as technical scientific descriptions.

Some YCs charge OCs with caving in to the evolutionary theory, alleging the "long ages" are synonymous with the evolutionary system. Macroevolutionary theory needs an old earth, but inferring that old-earth views are thereby macroevolutionary is to commit a logical fallacy (x and y regularly occur together, therefore x is the cause of y). By this same logic, YCs can be charged with accommodating naturalism for accepting "microevolution" (that species change over time); Darwinian macroevolution needs microevolution, but this does not entail the two are synonymous. Neo-Darwinists contend the various fossil strata constitute the main evidence for macroevolution. But YCs and OCs alike agree this very same fossil record, with its scarcity of credible transitional fossils, does not reveal a history of common biological descent. YCs typically understand fossils as depositions from Noah's flood, and OCs view them as artifacts of supernatural creative acts separated by long time spans.

Some YCs even contend that OCs have contributed to the demise of Western culture, but such contentions are historically unjustified. References by YCs to OCs as "evangelical evolutionists," "semi-creationists," or "compromisers" have clouded rather than clarified the debate. Indeed, YCs are not agreed as to just what is "evolutionary" in matters such as ice ages, star formation, and the origins of species.

A lesson from a past controversy may be helpful. Early in the twentieth century, some held the pretribulational rapture to be central to the faith. Great controversy followed, but eventually most Bible believers realized the issue was not worthy of such contention. Perhaps one day this will be true of the age-of-the-earth controversy. Creationist leaders should work hard to understand the data. And exploring, holding, and promoting various creationist views are legitimate projects. But promoting the controversy as a basis for disunity in the church is another matter altogether.

Can God's Actions Be Detected Scientifically?

C. John Collins

"I'll believe in God if you can prove scientifically that He does things!" How can we respond to such a challenge?

The first thing we must do is disentangle the questions. First, what do we mean by "God's actions"? Second, what do we mean by "science"? And third, can science detect events as *God's* actions? Let's take them one at a time.

To begin with, we recognize that, after the creation, God works in two ways. First, He maintains the things He created, along with their powers to cause things. Apples keep on tasting good and nourishing us because God keeps maintaining their properties. A soccer goalie deflects the ball because God maintains the properties of the ball, the air, and the goalie's body. Second, God is not limited by the powers of created things: sometimes He goes beyond their powers if it suits His purpose. We can call the first kind of action the *natural* (since it works with created natures), and the second the *supernatural* (since it goes beyond natural powers). Let's be clear about this: *Both* kinds are God's actions and both serve His purpose.

The sciences study aspects of the world around us, in hopes of understanding how they work. Some scientists study the regularities of the world (such as "the angle of incidence equals the angle of reflection"), while others study specific events, trying to reason backwards from effects to cause (like Sherlock Holmes, the "scientific detective").

Can God's actions be detected scientifically? It depends on which ones. Because God made His world "very good" (Gn 1:31), it needs no tinkering to keep in operation: so we don't expect that the sciences will "detect" God's natural actions. The reason that an atom's electrons don't crash into the nucleus is not that God holds them apart by a miracle, but that He made their properties so that they don't crash.

On the other hand, the sciences may sometimes help us detect a supernatural event because in knowing the properties of natural things, we can tell when these have been transcended. For example, the more we know about how babies come about, the more clearly supernatural becomes the conception of Jesus: there is no natural explanation for it. As C.S. Lewis put it, "No doubt a modern gynecologist knows several things about birth and begetting which St. Joseph did not know. But these things do not concern the main point—that a virgin birth is contrary to the course of nature. And St. Joseph obviously knew *that*." Advances in medical science have only sharpened the point. We could say the same about Jesus' resurrection: Dead bodies stay dead unless someone with extraordinary power interferes.

This kind of detection works best when it's based on knowledge, not ignorance: it's not just that we don't know how it could happen; rather, we have every reason to believe that it *can't* happen, unless something else is added. The sciences can help us know better the natures of the things involved, and thus to know when "something else" is needed to explain what we see.

But can this prove that it is God's action that has gone beyond nature? Not if we only look at the things involved, and not at the bigger picture. For example, if we just look at biology we can say that Jesus' virgin conception goes beyond the powers of His mother's body to produce, but we can't say that it was God who produced it. To say God had a role, we have to look at things such as the prophecy (Is 7:14), the angel's announcement (Lk 1:35), the purity of Mary, and the truthfulness of her religion. In other words, we have to look beyond what most people mean by "science," in order to use all the data available to us (you can see that we are still using logic and evidence).

Does the "New Physics" Conflict with Christianity?

Jeremy Royal Howard

The Bible portrays God as a rational Being who created the world from nothing and rules over it as Sovereign. Logic, order, purpose, natural law—these qualities are etched into the universe as reflections of the will and mind of God. Moreover, God made humans in His own image, which means our minds are equipped to operate according to God's rationality. Finally, since God is the author of the world and humanity, we are intellectually ready-made to understand truth about God and the world He made.

Some people say quantum mechanics (QM) refutes these beliefs. QM studies the bits of matter that are the size of atoms and smaller. It was long assumed that these micro-objects would follow the physical laws Newton described, but modern research shows that quantum entities behave far differently than the objects of our everyday experience. For example, photons (light) can take the form of particles or waves. Problem is waves and particles are contrary things. Waves cover a wide zone, but particles can only be at one tiny place at a time. Physicists are baffled that photons can do both. Next, tests reveal that in laboratory settings, quantum particles separated by a vast expanse can still affect one another as if they are in direct contact. This is like scratching your mom's back from 2,000 miles away. Finally, experiments suggest that quantum entities behave lawlessly, meaning there are no "rules" for their actions.

These oddities prompt some observers to conclude that QM overturns natural law and rationality, leaving us with an incomprehensible, uncreated universe. Standard physics says matter can be neither created nor destroyed by natural means, but some scientists (falsely) claim that quantum particles naturally pop in and out of existence. From this, leading atheists claim the whole universe "sprang" into existence naturally. No Creator necessary. Furthermore, they say even if God exists and created the universe, QM shows He made a world He cannot control. Once He uncorked this world, not even God knows what will come of it. Theologians who favor science fads over Scripture conclude the same thing: QM implies God cannot govern creation or know the future.

Scientists have historically taken the appearance of mystery or irrationality in nature as a sign that they do not yet know enough about the object under study. However, following the lead of Niels Bohr's Copenhagen Interpretation

(CI) of QM, many physicists refuse to count their inability to understand or predict quantum action as a sign of ignorance. Rather, they claim QM is basically a finished science that reveals a genuinely lawless and irrational world—a brooding cauldron of chance actions and purposeless conclusions. This fits well with non-Christian concepts of the universe. In fact, Bohr and his colleagues enthusiastically asserted that QM endorses Eastern worldview images. Today, popular science opinion is captive to Bohr's CI, and thus holds that QM supports New Age or atheistic worldviews.

I suggest the following starting points for the Christian response: First, for all the wild attributes that may hold true in QM, we note that macroscopic reality behaves in a predictable, law-like fashion and everywhere presents us with evidence of its fundamentally rational construction and operation. So even if quantum particles could do lawless things like pop in and out of existence naturally, no such thing happens in the realm of everyday objects. Quantum oddities, whatever you make of them, are detained at the door to the larger realities we experience. Second, many of the astounding behaviors attributed to QM occur only in highly artificial laboratory settings. There is no certainty that these things can actually happen in real-world settings. Thus, we are justified in casting an indifferent eye on many of the zany headlines coming from physics laboratories. Third, science's ability to penetrate the microphysical world is still very rudimentary. This leaves room for exceptionally high degrees of speculation and error. In this light, Christians should join the chorus of noteworthy scientists (like Einstein) who have insisted that QM should not be the basis for worldview assertions. This problem will apparently not be fully alleviated in the future, for scientists acknowledge that the mega-scale facilities and energies needed to verify the most important claims of QM will forever lie outside our reach. Fourth, science would be impossible if this world were not created by a personal, rational Being who designed both physical reality and human beings to reflect His rationality. Any scientific theory that supports non-rational worldviews is self-defeating. After all, the deliberations involved in reaching the conclusion that "this world is fundamentally irrational" have relied on the very rationality whose legitimacy is denied in the conclusion. Finally, a growing body of experts believes the CI will someday fall from scientific prominence, thus shifting the dominant paradigm of QM to models supporting rationality and natural law. Whether or not this happens, Christians can rest assured that this world is the creation of a rational God who rules as Sovereign over all things, including the wily objects of the quantum realm.

Besides QM, some suggest Chaos Theory and Special Relativity impinge on the Christian worldview. Special Relativity shows there are no fixed reference points in the universe. All motion or apparent non-motion is relative to a specific frame of reference. Some have imagined that this undermines our ability to form fixed judgments that apply universally, but of course our inability to do this in physics is irrelevant to our assurance about unalterable, universal truths revealed by God. As for Chaos Theory, the name itself is deceptive. Properly understood, it only says that many deterministic physical systems are so sensitive to initial conditions that we cannot fully predict their future behaviors unless we perfectly comprehend all of those conditions. Hence it is our ignorance, not creation itself, which sets up the appearance of chaos in physics.

In summary, the new physics highlights human finitude but does nothing to overturn God as Author and Ruler of creation.

Are Biblical Miracles Imitations of Pagan Myths?

Gary R. Habermas

F requently the complaint is made that biblical miracles, especially those of Jesus, were motivated or even inspired by pagan accounts from the ancient world. We are told that healings, demon possession, virgin births, and resurrections were all common fare in ancient times. So the implication is that the Bible is no different from other religious documents. Perhaps Christians simply plagiarized other accounts.

While it is true that myriads of miracle stories adorned the ancient world, it does not follow that Scripture duplicated them. Although promoted in some popular circles, this assumption is mistaken, and on several levels.

It is true that some scholars emphasize the similarities between pagan and biblical miracle accounts. But we must also accent the more common (and profound) differences . For example, there is usually an immense philosophical gulf between the pagan and biblical backgrounds for their respective miracle accounts. The pagan mindset most commonly incorporated cyclical, repetitive patterns in nature, marked by the seasonal cycles. In contrast, the Jewish philosophy of history moved in linear patterns, from one event to the next, culminating in God's grand climax.

Further, these pagan stories often concern persons who never even lived in history, such as Hercules of ancient Greek mythology, while Jesus and other miracle workers undoubtedly did. Moreover, scholars note that these stories were never very influential in Palestine, where a far different outlook prevailed.

Surprisingly, virtually no miracle stories in the ancient world are even candidates for inspiring Jesus' miracles. Few of these tales both predate the NT and closely approximate Jesus' miracles. So it is very difficult to prove a parallel.

Regarding Jesus' resurrection, the inadequacy of this proposed solution grows even more apparent. Writings clearly claiming that prominent pagan heroes were resurrected postdate the NT accounts of Jesus' resurrection.

Scholars know that some ancient religious teachings copied from Christianity, and Jesus' resurrection may be an example of what was copied!

So there are many reasons why the NT accounts were not derived from pagan texts. The most crucial response, stated simply, is that we have many reasons for believing that Jesus actually performed miracles during His ministry. Indeed, virtually all contemporary critical scholars agree that Jesus performed many acts that might be termed "miracles" or "exorcisms."

Most of all, there is an incredible amount of evidence arguing that Jesus was really raised from the dead. For instance, we have reliable reports from various authors regarding many who thought that they had actually seen the risen Jesus. The most crucial witness is Paul, an eyewitness who provides very early testimony. So we must not miss the clear point that if a number of early, credible witnesses (including previous skeptics Paul and James) were proclaiming their conviction that they had seen the risen Jesus, for which they were willing to die, then this belief is not paralleled in pagan stories. Far from being inspired by far-away tales, many Christians died for their honest belief that *they* had *really seen* the risen Jesus. Pagan stories do not explain this conviction.

Can We Still Believe in Demons Today?

Clinton E. Arnold

M any modern scholars regard belief in demons as a primitive worldview that includes elves, dragons, and a flat world. They contend that the advent of modern science, especially advances in understanding body chemistry, psychology, and neurology, enables better understanding of the phenomena the ancients attributed to the work of demons.

Skepticism about the existence of angels and demons is at odds with the direct and explicit testimony of Scripture. From the Garden of Eden in Genesis to Satan's doom in Revelation, the pages of Scripture are filled with references to evil supernatural beings who oppose God and His purposes. Their frequency of appearance actually heightens during the ministry of Jesus and the apostles. In fact, we learn most about their nature, character, and activities from Jesus and Paul.

Besides the biblical assumption of demonic reality, other matters must be considered:

Science is inherently incapable of answering this question. Some critics grant science authority to make judgments on issues it is incapable of judging. Just as science is incompetent to adjudicate on morality, so `it is also beyond its jurisdiction to decide the question of demonic existence. Scientific advances can give us insight into the origin and characteristics of certain natural phenomena, but there is no reason to assume it has power to answer questions regarding the existence of spiritual and supernatural beings.

Purely naturalistic explanations are not adequate for describing many forms of evil in the world. Indeed, although the impact of sin on the human soul explains much of the proliferation of evil, some situations are still so abhorrent or inexplicable, that they suggest a demonic origin. The killing horrors of an Auschwitz or a mother roasting her own child to death imply a powerful force leading humanity to destruction.

Some therapeutic situations are best explained by the work of a spirit being. While true that symptoms produced by schizophrenia, dissociation, and other psychological and chemical disorders were often wrongly attributed to demons, some conditions are best explained by the direct influence of a spirit entity. The international community of mental health professionals recognizes this and labels it "Trance and Possession Disorder," an especially common diagnosis in non-Western cultures.

We need to learn from the broader sweep of human history and cultures. The last 300 years in western history represents the only time that the existence of evil spirits has been viewed with widespread skepticism. Furthermore, an exploration of other cultures reveals throughout Asia, Africa, the Pacific Islands, and elsewhere, belief in evil spirits continues to be integral to the worldview of many people groups.

Belief in the reality of evil spirits need not lead to uncritical or unwarranted beliefs about demons nor the bizarre and dangerous practices of extremist individuals and groups. Our task should be to integrate this more complete view of reality into our functional worldview with constant sensitivity to biblical teaching on this topic. At the beginning of the *Screwtape Letters*, C. S. Lewis warned that we can err in two ways as regards the devil. We can fail to take account of him or we can give him too much attention.

SECTION 7

Ethics

Is the Old Testament Ethical?

Christopher Wright

The prevailing prejudice against Scripture is that the OT portrays a violent God of a violent people, and is filled with narratives recounting horrendous events with disreputable people playing major roles. Is the OT ethical? Here are some reasons why it is.

It was ethical enough for Jesus. Jesus accepted the truth and ethical validity of the OT ("the Scriptures") in His own life, mission, and teaching. His "you have heard it said . . . but I tell you" (see Mt 6–7) sayings don't contradict or criticize the OT, but either deepen its demands or correct distorted popular inferences. "Love your neighbor" meant "Hate your enemy" to many in Jesus' day, even though the OT never says any such thing. Jesus reminded His hearers that in the same chapter (Lv 19) it says you must love the foreigner as yourself (v. 34); Jesus extended this to include "love your enemy" (Mt 5:44). Jesus thus affirmed and strengthened the OT ethic.

Narratives describe what simply happened, not what was necessarily approved. We assume wrongly if a story is in Scripture, it must be "what God wanted." But biblical narrators deal with the real world, "telling it like it is," with all its corrupt and fallen harshness. We shouldn't mistake realism for ethical approval. OT stories often challenge us to wonder at God's amazing grace and patience in continually working out His purpose through such morally compromised people, and to be discerning in evaluating their conduct according to standards the OT itself provides.

The conquest of Canaan must be understood for what it was. This event, rightly, is most troubling to sensitive readers. We can't ignore its horror, but some perspectives can help us evaluate it ethically.

- It was a limited event. The conquest narratives describe one particular period of Israel's long history. Many of the other wars that occur in OT narrative had no divine sanction, and some were clearly condemned as the actions of proud, greedy kings or military rivals.
- Allow for the exaggerated language of warfare. Israel, like other

ancient Near East nations whose documents we possess, had a rhetoric of war which often exceeded reality on the ground.

- It was an act of God's justice and punishment on a morally degraded
society. The conquest shouldn't be portrayed as random genocide or
ethnic cleansing. The wickedness of Canaanite society is anticipated
(Gn 15:16), and described in moral and social terms (Lv 18:24; 20:23;
Dt 9:5; 12:29-31). This interpretation is accepted in the NT (e.g.,
Heb 11:31) speaks of the Canaanites as "the disobedient," imply-
ing awareness of choosing to persist in sin—as the Bible affirms of
all human beings. There's a huge moral difference between violence
that's arbitrary, and violence inflicted within the moral framework
of punishment (this is true in human society as much as in divine
perspective). It doesn't make it "nice," but changes the ethical evaluation significantly.

- God threatened to do the same to Israel—and did. In the conquest,
God used Israel as the agent of punishment on the Canaanites. God
warned Israel: if they behaved similarly, God would treat them as
His enemy in the same way and inflict the same punishment on them
using other nations (Lv 18:28; Dt 28:25-68). In the course of Israel's
long history in OT times, God repeatedly did so, demonstrating His
moral consistency in international justice. It wasn't a matter of favor-
itism. If anything, Israel's status as God's chosen people, the OT
argues, exposed them all the more to God's judgment and historical
punishment than Canaanites who experienced the conquest. Those
choosing to live as God's enemies eventually face God's judgment.

- The conquest anticipated the final judgment. Like the stories of
Sodom and Gomorrah and the flood, the story of Canaan's conquest
stands in Scripture as a "proto-typical" narrative. Scripture affirms
that ultimately, in the final judgment, the wicked will face the awful
reality of God's wrath, in exclusion, punishment, and destruction.
Then God's ethical justice will be finally vindicated. But at certain
points in history, such as the Conquest, God demonstrates the power
of His judgment. Rahab's story, set in the midst of the conquest narrative, also demonstrates the power of "repentance" and faith, and
God's willingness to spare His enemies when they choose to identify
with God's people. Rahab thus enters the NT hall of fame—and faith
(Heb 11:31; Jms 2:25).

An eye for an eye. Unfortunately, this phrase sums up for many what
OT law and ethics is all about. Even then, they misunderstand that this
expression—almost certainly metaphorical, not literal—wasn't a license for
unlimited vengeance, but precisely the opposite. This law established the fundamental legal principle of proportionality: punishment mustn't exceed the

gravity of the offence. The rest of OT law, when compared with law codes from contemporary ancient societies (e.g., Babylonian, Assyrian, Hittite), shows a remarkable humanitarian concern, especially for the socially weak, poor, and marginalized (the classic trio of "the widow, the orphan, and the alien"). Israel's laws operated with ethical priorities of human life above material property and of human needs over legal rights. Not surprisingly, then, Jesus (who clearly endorsed the same priorities) could affirm that He had no intention of abolishing the Law and the Prophets, but rather of fulfilling them.

Does the Bible Provide Ethical Guidance for Business?

Scott B. Rae

S cripture has much to say about economic life and it encompasses more than simply personal finance. Here's a summary of the Bible's ethical guidance for business.

First, God calls men and women to business. In Genesis 1–2, God ordains work as part of His calling to Adam and Eve. They were intended to work the garden as a part of their role in exercising dominion over creation. As a result, work has intrinsic value and is the way in which human beings fulfill the ongoing mandate to subdue the earth. Work wasn't instituted as a consequence of the entrance of sin into the world, though sin did serve to make work more taxing and difficult. From the beginning, work is blessed by God. Thus, His people working in business are doing His work in the world in the same way that the pastor is doing His work in the church. The Bible also calls people to work in order to support themselves and their families (2Th 3:6-12; 1Tm 5:8), take care of the poor (Eph 4:28), support the church and its outreaches (1Co 9:1-15), and to provide a platform for sharing one's faith.

Second, the Bible teaches that business is to be run with integrity. The Bible makes it clear that business is to be conducted honestly and that business isn't to be used as a mechanism to exploit others, specifically the vulnerable. The Mosaic Law contains numerous mandates to business integrity. For example, Leviticus 19:35 mandates that one's weights and measures be accurate, something that was very important in an agricultural society. Further, Proverbs makes clear that God demands integrity in one's business dealings (Pr 10:9; 11:1). The prophets demanded that those in business not use their resources to exploit the poor (Am 2:6-7; 4:1; Mc 7:10-12). The command "to act justly, to love faithfulness, and to walk humbly with your God" applies to business and establishes values of justice, love, and humility that should govern one's business dealings (Mc 6:8). Jesus continues this emphasis in the NT. He instructed the tax collectors to collect only what was prescribed (Lk 3:12-13; 19:1-10), that they continue to take care of the poor (Mt 25:31-46), and taught that business is a legitimate enterprise if conducted with integrity (Mt 25:14-30). Likewise, the apostles suggested that work is necessary, idleness is sinful, and generosity for the poor is not only virtuous but mandatory.

Third, the Bible condemns greed and condones ambition with contentment. Greed motivates most of the unethical behavior in business. The Bible is clear that greed is a vice that needs to be put away once someone comes to faith in Christ (1Co 6:10; Col 3:5). By contrast, contentment is the virtue to be cultivated (1Tm 6:6-8). Paul makes it clear that the *love* of money is the root of all kinds of evil, not the mere *possession* of wealth. In the ancient world, it was not uncommon for someone to have acquired wealth through means that exploited others. The notion that someone could *do well* financially and also *do good* for the community is relatively new, coming as a result of the emergence of capitalism—a system that itself cannot function well without a proper ethical foundation.

Does the Bible Affirm that Animals Have Rights?

Steve W. Lemke

No, Scripture never specifically grants rights to animals. The Bible doesn't assume animals have intrinsic rights, even the right to life. Unlike humans, animals were not created in the image of God. God made humans the pinnacle of His creation, with inherent worth and greater capacities than animals. He appointed humans to subdue and rule over all the animals (Gn 1:20-31). God specifically approved the use of animals as a source of food for humans (Gn 9:1-3; Lv 11:2-3). Since animals have lesser value than humans, they shouldn't be given the rights accorded to human beings, and human life should never be sacrificed to save animal life.

Yes, the Bible affirms that humans do have a moral obligation to treat animals humanely. Although animals are clearly not equal in worth to human beings, they have value since God created them as "good" (Gn 1:20-25). So, as part of our God-given stewardship, we shouldn't abuse or pointlessly harm animals. Scripture uses the same word to describe the animating force that God gave animals (*nephesh*, Gn 1:20,21,24,30), as it does in describing how He breathed a living soul into persons (Gn 2:7). Unlike animals, human souls have unique capacities: self-awareness, abstract reasoning, an orientation toward the future, freedom, moral responsibility, and the capacity to have a relationship with God. Animal sacrifices presuppose animals have value (Lv 4–6; Heb 9:11-28). Animal pain is a matter of moral concern because God cares for animals (Gn 7:2-4; Ps 104:10-30; 147:7-9; 148:7-10; Mt 6:26; Lk 12:6-7,24).

Although God gave permission to eat animals for food after the flood (Gn 9:1-3), this may have been a concession to human sinfulness. Vegetarianism practiced in the Garden of Eden (Gn 1:29-30; 2:16), and the prophecy that natural predators will live together in peace in the future (Is 11:6-8) suggest that the eating of animal flesh isn't God's ideal.

Scripture calls upon humans to treat animals humanely. The Mosaic law forbade the heartless treatment of birds, promising long life to those who don't abuse animals (Dt 22:6-7). Other regulations were given for the welfare of farm animals (Dt 22:1-4,10; 25:4). Humane treatment of animals is a characteristic of godly living (Pr 12:10).

Does the Bible Demean Women?

Sharon James

If there is an unforgivable sin today, it is that of sexism. We are conditioned by modern presuppositions about equality to react against any role distinctions for men and women. When we read that God created woman as the "helper" (Gn 2:18), that "the man is the head of the woman" (1Co 11:3), that wives should submit to their husbands (Eph 5:22), or that only men are to lead the church (1Tm 2:12), we instinctively think, *How unfair!* The issue is even more serious because throughout history men have used their superior physical strength to exploit women, and sometimes the Bible has been misquoted to justify abuse of women.

It is sadly true that, since the fall of humanity into sin, male leadership has often been expressed in sinful oppression (Gn 3:16). We admit that often in church history, the gifts of women have not been properly affirmed. Yet historically, wherever Christianity has spread, the status of women has improved. Those countries where women are most exploited today are those with least exposure to the gospel. The Bible teaches that men and women were made equally in God's image (Gn 1:27-28), and that all human life is sacred. Christians have been among the first to provide education and other rights for women.

What about the intrinsic patriarchy of Scripture? Evangelical feminists (egalitarians) reject role distinctions. They argue that the Bible was written in a patriarchal context but that we have moved beyond that today. So marriage is an equal partnership with mutual submission (see Gn 2:24; Mt 19:4-5; Eph 5:31), and that women should engage in every ministry in the church. But their efforts to explain away the "difficult texts" (for instance, 1Tm 2:8-15) are unconvincing. Feminist scholars who reject the authority of Scripture are more consistent, simply saying that the Bible is wrong on this issue.

In response to these views, we should be willing to challenge contemporary presuppositions in the light of Scripture:

Presupposition 1: Equality means sameness. Talk of different roles is discriminatory.
Response: Equality does not mean sameness. The three Persons of the Trinity are equal in deity, but different in role.

Presupposition 2: Difference in role relates directly to personal worth. Submission equals relegation.
Response: Submission does not mean being of lesser worth. The Son submits to the Father, while being equal in deity, and His submission is His glory.

Presupposition 3: Women will only be empowered when they have become the same as men (filling the same jobs and reaching the same status).
Response: Women do not have to fill the same jobs as men in order to be empowered. This idea insults the majority of women who regard relational success as of greater importance than career success. The Bible honors those women who were wives, mothers, and homemakers (Pr 31; 1Tm 5:9-10,14) as well as women who ministered and worked in other ways.

If we abandon false presuppositions, we can see that the Bible affirms women. God wonderfully designed them to bear and nurture new life, and equipped them in a multitude of ways (physical, emotional, psychological) for that task. The calling of wife and mother is an exalted one. A wife is honored, not demeaned, when her husband takes responsibility for protection and provision in a Christlike way (Eph 5:25-33). The Bible also affirms the calling of single women (1Co 7:34), and those who are unable to have biological children: they can be "spiritual mothers" to many. God equips women with distinctive strengths that can be used not only in the family, but in many areas of ministry, as well as in the workplace.

Those men who lead the church are responsible for equipping other members, including women, for ministry (Eph 4:12). The NT mentions many women who were involved in important ministries. Mary Magdalene, Joanna, and Susanna traveled with Jesus and the Twelve and supported His ministry financially (Lk 8:1-3). While all but one of the disciples was in hiding following Jesus' arrest, several women witnessed Jesus' death and prepared His body for burial (Mt 27:55). Jesus first appeared to women following His resurrection (Mt 28:1-7). The church at Jerusalem met at the home of Mary, mother of John Mark, apparently a woman of means (Ac 12:12). Paul commended Phoebe and other female co-workers (Rm 16); Euodia and Syntyche contended with him in the cause of the gospel (Php 4:3); Priscilla and her husband taught Apollos (Ac 18:26); women prayed and prophesied in the meetings of the Corinthian church (1Co 11:5); godly widows were placed on an official list—probably to receive aid and for a ministry of prayer and practical service (1Tm 5:3-10). Many believe that female deacons were involved with mercy ministries (1Tm 3:11). Elders were to equip mature women to teach younger women (Ti 2:3-5).

Those who see defined gender roles in Scripture maintain that the Bible explains the meaning behind gender distinctions. Masculine strength can be for *protection* and *provision*. Many women are gifted with a "helper design"— relational capacities to *nurture* and *care*. These distinctive qualities, and the way we relate to each other, reflect something deep within God Himself. In short, a closer look at Scripture shows that women are honored and affirmed in the Bible. They are not second class in His eyes.

What Does the Bible Say About Euthanasia?

Nigel Cameron

E uthanasia is any act or omission, in the context of sickness or disability, that intentionally causes death. As such, it has become a topic of contemporary debate. But it is nothing new. The killing and abandonment of the sick and elderly have been common practices in cultures around the globe, and one of the most powerful impacts of the gospel has been to defend the defenseless and to devalue those without economic benefit to society.

In the Greco-Roman world of the early church, euthanasia was common and widely approved. The powerful pagan protest against physicians who had taken the Hippocratic oath, repudiating euthanasia and assisted suicide, came in a context in which euthanasia could be an appealing option in the face of chronic disease or uncontrollable pain. What is remarkable about the resurgence of interest in this primitive approach to sickness and suffering in our own day is that we now have far greater medical and other resources with which to cope with these challenges. It is perhaps the surest indicator that our understanding of human nature is being reinvented as the culture turns its back on its Judeo-Christian roots.

The starting point for a biblical understanding of human nature is the idea that human beings are made in the image of God. It is clear from Genesis 1:26-27 that this applies to all members of the human species. *Homo sapiens* is distinguished from all other "kinds" by our bearing the likeness of our Maker. The *imago Dei* (image of God) is what makes us the beings we are, and it is in place wherever there are members of our species. This godly image plainly applies to those who are sick and disabled as well as those in the flower of human giftedness. Those with severe mental impairments, including the so-called persistent vegetative state, remain full members of the human species and therefore bear God's image.

A definition of euthanasia that focuses on the intent to cause death is important, and in principle it distinguishes euthanasia from health care decisions affecting terminal patients when there is no intent to end life. The term "physician-assisted suicide" has been coined to promote voluntary euthanasia, but it is misleading. Voluntary euthanasia does entail a suicidal motive, and suicide is a sad but immoral case of homicide—the homicide of the self. But euthanasia always involves a homicide on the part of the physician, whether it comes through the prescription of lethal drugs or another method. And if it is legal, it involves a community policy decision which states that such lives are not worth living.

A distinction is often made between "active" and "passive" euthanasia, but this distinction can be misleading. If the intent is to bring about death, the moral accounting is the same. A more useful distinction lies among voluntary, involuntary, and nonvoluntary euthanasia. Voluntary euthanasia is the public policy goal of some activists and intellectuals who deny that they favor involuntary killing. Yet there are problems in defining adequate consent in the case of the seriously ill. For example, even some who favor voluntary euthanasia would consider the late Dr. Jack Kevorkian a serial killer, since even though he secured "consents," he preyed on the fears of lonely people. Moreover, there is the problem of "nonvoluntary" killing—the euthanasia of those who are not competent, such as Alzheimer's patients or infants, who constitute some of the prime candidates for an induced death.

The biblical doctrine of the sanctity of life of those in God's image offers a fundamental protection for patients, aging relatives, the handicapped, and the poor by ruling out the option of acting to bring about death. Job—the OT's great example of suffering and faithfulness—was challenged by his wife to take the euthanasia option: "Curse God and die!" (Jb 2:9). But he maintained his integrity and proclaimed in response, "Should we accept only good from God and not adversity?" (2:10).

Does the Bible Teach the Abuse of Nature?

Steve W. Lemke

The answer to this question requires balancing and blending two truths.

1. God expects us to use nature. God commanded humans to have dominion over all of nature, subduing it and ruling over it (Gn 1:20-31). God gave persons broad latitude in their dominion over nature, including permission for humans to eat plants and animals for food (Gn 1:29-30; 9:1-3). Jesus demonstrated His absolute control over nature in events such as calming a storm (Mt 8:24-27) and causing a fig tree to wither (Mt 21:18-27). We thus have divine approval to use nature for our own needs and purposes. Good stewards are expected to maximize production by shrewd management of God-given resources (Mt 25:14-30).

2. God opposes the abuse of nature. Our having dominion over nature should not be confused with our owning nature. Humans do not own nature, because the earth is the Lord's (Lv 25:23; Ps 24:1; 50:10-11). We are given the natural world as a stewardship, not as a possession.

Scripture teaches that, as stewards of God's good creation, we should apply sound principles of land and resource management. In the agricultural regulations of OT law, for instance, the land was to lie fallow in the seventh year so its minerals could be replenished (Ex 23:10-11; Lv 25:1-22). In two key NT parables—the parable of the vineyard (Mt 21:33-44; Mk 12:1-12; Lk 20:9-19) and the parable of the talents (Mt 25:14-30)—human beings are depicted as stewards or managers of God's property. These parables emphasize that God will hold us accountable for our management of these resources.

Nature is good because it was created by God and pleases God (Gn 1:1-31). God designed the natural world with an orderly structure, and violating that natural order is sinful (Rm 1:26-27). The natural world shares the burden of the curse of the fallen world (Gn 3:17-19), but Scripture repeatedly affirms God's providential care for the world of nature (Ps 104:1-35; 147:7-9; 148:1-10). Scripture also suggests that all of creation will share in redemption (Rm 8:20-22), promising the creation of the new heavens and the new earth (Rv 21:1).

Does the Bible Provide Guidance Regarding Human Cloning?

R. Albert Mohler Jr.

W hen "Dolly" the cloned sheep was born in 1997, few thoughtful persons could avoid wondering whether this stunning new technology would soon be used to clone a human being. Now, human cloning has become an issue of immediate, urgent, and universal importance. The cloning of a human being represents a radical break with the human past and with the established patterns of human life. It also raises a host of ethical quandaries: Who would be the "parents" of a cloned child? In an age of patented forms of life, could a cloned being be "owned," at least in genetic pattern? Will parents seek to clone children in order to provide organs for transplant into another child?

These are but a few of the many pressing questions that will demand address, and the worldview of secular humanism provides only tentative and provisional answers. The fact is that *only* the Christian worldview—revealed in God's Word—can provide us with an ethical context and authority adequate to such questions.

The biblical creation account presents the creation of human beings as the pinnacle of God's creative purpose. After creating the world and filling it with living creatures, God purposed to create human beings. The human creature—set apart from all other creatures—would bear the *Imago Dei,* the image of God.

Though the image of God in human beings has been corrupted by sin, it has not been removed, and this image is an essential mark of true humanity.

Each human being is a special creation of God, made in His own image. Each is unique by the design of the Creator. The status of human beings as created beings, each unique but all bearing the image of God, establishes a foundation for theological understanding—and for answering the questions raised by human cloning.

This understanding also makes clear the decisive distinction between the biblical and secular conceptions of human nature and value. The naturalistic understanding of humanity rejects any conception of divine purpose. Human beings are cosmic accidents—the fortuitous by-products of blind evolutionary process. Any value thus ascribed to human life is arbitrary and tentative, and necessarily self-centered.

The Bible, on the other hand, teaches that human beings, like all of creation, were created in order to glorify God. But humans were created with a distinct and unique capacity to know, reverence, worship, and glorify the Creator. He made human beings, male and female, of His own good pleasure, in His own image, and to His own sovereign purpose. Thus, human beings are not mere biological artifacts, nor accidental forms of life.

Human cloning represents an effort to redefine human identity and human reproduction by allowing individuals to replicate themselves. This reality cannot be separated from the related questions of "designer" children, human-enhancement technologies, eugenics, and sexuality. Furthermore, the use of cloning technology in human embryonic stem cell research undermines human dignity and will eventually lead to an expansion of cloning for other purposes.

The artificiality of cloning technology undermines marriage by further separating sex and reproduction. Human cloning—whatever its form—violates the sanctity of human life as revealed in Scripture.

What Does the Bible Say about Abortion?

Nigel Cameron

The intentional taking of life before birth is not new. Though adoption of "abortion rights" as a progressive political cause in Western societies is recent, abortion has been practiced in every culture from ancient times. Indeed, one of the signal achievements of the spread of the gospel in the Greco-Roman world was to push this practice, and its close sibling, infanticide, to the margins of society. In classical paganism, while it was sometimes controversial, abortion (like euthanasia) was common and widely approved. The Hippocratic physicians, whose medical vision was powered by pagan defense of the sanctity of life, were swimming upstream. It was the church of Jesus Christ which swept through late antiquity as the greatest pro-life movement, setting standards in medicine, culture, and public policy that still condition the thinking of fractured Christendom in the twenty-first century.

Readers who seek *abortion* in a Bible concordance are unlikely to find it, and as a result dissident believers have sometimes suggested that Scripture is silent on the subject, so we may do as we please. Such a conclusion depends on some serious misunderstandings. The biblical foundations of a comprehensive prohibition on induced abortion lie very deep, in the doctrines of creation and incarnation.

The starting point for a biblical understanding of human nature is that human beings are created in God's image. It is clear from Genesis 1:26-27 that this applies to all those who are members of the human species. *Homo sapiens* are distinguished from all other "kinds" by our bearing the likeness of our Maker. The image is specifically stated to be given to women as well as men, and is said to remain after the Fall (Gn 9:6). And it applies to Jew and Gentile, religious and irreligious, young and old, those in the flower of youth, and the most sadly disabled and sick. The *imago Dei* is what makes us the beings we are; and it is in place wherever there are members of our species. The question of which beings bear the image is one of species membership and, therefore, genetics.

While extraordinarily difficult issues are raised by the prospect of human-animal hybrids (and also, perhaps, humanoid robots), the issue here is simple. If this is a member of the human species, this being bears the divine image. It is therefore a he or a she, and his or her life is sacred. With this single recognition, we find the basis of a biblical bioethics, and immediate answers to many of the most pressing questions in contemporary medicine and bioscience. It provides a straightforward response to the issue of induced abortion, since the commandment "Do not murder" (Ex 20:13) applies to all human beings, from the beginning of life to its end. And this command is explicitly rooted in the bearing of the divine image in Genesis 9:6, in the ironic context of the Noahic provision of the capital sentence: "Whoever sheds man's blood, his blood will be shed by man, for God made man in His image."

This species principle is of central importance to debate about human embryos, as researchers have developed techniques using in vitro fertilization and cloning making it possible to use embryos for destructive research. The biblical position is unambiguous: those who are a part of the species, made in the divine image, should not be murdered.

The second foundation lies in the doctrine of the incarnation. As if to illustrate this creation principle of the species-wide bearing of the image, in His incarnation the Son of God, the Second Person of the Trinity, takes human form, and does so from the beginning of human biological existence. When in the "sixth month" (Lk 1:36, a reference to the advanced state of her cousin Elizabeth's pregnancy) Mary was told by the angel that she will conceive by a miracle, the human life of the Son of God began. Shortly afterwards she visits Elizabeth, and we witness John the Baptist's first testimony to his kinsman and his Lord, for as a six-month fetus he leaped in his mother's womb at the presence of the days-old embryonic Jesus (Lk 1:39).

In light of these basic theological affirmations, the many incidental references to unborn life in the OT—in the prophets, Job, and especially Psalms—take on powerful significance (for example, Ps 139:13ff).

The one biblical text sometimes offered as a counterargument is Exodus 21:22, which refers to the appropriate punishment to be applied if men, while fighting, accidentally hit a woman and cause her to miscarry. There are varying translations of the passage, but it's not relevant to the abortion debate. It refers only to the manslaughter of the unborn child, not a deliberate killing.

Is the Bible Sexually Oppressive?

Josh D. McDowell

Let's clear up one misconception. God is pro-sex! He invented it and thinks it's beautiful when enjoyed within the correct framework.

Proverbs tells us, "Take pleasure in the wife of your youth. . . . let her breasts always satisfy you; be lost in her love forever" (Pr 5:18-19). The context here is speaking of sex within the parameters of a lifelong marriage commitment (i.e., "the wife of your youth"). Another example of God's perspective on sex is the Song of Songs, an OT book that uses the beauty of the sexual experience to express one's very spiritual experience.

There is not a single verse in the Bible that decries the experience of sex as sinful, dirty, or wrong. It's only the *misuse* of sex (when it is experienced outside a loving, intimate commitment between a husband and wife) that is so often spoken against in the Scriptures. Sex as God intended it is a beautiful thing.

So why the limits? Simply put, it's because God loves us. Love is defined in Ephesians 5:28-29 as providing and caring for, which includes protection. God's motivation behind every command in the Bible is to protect us and provide us with His best. Even in the "do nots" (commandments which may, at first glance, seem imposing and prohibitive), we can know that God has our best interests at heart. How can we be sure of His loving intentions? We need only look at the life of Christ as recorded in the Gospels. Everything He did—from healing the sick and teaching the multitudes to giving His life on the cross to pay for our sins—was a clear picture of God's love in action.

True to His loving nature, God's instruction to reserve sex for the marriage relationship is given out of love for us. In this case, His boundaries protect us from unwanted pregnancies, agonizing and even deadly diseases, unhealthy emotional attachments, feelings of guilt, and many other dangers. They provide us with good health and safety, freedom from fear, true intimacy and trust in marriage, and many other benefits.

Just like the lanes in a swim meet protect the swimmers from hindrances and give them every opportunity to win, so God's laws are intended for our good. They are not there to frustrate us, but to reflect the freedom we have in Christ. Without the parameters, one cannot experience sex in the way God intended. And when we recognize His loving plan for us—a positive plan for our good and not a negative plan to limit us unfairly or frustrate us—our response should be one of loving obedience.

Does the Bible Support a Just War?

Norman L. Geisler

W hile the Bible doesn't approve of war for every cause and encourages peace with all persons (Rm 12: 18), nonetheless, peace and justice are sometimes unobtainable without war (Mt 24: 6). This is made clear from many considerations. First, the Bible does not prohibit all taking of life. Killing in self-defense is justified (Ex 22:2), as is killing in capital punishment (Gn 9:6). Government is divinely authorized to use "the sword" (Rm 13:4), which Jesus Himself recognized (Jn 19:11). Second, under the law, God spelled out the rules of warfare for Israel (Dt 20). Third, while Jesus forbade His disciples from using a sword for spiritual purposes (Mt 26:52), He urged them to buy a sword if necessary for protection (Lk 22:36-38). Fourth, John the Baptist did not call for repentance from serving in the office of soldier (Lk 3:14).

The Bible commands Christians to obey their government (Rm 13:1-7; Ti 3:1; 1Pt 2:13-14). However, there are limitations to such obedience. When the government commands worship of idols or a king (Dn 3:6), forbids preaching the gospel (Ac 4–5), or orders killing children (Ex 1), then it is a believer's duty to disobey. Likewise, if government engages in unjust war, believers may dissent. However, like Daniel (Dn 6), the three young Hebrew men (Dn 3), and Peter (Ac 4-5), those who disobey government must accept the consequences meted out by the state.

Several conditions for a just war are given in the Bible. (1) It must be declared by one's government (Rm 13:4); (2) It must be in defense of the innocent and/or against an evil aggressor (e.g., Gn 14); and (3) It must be fought by just means (Dt 20:19).

Who Are You to Judge Others?

Paul Copan

H ands down, Matthew 7:1 is the most frequently quoted Bible verse today: "Do not judge, so that you won't be judged." It's been twisted to mean we can't say someone's action or lifestyle is wrong. However, when someone says, "Don't judge," he's judging you for judging someone else. You've done wrong by saying someone else has done wrong! Clearly, we can't escape making moral judgments. Furthermore, in the same context of the oft-quoted verse, Jesus made a moral judgment about certain persons, using metaphors about "dogs" and "pigs" (Mt 7:6), stressing that we shouldn't continue to present God's grace to those who persistently scoff and ridicule. At some point, we must shake the dust off our feet and move on to the more receptive (Mt 10:14; Ac 13:51). On the other hand, Jesus commanded: "Stop judging according to outward appearances; rather judge according to *righteous judgment*" (Jn 7:24, emphasis added).

How do we resolve the apparent tension? By taking note of the spirit in which we make judgments. Do we think we're superior (the attitude Jesus condemned), or are we assessing actions and attitudes with a spirit of humility and concern, recognizing our own weaknesses (1Co 10:13; Gl 6:1)? In Matthew 7:5, Jesus told us first to examine ourselves (removing the log from our own eye); then we can help our brother or sister (taking the speck out of his or her eye). So there *is* a problem to be dealt with—but only after self-examination. The wrong kind of judging is condemning. The right kind of judging is properly evaluating moral (or doctrinal) matters—with a humble, helpful attitude. (In 1Co 5:5, "judging"—even excommunication—is required in light of a church member's shameless sexual misconduct). We should treat others the way we would want to be treated (cp. Mt 7:12), thinking, *There—but for the grace of God—go I.*

So when discussing judging with others, first clarify what you mean by the word "judge." This can serve as the context for clarifying right and wrong kinds of judgment. Further, we must take care to avoid the "Who am I to say So-and-So is wrong?" mentality. We can't shrink back from making moral judgments, nor can we escape them—lest we declare it wrong to say another is wrong.

What Does the Bible Teach About Homosexuality?

Scott B. Rae

I n the OT, homosexuality is unequivocally condemned. Homosexual sex is prohibited in the law (Lv 18:22; 20:13) and is called an abomination. However, of all the illicit sexual relations listed in Leviticus 18, homosexuality is not singled out as being more worthy of condemnation than other varieties of sexual sin. God's attitude toward homosexuality is portrayed in the judgment on Sodom and Gomorrah (Gn 19). Ezekiel includes among the sins of Sodom the "immoral acts," using the same term as in Leviticus 18 to describe homosexual acts (Ezk 16:43; cp. Jd 7). The law condemns all homosexual sex and does not distinguish between perverted and wholesome homosexual relationships.

The central NT passage that addresses homosexuality is Romans 1:24-27 (cp. 1Co 6:9; 1Tm 6:10). It's set in the context of the condemnation of those who reject God as revealed in creation, or through natural law. It's part of Paul's broader argument for the universality of sin and judgment, setting the need for the believer to be justified by faith in Christ's atoning death on the cross, outlined in Romans 4–5. Those who reject the available knowledge of God and choose instead to worship the Greek and Roman idols faced life-style consequences. One of these consequences is homosexual behavior. Paul appealed to the natural order of creation to condemn homosexual behavior (Rm 1:27).

What's natural is objective and based on creation, not dependent upon an individual's sexual orientation. Male and female were created with an innate tendency toward opposite sex attraction, but because of sin, the human race developed the potential for homosexuality. This potential is often realized when certain developmental factors are present. Because of the reality of sin, every person has the potential for homosexuality, in the same way that we have the potential for any other kind of sin Scripture describes.

Some have suggested that Paul intended to condemn only certain types of homosexuality. For example, given the context of idolatry, some have argued that Paul was only condemning homosexuality in the context of idolatrous worship. Others have suggested that Paul intended to condemn perverse homosexuality, such as multiple partners and nonconsensual homosexual sex. Still others argue that Paul was objecting to persons' reversing their natural sexual orientation and acting sexually in ways that violate their orientation.

There is little evidence in the text that Paul actually intended to limit his teaching to certain kinds of homosexual activity. Rather, Paul's appeal to a universal truth about sexual relations linked to the order of creation (cp. Jesus' teaching in Mt 19:4-6) should prevents us from seeing this passage as limited to certain kinds of homosexual behavior and from seeing Paul as culturally outdated in his teaching. Rather, it provides an appropriate context for a judgment on all homosexual sexual relationships

In applying these passages that forbid homosexuality, some suggest it is important to make a distinction between homosexual *attraction* and homosexual *sexual relations*. And indeed there is a difference between being attracted to a person of the same sex and acting sexually on that attraction. For a straight, married person to be attracted to someone of the opposite sex other than his or her spouse, it is not sin per se. It becomes sin when that attraction is acted upon, either in lust (the process of mentally having sex with a person) or in sexual overtures. Likewise, it may be that the homosexual attraction is not sin per se, though at variance with the order of creation. But when that attraction gives way to lust and ultimately to sexual activity, it is sin.

Some argue that what the Bible condemns in homosexual relationships is what it also condemns in heterosexual relationships—that is, lust and sexual involvement outside marriage. Thus the options for the Christian homosexual would be the same as the Christian single person: either abstinence or heterosexual sex in marriage. Some Christians who struggle with their sexual identity have grasped this distinction and rejected the gay lifestyle while attempting to work out issues related to their sexual identity.

It may be that failure to recognize a distinction between feeling a homosexual attraction and acting homosexually has kept the church from being a more accepting place for those struggling with their sexual orientation.

How Should a Christian Understand the Role of Government?

Charles Colson

C hristianity's about much more than just salvation; it speaks to *all* of life. "Jesus is Lord" was the earliest baptismal confession. Scripture mandates taking dominion and cultivating the soil (Gn 1) and being salt and light (Mt 5:13-16). Abraham Kuyper, former Dutch Prime Minister and theologian, famously said, "There is not a square inch in the whole domain of human existence over which Christ, who is sovereign over all, does not cry out 'Mine!'"

No area of cultural engagement is more important than government and politics: we're commanded to submit to governing authorities (Rm 13); Jesus Himself said, "Give back to Caesar the things that are Caesar's" (Mt 22:21). This means Christians must be good citizens, pay taxes, obey laws, and serve (as called) in government. Augustine argued that Christians are to be the *best* citizens: what others do only because the law demands, we do out of love for God.

Because government is ordained by God to preserve order and do justice, we're instructed to honor the king (1Pt 2:13-17) and pray for those in authority that we might live peaceful lives (1Tm 2:1-22). The only thing worse than bad government is anarchy.

The authorities are established by God, Paul says. Hence, John Calvin accorded the magistrate's office as having one of the most important roles in any society—working as a servant for good (Rm 13:4). It's a noble calling for Christians to enter public service. Contrary to common caricatures of politicians, some of the finest public servants I've known are serious believers who live out their faith in office without compromising their convictions.

The cultural mandate means the church has an important role to play in respect to political structures—working for justice, speaking prophetically, and often being the conscience of society, even when this means persecution, prison or death, as it did for many in the confessing church in Nazi Germany.

Though there have been times when the church failed in this responsibility, thankfully today it's at its post, the strongest voice in American society in defense of life and human rights. The church is also the agency which, in this age of terrorism, prophetically holds government to the moral boundaries of the just war tradition.

Though in America we observe a strict separation of church and state—the state shouldn't establish a state church or restrict the free exercise of religion—there should never be a separation of religion and public life. The public square needs religious influence; indeed, the Christian faith has played a critical role in shaping our institutions. Reformation doctrines like Sphere Sovereignty (government doesn't rule alone; all structures—the family, the church, private associations—have ordained responsibilities) and the Rule of Law made Western liberal democracy possible. Our founding fathers respected the "laws of nature and nature's God," recognizing that without a moral consensus resting upon Judeo-Christian tradition, virtue could not be maintained and self-government would fail. Noted historian Will Durant wrote that he could find no case in history where a nation survived without a moral code and no case where that moral code was not informed by religious truth.

But the church must approach its public role with caution and sensitivity. Pastors/church leaders, for example, should never make partisan endorsements of candidates (which can divide our ranks and politicize the faith) or allow themselves to be in the hip pocket of either political party. That said, the pastor should never hesitate to speak boldly from the pulpit about pressing moral concerns.

There are clear dangers in dealing with politics. Among my duties as special counsel to President Nixon was winning the support of special interest groups. I found religious leaders easily impressed with the trappings of office. And later watching from the outside, I saw Christian leaders succumb to these blandishments. There's a fine line here. It was wrong when, for most of the twentieth century, evangelicals stood apart from politics; so too it's wrong to allow ourselves to be married to a political party.

Christians individually and through organizations must engage in the political process, but always preserving their independence and fulfilling the prophetic office (which may mean calling friends to account.) Though Christians are to be the best of citizens, our first loyalty is not to the kingdom of man but to the kingdom of God.

What Did Jesus Have to Do With Violence?

Mark Durie

T he conquest of Canaan, as described in the Bible, was a bloody one. Some cities like Jericho were put to the sword. Isn't it dangerous to have such material in the Bible? Might not these stories incite Christians to acts of bloodshed or even genocide against others? The answer to this question is a very emphatic "No!"

There are a number of reasons why the conquest of Canaan, and other stories of conflict in the Bible, do not incite Christians into violent acts of insurrection, murder, and genocide.

One is that the account of the conquest of Canaan was entirely situation-specific. Yes, there is a divine instruction reported in the Bible to take the land by force and occupy it, driving out the inhabitants (Nm 33:52). However this was not an eternal permission for believers to wage war. It was for a specific time and place. According to the Bible, the Canaanites had come under divine judgment because of their religious practices, above all child sacrifice (Dt 18:12).

The sacrificing of firstborn children by immolating them before an idol (Dt 18:10) was a persistent trait of Canaanite religion. The Phoenicians were Canaanites, and as late as the second century B.C. the people of Carthage, a Phoenician colony, were sacrificing children to their goddess Tanit. Archeologists have found charred remains of tens of thousands of newborn infants and fetuses buried in Carthage. The practice of child sacrifice made the Romans despise the Carthaginians.

The Bible's stories of the use of force against the Canaanites are more than balanced by the accounts of the destruction of Israel and Judah by foreign armies. These violent invasions are also described as being God's judgment, now turned against the Israelites because they did not distance themselves from Canaanite religious practices. Even the kings of Israel and Judah are charged with practicing child sacrifice (2Kg 17:17; 21:6; Ezk 16:21).

Although the OT does condone the use of force to purge a land of violence and injustice, the Bible's attitude to such violence is not that it is sacred or holy. On the contrary, King David, who fought many wars with God's active support and guidance, was not allowed to be the one to build God's temple in Jerusalem because there was so much blood on his hands (1Ch 28:3).

Violence is regarded by the Bible as an inherently evil symptom of the corruption of the whole earth after the fall: "the earth was filled with violence" (Gn 6:11). In contrast, the prophet Isaiah looked forward to the day when the days of violence would be no more. Isaiah describes the Lord's anointed as unacquainted with violence: "They made His grave with the wicked, and with a rich man at His death, although He had done no violence and had not spoken deceitfully"(Is 53:9).

In this way the OT sets the scene for the revelation of Jesus Christ. The key question for Christians is "What did Jesus have to do with violence?" When we turn to consider Jesus and His followers, we find a systematic rejection of religious violence. Jesus' message was that His kingdom would be spiritual and not political. Jesus explicitly and repeatedly condemned the use of force to achieve His goals: "Put your sword back in place because all who take up a sword will perish by a sword" (Mt 26:52).

As Jesus goes to the cross, He renounces force, even at the cost of His own life: "My kingdom is not of this world. . . . If My kingdom were of this world, My servants would fight, so that I wouldn't be handed over to the Jews. As it is, My kingdom does not have its origin here" (Jn 18:36).

At one point Christ says "Don't assume that I came to bring peace on the earth. I did not come to bring peace, but a sword" (Mt 10:34). This is sometimes cited by anti-Christian apologists as evidence for Jesus' militancy, but the statement occurs in an extended passage where Jesus is advising His disciples on the inevitability of persecution. The sword He refers to is the one which will be raised against them.

Jesus' take on violence was reinforced by the Apostles Paul and Peter, who urged Christians to show consideration to their enemies, renounce retaliation, living peaceably, return cursing with blessing, and show humility to others (Rm 12:14-21; Ti 3:1-2; 1Pt 2:20-24). They also allowed that the (most likely pagan) civil authorities would need to use force to keep the peace and this role should be respected (Rm 13:1-7; 1Pt 2:13-17). This was an extension of the earlier Jewish position that Jews should submit to the rule of law in whichever country they were in, even if the king was a pagan (Jr 29:4-7).

The NT supports the just use of force as a proper function of the state, whatever its religious identity. Thus it is not a specifically religious or sacred act to go to war or to use force to implement justice. It is just a matter of public duty, one aspect of the ordering of society which God has established for the common good. Fighting may be considered just, not because it is advancing any one faith over another, but because it is warranted and conducted according to principles of justice applicable to all people.

If only Christians had maintained this NT position through the centuries, the world would have been a better place. The invention of "Christendom" in the fourth Christian century, and the later influence of a centuries-long struggle against the Islamic jihad, ultimately led Christians to develop aberrant theologies which regarded warfare against non-Christians as "holy," and soldiers who died fighting in such wars were regarded as "martyrs." Thankfully, this view of warfare has been universally denounced in the modern era as incompatible with the gospel of Christ.

SECTION 8

Heaven, Hell, and the Spiritual Realm

What Does the Bible Teach About Angels?

Ron Rhodes

The Bible's teaching about angels can be summarized by the following points:

- The NT speaks of angels more than 165 times; the OT more than 100 times.
- The angels were created prior to God's creation of the earth (Jb 38:7; Ps 148:2-5).
- Humans do not become angels at the moment of death (1Co 6:3; 13:1).
- All the angels were created by God as good angels (Gn 1:31).
- The angels were apparently subjected to a period of probation. Some angels remained committed to God; others did not.
- An angel rebellion, headed by the evil one, arose against God. Apparently the evil one became so impressed with himself that he wanted to take God's place. He came to be referred to as Satan, meaning "adversary." One-third of the angels followed him in this rebellion (Ezk 28:11-19; 2Pt 2:4; Rv 12:3-4,10) becoming what the Bible calls demons.
- The holy angels live in heaven (Is 6:1-6; Dn 7:10; Heb 12:22). When they are assigned a task by God, they leave heaven, complete their work on earth, and then return to heaven.
- Angels are personal beings, with minds (2Sm 14:20), emotions (Heb 12:22), and wills (Rv 22:8-9).
- Angels are incorporeal (lacking material form) and invisible (Heb 1:14). We are thus generally unaware of their activities around us (2Kg 6:17).
- Angels can nevertheless take on human appearance when their assigned task calls for it (Gn 18:1-8; Heb 13:2).
- Angels are localized beings. They are not "omnipresent" like God. They have to move from one place to another (Dn 9:21-23).

- Angels are extremely powerful; they are described as "mighty" (Ps 103:20).
- God's angels are holy ("set apart"). They are set apart from sin and set apart unto God to do His bidding (Jb 5:1; Ps 89:7).
- The holy angels are unreservedly obedient to God (Ps 103:20).
- Angels are immortal, though created. Once created (Ps 148:2-6), they never cease to exist (Lk 20:36).
- The angels are innumerable (Rv 5:11). Daniel 7:10 makes reference to "ten thousand times ten thousand" angels (100 million angels).
- Angels are called "ministering spirits" (Heb 1:14). The word "ministering" comes from a Greek word meaning "serve." Angels, then, are spirit servants who render aid to the heirs of salvation in the outworking of God's purposes on earth.
- This service takes many forms, including being used by God in answering believers' prayers (Ac 12:7), bringing announcements and warnings to God's people (Lk 1:13; Ac 10:3-33), giving encouragement (Ac 27:23-24), providing protection (Ps 91:11), giving guidance (Gn 19:17), providing deliverance (Ac 12:7), and caring for believers at the moment of death (Lk 16:22).
- Many believe that every Christian has a specific guardian angel throughout life (Mt 18:10; Ac 12:15). Others believe that angels are charged with different assignments as God directs (Ps 91:11).
- Angels are organized by rank, including thrones, powers, rulers, authorities, and dominions (Eph 1:20-21; Col 1:16), but the details and nature of these ranks are not revealed to us.
- Among unbelievers, angels restrain wickedness (Gn 19:1-15), announce God's judgments (Rv 14:7-10), execute God's judgments (Ac 12:23; Rv 16:1-18), and in the end times cast them "into the blazing furnace" (Mt 13:37-43).
- In the afterlife Christians will judge angels (1Co 6:3).

Is There Evidence for Life After Death?

Hank Hanegraaff

P hilosophical naturalists (including most evolutionists) believe that death is the cessation of being. In their view, humans are merely bodies and brains. Though they reject metaphysical realities such as the soul, there are convincing reasons to believe that humans have an immaterial aspect to their being that transcends the material and thus can continue to exist after death.

From a legal perspective, if human beings were merely material, they could not be held accountable this year for a crime committed last year, because physical identity changes over time. We are not the same people today that we were yesterday. Every day we lose millions of microscopic particle. In fact, every seven years or so, virtually every part of our material anatomy changes, apart from aspects of our neurological system. Therefore, from a purely material perspective, the person who previously committed a crime is presently not the same person. Yet, a criminal who attempts to use this line of reasoning as a defense would not get very far. Such legal maneuvering simply does not fly even in an age of scientific enlightenment. Legally and intuitively, we recognize a sameness of soul that establishes personal identity over time.

Finally, freedom of the will presupposes that we are more than mere material robots. If I am merely material, my choices are merely a function of such factors as genetic makeup and brain chemistry. Therefore, my decisions are not free; they are fatalistically determined. The implications of such a notion are profound. In a worldview that embraces fatalistic determinism, I cannot be held morally accountable for my actions, since reward and punishment make sense only if we have freedom of the will. In a solely material world, reason itself is reduced to the status of a conditioned reflex. Moreover, even the very concept of love is rendered meaningless. Rather than being an act of the will, love is relegated to a robotic procedure that is fatalistically determined by physical processes.

While the legal and freedom arguments are convincing in and of themselves, there is an even more powerful and persuasive argument demonstrating the reality of life beyond the grave. That argument flows from the resurrection of Jesus Christ. The best minds of ancient and modern times have demonstrated beyond a shadow of doubt that Christ's physical trauma was fatal; that the empty tomb is one of the best-attested facts of ancient history; that Christ's followers experienced tangible post-resurrection appearances of Christ on several occasions; and that within weeks of the resurrection, not just one Jew, but an entire community of at least 3,000 Jews experienced such an incredible transformation that they willingly gave up sociological and theological traditions that had given them their national identity.

Through the resurrection, Christ not only demonstrated that He does not stand in a line of peers with Abraham, Buddha, or Confucius but also provided compelling evidence for life after death.

More Evidence for Life After Death

J.P. Moreland

The case for life after death consists of empirical (observable) and nonempirical (theoretical) arguments. The empirical arguments are two: near-death experiences (NDE's) and the resurrection of Jesus. A sufficient body of evidence exists for the view that people have died, left their bodies, had various experiences, and returned to their bodies. Attempts to explain NDEs naturalistically fail in those cases where the disembodied person gained knowledge about things miles away (e.g., conversations of family members). One must be cautious about theological interpretations of NDE's, but their reality is well established. Some argue that, even if true, NDE's only provide evidence for temporary existence beyond death. Strictly speaking, this is correct. However, if biological death does not bring the cessation of consciousness, it is hard to see what could do so after death.

Jesus' resurrection is defended elsewhere in this collection of essays. Suffice it to say that if Jesus rose from the dead, this qualifies Him to speak about life after death because His resurrection provides evidence that He was the Son of God, and means He has returned from the afterlife and told us about it.

The nonempirical arguments divide into theistic-dependent and theistic-independent ones. The former assume the existence of God and therewith argue for immortality. If God is who He says He is, the case is proven beyond reasonable doubt. Three such theistic dependent arguments are especially important.

The first is two-pronged and argues from the image and love of God. Given that humans have tremendous value as image bearers and God is a preserver of tremendously high value, then God is a preserver of persons. Moreover, given that God loves His image bearers and has a project of bringing them to full maturity and fellowship with Him, God will sustain humans to continue this love affair and His important project on their behalf.

The second argument, based on divine justice, asserts that in this life goods and evils are not evenly distributed. A just God must rectify these inequities, and an afterlife is thus required.

Finally, there is the argument from biblical revelation: It can be established that the Bible is the truthful Word of God, and it affirms life after death. For this to be an argument, rational considerations must be marshaled on behalf of the Bible's divine status.

Two non-theistic dependent arguments exist for immortality. The first is the argument from desire: (1) The desire for life after death is a natural desire. (2) Every natural desire corresponds to some real state of affairs that can fulfill it. (3) Therefore, the desire for life after death corresponds to some real state of affairs—namely life after death—that fulfills it.

Critics claim that the desire for immortality is nothing but an expression of ethical egoism. People do not universally desire it, and even when they do, it is a learned, not a natural, desire. Further, even if it is a natural desire, sometimes such desires are frustrated. While adequate responses exist for these rebuttals, they weaken the force of the argument, though it is hard to say precisely how much.

The second argument claims that consciousness and the self are immaterial, not physical, and this supports belief in life after death in two ways: (1) It makes disembodied existence and personal identity in the afterlife intelligible.

(2) It provides evidence for the existence of God. This, in turn, provides grounds for reintroducing the theistic-dependent arguments for life after death.

The argument for consciousness being nonphysical involves the claim that once one gets an accurate description of consciousness—sensations, emotions, thoughts, beliefs—it becomes clear that it is not physical. Conscious states are characterized by their inner, private, qualitative feel made known by introspection. Since physical states lack these features, consciousness is not physical.

The case for an immaterial self is rooted in the claim that in first person introspection, we are aware of our own egos as immaterial centers of consciousness. This awareness grounds intuitions that when one has an arm cut off, has a portion of one's brain removed, or gains/loses memories and personality traits, one does not become a partial person or a different person altogether.

While these two arguments provide some grounds for belief in an afterlife, they are far from conclusive. At the end of the day, the justification of belief in life after death is largely theistic dependent.

What Should a Christian Think About Near-death Experiences?

Gary R. Habermas

R eports of near-death experiences have occasioned much interest. These reports abound from those who claim to have hovered above their nearly dead bodies, journeyed down dark tunnels towards a beautiful light, often in the presence of deceased loved ones.

The most interesting near-death accounts are the dozens which claim that the dying person, during their turmoil, actually observed events that were later reported and verified. These events may have taken place some distance away and could not have been observed from the individual's location even if they had been completely well. Sometimes the near-death individual had extended periods without a heartbeat during these observations. On a few rare occasions, no brain activity was reported. A number of blind persons have also produced accurate descriptions of their surroundings.

Attempts have been made to explain these experiences naturally, especially by medical or psychological factors, such as hallucinations. However, none of these subjective approaches can account for the evidential cases just mentioned. For example, internal brain phenomena cannot explain accurate descriptions of events, particularly a distance away, especially when the person's heart or brain has failed!

How should Christians think about such accounts? To be sure, some tough questions surround this topic. For example, some non-Christians have declared that they had wonderful experiences during a near-death state.

But negative experiences, including graphic visions of Hell, have also been reported. Further, these persons were not biologically (irreversibly) dead, but only near-death. So how can we be sure of their final state? Last, we are dealing here not with the experiences themselves, but with personal interpretations of the experiences, which are notoriously inaccurate during highly emotional times. In these cases, serious evidence is lacking.

What about reports of satanic or occultic aspects? Undeniably, such do exist and caution is definitely necessary. But it appears that there is nothing inherently occultic about near-death experiences. People are simply reporting their perceptions.

The carefully observed and well documented cases provide some evidence for at least the initial moments of afterlife. This is contrary to the dictates of naturalism, which claims that the natural world is all there is to reality. So near-death experiences can be both well evidenced and valuable. At the same time, Christians must be careful not to endorse non-biblical interpretations of these experiences or accept them as revealing truth on a par with the Bible.

Does the Bible Teach That There Is a Purgatory?

Chad Owen Brand

S ome Christian traditions teach that Christians who die in good fellowship with the Church but who are still not in a state of perfection will go to an intermediate place after death that is neither heaven nor hell, known as purgatory. Unbaptised adults and those who have committed mortal sins, according to this tradition, go to Hades or hell. A few perfected persons (saints) go directly to heaven.

Defenders of purgatory teach that it will be a time and place of suffering, something akin to the lake of fire, but not as severe and only temporary. The amount of time one spends there depends on the degree of purging needed, based on one's sins. Pope Gregory I taught that baptism absolves us of original sin, but we have to remit payment for our actual sins. This purging is a preparation of the soul for heaven.

Is there any biblical justification for the doctrine of purgatory? Supporters of the doctrine generally go to 2 Maccabees 12:39-45 to defend their position. But this text says nothing about purgatory, and those who do not accept the authority of the Apocryphal writings would not find it compelling even if it did. The other text that is sometimes cited is 1 Corinthians 3:10-15, where the concluding phrase is "yet it will be like an escape through fire." But again there is nothing in the text which indicates that there will be a time and place after death in which individuals will be purged of the sins committed in this life.

The doctrine of purgatory fails the biblical test both in terms of direct interpretation of the specifically cited texts and in terms of the overall teaching of Scripture. Neither of the classically cited passages even mentions purgatory, by name or by concept. Even more, this doctrine denies one of the fundamental teachings of the NT—that Jesus' death on the cross atoned for all of our sin, not simply original sin (Rm 3:21-26 ; 2Co 5:21). Because of that atonement, though we will all stand before the judgment seat of Christ, those who have placed faith in Christ will never face condemnation (Rm 5:1; 8:1; 2Co 5:10).

Why Would a Good God Send People to an Everlasting Hell?

Paul Copan

The essence of hell is to be away from the "Lord's presence" (2Th 1:9). Hell's differing images of darkness, fire, and decay express the anguish of being cut off from intimate union with God (Rv 21:3; 22:4). God genuinely offers salvation to all and thus commands all without exception to repent (Ezk 33:11; Ac 17:30; 2Pt 3:9), but He will not hold up the final celebration because of those resisting His grace (Ac 7:51).

Let's address some hell-related questions that unbelievers and believers find troubling.

Isn't God unjust to punish persons forever for sins committed during a limited earthly existence? Those in hell have committed the ultimate, infinite sin—not simply a string of finite sins—rejecting a relationship with the self-giving God. Also, hell is the logical outcome of a mindset to live life apart from God—not simply committing individual sins. The punishment fits the crime. You want no God, you get no God. There are two kinds of people: those who say to God, "Thy will be done," and those to whom God says, "*Thy* will be done" (C.S. Lewis).

But wouldn't persons in hell really want to be with God if they knew what heaven was like? No. Those who have resisted God on earth continue in their hard-heartedness thereafter (just as those living for God on earth continue to enjoy Him). God's holy presence would truly be "hell" for those wanting their own way. We have no hint from Scripture of repentance in hell. Rebellion, hate, and selfishness continue. The rich man in hell (Lk 16:19-26) is remorseful, not repentant—not wanting to change but find relief!

But how can people be sent to hell without knowing its full implications? Even if one isn't fully aware of hell's full anguish, this doesn't mean our choice is too much to bear: God is ready to equip anyone for salvation (Jn 16:8). Though the full consequences of our embracing or rejecting God aren't fully apparent to us now, grace to choose responsibly is available to all. What prevents the salvation of everyone? Individuals freely choosing to reject God's grace. We can always resist the Holy Spirit (Ac 7:51). God doesn't *send* people to hell; they freely *reject* Him, condemning themselves by not acknowledging their guilt.

Why didn't God make the world in such a way that all people would love Him? While a world in which everyone loves God is theoretically possible, it is not feasible. Whatever possible world with free creatures God could create, it may be that none is sin-free, and God's love isn't *forced*. Hell—the absence of God's presence—exists because, like Milton's Satan, people would rather "reign in hell than serve in heaven." God isn't unloving, but has gone to great lengths to show grace to everyone. Should God not create at all because many will freely resist Him in any world God would make and thus deprive many others of the greatest good possible?

Why did God create people He knew would reject Him and be separated from Him forever? Despite God's desire that all be saved (1Tm 2:4; 2Pt 3:9), many still resist. What if some become more resistant no matter how loving God is (Is 5:4; Mt 23:37)? Should God not create those who would respond to His love simply because others would refuse it? What if God created a world in which a maximal balance of least condemned and most redeemed was realized? This is not unloving.

Why couldn't God, from the start, make us like heaven's saints—loving God while unable to sin? Robust freedom on earth—to embrace freely God's grace or resist it—is a requirement for arriving at one's final destiny. Our earthly direction is "sealed" in the afterlife; our heart's desire is finally granted—God or no God. So God couldn't have created a heaven-like state in which the redeemed no longer sin without damaging this vitally important freedom. (Or perhaps, rather than "sealing" us from sin in the afterlife, God simply foreknows that no saint will actually freely sin, guaranteeing a sin-free condition in the final state.)

Finally, because God has so fully given of Himself to make salvation freely available through His Son, we can confidently entrust any lingering questions about hell to His excellent character.

Does the Bible Teach Annihilationism?

J.P. Moreland

Does the Bible teach that the unsaved will suffer in hell for only a time and then be annihilated? Some argue from Scripture that the flames in hell are literal and point out that flames destroy whatever they burn. Morally, it is claimed that infinitely long punishment is disproportionate to a finite life of sin. Thus extinction is morally preferable to everlasting punishing.

The scriptural argument for this view is weak. Clear texts whose explicit intent is to teach the extent of the afterlife overtly compare the everlasting conscious life of the saved and the unsaved (Dn 12:2; Mt 25:41,46). Moreover, the flames in hell are most likely figures of speech for judgment (cp. 2Th 1:8; Heb 12:29). Otherwise, contradictions about hell are apparent (for example, it is dark despite being filled with flames).

The moral argument fails as well. For one thing, the severity of a crime is not a function of the time it takes to commit it. Thus rejection of the mercy of an infinite God could appropriately warrant an unending, conscious separation from God. Further, everlasting hell is morally superior to annihilation. That becomes evident from the following consideration.

Regarding the end of life, sanctity-of-life advocates reject active euthanasia (the intentional killing of a patient), while quality-of-life advocates embrace it. In the sanctity-of-life view, one gets one's value, not from the quality of one's life, but from the sheer fact that one exists in God's image. The quality-of-life advocates see the value of human life in its quality; life is not inherently valuable. Thus the sanctity-of-life position has a higher, not a lower, moral regard for the dignity of human life.

The traditional and annihilationist views about hell are expressions, respectively, of sanctity-of-life and quality-of-life ethical standpoints. After all, the grounds God would have for annihilating someone would be the low quality of life in hell. If a person will not receive salvation and if God will not extinguish one made in His image because He values life, then God's alternative is quarantine, and hell is certainly that. Thus the traditional view, being a sanctity-of-life and not a quality-of-life position, is morally superior to annihilationism.

Does the Bible Teach Reincarnation?

Paul Copan

T he simple answer is no. When proponents of reincarnation allege that certain biblical texts allegedly teach the soul's preexistence or reincarnation, those texts are being approached superficially and the case for teaching reincarnation from them dissolves under further scrutiny.

Reincarnation (Hinduism) or rebirth (Buddhism) is integral to Eastern philosophy. In the *Bhagavad Gita*, Krishna talks of having "passed through many births." And what we reap in this life (*karma*) comes from what we've sown in past lives. Biblical, theological, and philosophical reasons, however, undermine reincarnation.

If one acknowledges the Bible's authority and storyline, one will readily recognize the Eastern doctrine of reincarnation as unacceptable. Many claiming that reincarnation is in the Bible would go on believing in reincarnation anyway, with or without biblical support. They read reincarnation into isolated verses (e.g., statements about being "born again" in Jn 3) without respecting the biblical context or the worldview of the author. In doing so, they do not respect the biblical text as they would want their own Eastern texts respected. (What if we read bodily resurrection into *their* texts?)

Each of us must die and then be judged by God (Heb 9:27). When God tells Jeremiah He knew him before he was in his mother's womb (Jr 1:5), this doesn't demonstrate preexistence or reincarnation; it only indicates God's foreknowledge and sovereignty. Notice Jeremiah does *not* say, "Before *I* was in my mother's womb, *I* knew *You*, God!" *That* would make a persuasive case for preexistence! Also, the disciples' questioning whether the man born blind sinned before birth (Jn 9:2) does not express reincarnation, but the rabbinic belief that a fetus could sin while in his mother's womb (cp. *Genesis Rabbah* 63.6).

Furthermore, the historically supportable event of Jesus' bodily resurrection undercuts reincarnation. The biblical view of the afterlife is radically different than that of Eastern philosophies. True immorality is not the eradication or "snuffing out" (*moksha*) of the self or its absorption with the One, *Brahman,* like a drop in an ocean. To receive immortality is to receive an immortal, imperishable physical body (1Co 15:53-54). First Corinthians 15 calls it a *spiritual* body (that is, supernaturally animated by the Holy Spirit) rather than a *natural* body (animated by a human soul). Immortality means being forever in union with God and living in God's presence with this new body in the new heavens and new earth—without losing individual identity.

Theologically, God's grace and forgiveness undercut *karma.* We need not bear the heavy weight of guilt and shame because Jesus Christ has absorbed that for us. And if reincarnation be true, why help the underprivileged? Aren't they getting what they deserve—their *karma*?

Despite "evidence" for reincarnation, arguments for one's having lived previous lives could be explained by demonic activity (see Ac 16:16-18). A person having access to information about another's previous life does not imply that this was his own life. A psychic may purport to have knowledge of a crime, but this doesn't mean he committed it!

Philosophical problems with reincarnation are many. (1) Those "remembering" past lives tend to be clustered in the East (where reincarnation is taught), not throughout the world (as we'd expect if it were a true condition of all humans). (2) If we forget our past lives, what purpose does reincarnation serve for self-improvement? (3) Assuming reincarnation (with an *infinite* past series of rebirths), then we've all had plenty of time to reach perfection. Why haven't we? (4) Reincarnation doesn't solve the problem of evil as some claim, but only infinitely postpones it (and in some Eastern schools, evil's just an illusion anyway). (5) Reincarnation makes incoherent the idea of monism—everything is one without distinction—by presupposing distinctions between (a) individual souls, (b) the *karmas* of individual souls not having yet reached enlightenment, (c) the enlightened and unenlightened, and (d) individual souls and the One (ultimate reality).

SECTION 9

Cults and World Religions

Is Mormonism Compatible with the Bible?

Chad Owen Brand

Joseph Smith Jr., the founder of the Church of Jesus Christ of Latter-day Saints, claimed he was restoring the genuine church to the earth, a church absent since the first century. But is Mormonism truly Christian?

People who ask such questions often differentiate between denominations, sects, cults, and world religions. *Denominations* are movements that differ on doctrinal issues, but who hold to a common core of beliefs about God, Christ, and the Scriptures. They see God as trinitarian, Christ as unique in His human-divine person, and the Scriptures as the authoritative text passed down from the prophets and apostles. *Sects* agree with the denominations on these matters, but often have some characteristic that places them on the fringe of Christianity, such as the radical separatism of the Amish. *Cults* are connected to Christianity in that they employ Christian Scripture and appeal to Jesus, but they also differ from the traditional faith in certain core areas. They may deny or reinterpret the Trinity. They may have novel views about Christ. They may reject part of the Christian Scripture, add new texts to it, or claim to have an infallible interpretation that is new and that replaces traditional doctrine with a new approach. *World religions* are those historic traditions that include the Christian religion as well as others, such as Judaism, Islam, and Hinduism.

Is Mormonism Christian? If the question only asks whether Mormonism is connected to Christianity in some sense, the answer would be "Yes." But that is not enough. Religions such as Baha'i claim some connection to Christianity, and Muslims believe in the second coming of Jesus. In order for a faith to be Christian it must pass both the doctrinal and the experiential tests. Doctrinally, it must be orthodox on the key issues outlined above and experientially it must see salvation as a faith encounter with Christ alone as the pathway to being right with God. How does Mormonism stack up?

Mormonism is neither monotheistic nor, technically, trinitarian. In one of the Mormon scriptures, *The Pearl of Great Price*, we are told that the world was fashioned "by the Gods." In his famous King Follett sermon, Joseph

Smith stated that God was once as we are and that we may become as He is—a God. Mormonism teaches that Father, Son, and Spirit are all God, but it denies the historic Christian view on the Trinity. Mormon scholar Robert Millet has written that the Trinity is comprised of "Three Beings." Mormonism is not trinitarian, but tritheist. Mormon theology teaches that Jesus is an incarnation of Elohim, conceived as the *literal* son of God. But He is not the unique incarnation, since we also can be incarnations of the Father. Jesus is important to the whole of Mormon theology, but differently than for traditional Christians. We are not saved by the atoning work of Christ in Mormonism, but by lives of obedience to Mormon principles. Mormons follow the Bible as Scripture, but they have added three other texts which they place alongside the Bible—*The Book of Mormon*, *Doctrine and Covenants*, and *The Pearl of Great Price*. It is in the last two books in particular that the novel Mormon doctrines can be found.

Because of these departures from standard Christian teachings, Mormonism falls outside orthodox Christianity.

What Is the Occult?

Leonard G. Goss

The English word "occult" comes from the Latin *occultus*, which means things that are hidden, esoteric, concealed, or mysterious. For occult practitioners, the occult represents interference with physical nature by using hidden knowledge (*gnosis*), such as non-conventional practices including reciting formulas, making gestures, mixing incompatible elements, performing healing spells, or performing in secret ceremonies attempting to alter physical nature. What is the hidden knowledge? According to occultists, it is the force at the base of the universe, and it is obtained only through secret communication with that force. Is this hidden force God? Or the devil? Or the soul of the universe? That depends a good deal on what particular source their *gnosis* has tapped into, but one thing the force is not: It is not the God of Abraham, Isaac, and Jacob.

For those dabbling in the occult, occultic activities are considered harmless and fascinating—a real source of spiritual knowledge. For Christians, however, the practices making up the occult are destructive and spirit-threatening. Christians view as deeply evil things like alchemy, astrology, casting runes, crystals and crystal balls, divination, dowsing, ESP, fortune-telling, horoscopes, the I Ching, levitation, ouija boards, paganism, palm reading, the paranormal, pendulum divination, psychic phenomena, reading Tarot Cards, ritual abuse, satanism, séances, secret societies, sorcery, spiritualism, talking to dead spirits, Wicca (so-called White Witchcraft), and Witchcraft (Black Magic). The extent of occult involvement is universal. Spiritual warfare is all around us, and if Satan cannot keep us from knowing Christ, he will try containing us by drawing us into deception. The Enemy is a deceiver, liar, tempter, and devourer of human souls.

Why the interest in the occult? First, many churches have "watered down" the gospel of Christ, rejecting the church's central teaching of Christ's divinity and other essential truths. When this happens, a spiritual vacuum invites people to go to the occult to be satisfied, swinging the door to occultist practices wide open. Second, there is a certain mystery about the occult which appeals to our curiosity. Many, thinking the occult is harmless, go deeper and deeper until they can't get out without any bad effects. Third, we all want ultimate answers to life's basic questions, and the occult offers a sort of "reality" by providing these answers. Actually, occultist practices are a counterfeit of God's power, and as such they do reveal some amazing things—but these things are not the ultimate truth. Fourth, an increase in demonic activity is to be expected as a sign of the end times (see Mk 13:22; 1Tm 4:1).

Often, there is deliberate faking in the lucrative field of the occult. There is money to be made. There is also inaccurate reporting. When some people find a theory fascinating, they often care less about the facts. In addition, there is much auto suggestion. When it suits their wishes, some believe anything they want. There is, however, true demonic deception. The Bible teaches that there is a deceptive, dangerous spirit world which distorts reality and ruins human lives. Despite the reality that there is much outright fraud that is passed off as paranormal or occultic, all Christians need to know that the occult and the paranormal are real. The Bible is clear on this, as Saul discovered upon meeting the medium of Endor (1Sm 28), and we must not dismiss it. If God is real, His chief adversary is also real.

First John 3:8 says: "The one who commits sin is of the Devil, for the Devil has sinned from the beginning. The Son of God was revealed for this purpose: to destroy the Devil's works." Involvement in the occult is involvement in the devil's works, and as it can lead to very serious outcomes spiritually and psychologically, we must remember that the Bible denounces all occultic practices (see Dt 18:9-14; Ac 13:6-12). The road to the occult is broad and always destructive. The way of Christ is narrow but always leads to eternal life.

Aren't All Religions Basically the Same?

Craig J. Hazen

There is a very old and famous fable—of either Buddhist or Jain origin—that has been used through the centuries to illustrate what is thought to be a fundamental truth about the religions of humankind. Several blind men were led into a rajah's (or king's) courtyard where they encountered an elephant.

One felt a tusk and concluded an elephant is like a spear. Another touched a leg and thought an elephant was like a tree. Yet another bumped into the side of the beast and thought it was like a wall, and so on. The rajah heard the activity, came out on his balcony and told the blind men that they were each encountering only one small part of the magnificent whole.

The lesson by analogy, of course, is that the different religious traditions of the world are all stumbling upon only one particular aspect of ultimate reality and are blind to the total picture. But at the end of the day, all of the religious hands are touching the same essential truth.

It is easy to see the appeal of this unifying approach to the broad spectrum of religious beliefs. After all, exclusive claims to religious truth are seen by many to be the root of so much violence and suffering in the world as believers in one tradition fight those of other traditions—sometimes for centuries. If at their core all religions are the same, or each is heading toward the same end, then there is no real reason for conflict or quarrel.

Ironically, this fable has built into it an element that is not highlighted in the traditional interpretations but may be the most important issue in the story. How do the blind men discover the truth about their encounter with the elephant? It is revealed to them from above. The rajah steps out on his balcony and from his transcendent perspective and using his unimpaired sight he communicates to those below the full picture of their experience. The more profound real-world question that emerges from the fable is where is our "Rajah" who can see all and reveal to us the truth that is not accessible from our limited perspective?

Unless there is some word from above to tell us that all religions are basically the same, there is no good reason to conclude they are the same. After all, the evidence is stacked heavily against it. Although one can identify common beliefs and practices, some of the differences among the traditions are stark and irreconcilable. Compare for instance, basic Mormonism, Buddhism, and Christianity on the critical question of what is ultimately real. Mormon scripture teaches that ultimate reality is material or physical and that even God and spirits are material objects whose constituent matter has existed for all eternity. Mahayana Buddhists believe that ultimate reality is emptiness (*sunyata*) or beinglessness (*nisvabhava*)—no gods, no matter, no spirit, no self. Christians, by contrast, see ultimate reality in God who is an eternal, personal, triune being who created all there is—both physical and nonphysical—from nothing. By any measure these are dramatic differences.

The conflicting ideas are multiplied once other issues are addressed. What is a human being? Why do we exist? What is good? Why is there pain and suffering? Where is history going? How do I reach salvation or enlightenment? Given the deep divergence on such timeless questions, it is completely legitimate to wonder if the essential unity of all religions is really just a noble wish or a romantic hope. Indeed, without a word from the "Rajah" to tell us that the contradictions among the great faiths can be overcome, the notion that all religions are the same seems utterly untenable.

Another irony about the fable presented here is that there is excellent reason to believe that *there really is a Rajah* who has spoken to humankind and has given us the transcendent perspective we need to know the truth. Jesus Christ is a radical figure in the history of the great religious traditions in that He is the only leader who claimed to be the one eternal God in human flesh. He knows the beginning from the end and knows the deepest religious yearnings of all people. He said definitively that there was only one God and only one source of salvation: Jesus Christ Himself. Moreover (and this is very important), Jesus did not leave us with "blind faith" as the only means to know that His claims are true. Rather, He established the truth of His claims objectively through His glorious resurrection from the dead—the central miracle of human history.

The King has indeed spoken from on high. All religions are not the same. And although we are all blind in sin, we can still hear the Savior's words. He who has ears, let him hear the voice of the King.

How Does Christianity Relate to Hinduism?

Ravi Zacharias

I often think back with nostalgia to growing up in India and the late night conversations we would have of a Hindu play or some event that featured its thought. Now, through the lens of Jesus Christ, I have learned to see how deep-seated culture and religion can be, and that only the power of the Holy Spirit can take truth and gently reveal the error of an ingrained way of thinking. Consequently, whenever we speak with someone from another faith, it is essential to remember that one must not attempt to tear down another's belief system but rather to reveal the hungers of the human heart and the unique way in which Christ addresses them.

For the Hindu, *karma*—the moral law of cause-and-effect—is a life-defining concept. Life carries its moral bills, and they are paid in the cyclical pattern of rebirth until all dues are paid in full. Hinduism here conveys an inherited sense of wrong, which is lived out in the next life, in vegetable, animal, or human form. This doctrine is nonnegotiable in Hindu philosophy. Repercussions of fatalism (that is, whatever happens will happen) and the indifference to the plight of others are inescapable but are dismissed by philosophical platitudes that do not weigh out the consequences of such reasoning. Thus it is key to bear in mind that although *karma* is seen as a way of paying back, this payback is never complete; hence, life is lived out paying back a debt that one cannot know in total but must be paid back in full. That is why the cross of Christ is so definitive and so complete. It offers forgiveness without minimizing the debt. When that forgiveness is truly understood it issues in a loving heart of gratitude. There is a full restoration—in this life and for eternity.

The Christian should also understand the attraction of pantheism, the Hindu view of seeing the divine in everything. It superficially appears more compatible with scientific theorizing because there is no definitive theory of origins. Life is cyclical without a first cause. Pantheism also gives one a moral reasoning through karmic fatalism, one is trapped in the cycle until one escapes, without the need to invoke God. But in the final analysis, it is without answers when one needs to talk about the deepest struggles of the soul. Hindu scholars even admit this creation of a path of *bhakti* (love, devotion) to satisfy the inescapable human hunger for worship.

It is here that a keen understanding is needed. Krishna's coming to earth as an avatar—that is, one of the incarnations of the Hindu god Vishnu—in a way brings "God to man." But a huge chasm still remains. How does one bring man to God? For this there was only one way—the way of the cross. A profound and studied presentation of the cross, and what it means, is still the most distinctive aspect of the Christian faith. Even Gandhi said it was the most unexplainable thing to him and was unparalleled. For the Christian, the cross of Jesus Christ is the message "first to the Jew, and also to the Greek" (Rm 2:9)—to the moralist and the pantheist, to the religious and the irreligious. We can communicate this message with a Hindu acquaintance or friend only through a loving relationship. The love of Christ, patient listening and friendship, and the message of forgiveness provide the path to evangelism.

How Does Christianity Relate to the Baha'i Faith?

Douglas Groothuis

The Baha'i religion began when a Persian man calling himself Baha'u'lah (Arabic for "the glory of God") declared in 1863 that he was the latest revelation of God. Several million Baha'is worldwide believe that Baha'u'lah (A.D. 1817–1892) is the latest in a long line of "manifestations" of God, and that he fulfills prophecies from the world's religions, including the biblical prophecies concerning the Second Coming of Christ.

Baha'is assert the unknowability and oneness of God, the unity of religion, the unity of humanity, and the unity of science and religion. They believe that Baha'is will eventually lead the world into a state of global harmony. Baha'is believe that all major religions are inspired by God and that they develop in a progressive manner. Baha'u'lah will not be succeeded by another manifestation until a thousand years after his death.

The Baha'i religion, despite its lofty goals, is incompatible with biblical Christianity and lacks evidence to support its claims. All religions cannot be from God, since they contradict each other on essential truth-claims. The teachings of Buddha, for example, exclude a personal God. But Judaism, Christianity, and Islam are monotheistic. Baha'is attempt to account for these discrepancies in two ways.

First, they claim that religious truth is relative to historical periods. This argument fails because it renders an omnipotent God unable to reveal even the most basic divine truths consistently. Moreover, if God is unknowable, as Baha'is claim, there is no basis for any divine revelation (knowledge), Baha'i or otherwise. Second, they argue that the original teachings of the world religions (except the Baha'i religion) have been corrupted. For example, they say original Christianity did not teach that Jesus was uniquely divine or that He physically rose from the dead. Baha'is deny these well-attested facts because they would place Jesus in a position far beyond what Baha'is allows for a manifestation of God (Rm 1:4; 1Tm 2:5). But neither history nor logic supports these revisionist claims. Christians should challenge Baha'is to read the NT for themselves and to investigate the many reasons for its reliability. They should also challenge Baha'is to consider that their doctrine of the progressive unity of all religions has no logical or factual basis and can be held only on the purported authority of Baha'u'lah, who, unlike the resurrected Jesus, died, and remains dead.

Don't Religious Beliefs Just Reflect Where One Was Raised?

Paul Copan

B ehaviorist B.F. Skinner declared: "my behavior at any given moment has been nothing more than the product of my genetic endowment, my personal history, and the current setting." If correct, Skinner's philosophy was the product of his genes and background—a purely accidental (rather than reasoned-out) conclusion.

Many apply this to religion. "If you grew up in Saudi Arabia, you'd probably be a Muslim," claims the religious pluralist (who believes all religions are capable of saving/liberating). "Therefore, particular religious beliefs are just the arbitrary product of one's environment." But the pluralist is in the same fix. One growing up in a pluralistic culture will likely believe in pluralism. Presumably, his belief is just the product of *his* upbringing and just as arbitrary as another's. What's more, if he'd grown up in medieval Italy, he likely wouldn't have been a pluralist. But the pluralist would have us believe his views are rationally concluded, not the accidents of history or geography!

Politically speaking, if you'd grown up in the Soviet Union, chances are (statistically) you'd be part of the Communist Youth. But should we therefore conclude all political systems are morally equivalent (Communism vs. democracy)? Certainly not! Similarly, the diversity of religious systems doesn't mean that (1) all belief-systems are equally plausible or (2) one religion can't be true. Our ability to step back and reflect upon cultural influences and even resist them indicates we are thinking, choosing beings made to seek truth whatever our limitations. In both creation and conscience, God hasn't left human beings without a witness (Ps 19:1-6; Ac 14:17; Rm 1:20; 2:14-15). And if anyone is separated from God, it's because he freely resists God's grace, not because of his location.

If a good God exists, it's likely He would cut through the mire of sin and the haze of religious ambiguity by revealing Himself in human history. Jesus of Nazareth made radical claims other world religious leaders would never have made. Further, He rose from the dead, confirming those claims—further reasons to reject pluralism.

Appealing to geographical statistics doesn't settle anything. History, philosophy, experience, and revelation are some important reasons for considering a religion to be true.

How Does Christianity Relate to Other Eastern Religions?

Winfried Corduan

Let's be clear about one point from the outset: unlike biblical religion, Eastern religions usually have flexible boundaries, and persons may combine elements from several religions in their lives. For the five religions below, we will give a brief summary and a response from a biblical perspective.

Jainism is a popular Indian religion, similar to Hinduism and Buddhism. It was founded by a man named Mahavira in the sixth century B.C., (roughly a contemporary of Jeremiah and Daniel in the Bible). Mahavira taught that human beings need to escape from reincarnation, and that they can do so by living a rigorous life of self-deprivation. The highest obligation is never to harm any living being, whether it be animal, insect, or plant. Someone who observes this duty faithfully will attain a higher state of life and, ultimately, release from reincarnation altogether. Jains venerate Mahavira and his mythological predecessors, the Tirthankaras.

Response to Jainism: The Bible teaches that humanity's main problem is not reincarnation, but separation from God due to sin. Salvation cannot be earned by an ascetic life; it can only be received by faith through God's work of redemption in Christ. Christians agree with Jains that all life deserves respect, but they do so because life was created by God, not because it is inherently divine.

Sikhism was founded by Guru Nanak in India around A.D. 1500, contemporary with the Protestant Reformation in Europe. He sought to establish harmony between Hindus and Muslims by teaching that God is beyond any human name or attribute and that true devotion to God will bring about union with him. There were nine successive gurus after Nanak, but the last of the line declared that the Sikh holy book, the *Adi Granth*, would henceforth be the true guru. It has been the focus of veneration among Sikhs ever since.

Response to Sikhism*:* Christians who believe that the Bible is the inspired Word of God can appreciate the Sikhs' veneration for books thought to be from God. However, whereas for Sikhism the holy book itself (their *Adi Granth*) is regarded as a sacred object, for Christians the Bible is seen as the revelation of God's message but not as an object to be worshiped. The Bible offers to Sikhs (and anyone else) a hope for the future and an assurance of salvation that is absent from Nanak's message.

Daoism (formerly spelled "Taoism") is part of popular Chinese religion, originally based on some fairly esoteric philosophical writings. Its founder, the legendary Laozi (roughly sixth century B.C.), taught that the true "Way," the *Dao* could be found by allowing the opposing forces of the universe—the *yin* and *yang*—to find their balance. This philosophy eventually metamorphosed into a religion devoted to the service of many gods and spirits, presided over by the "Jade Emperor" in heaven. Religious Daoism emphasizes ancestor veneration.

Response to Daoism: In contrast to philosophical Daoism, the Bible asserts that good and evil are genuine realities, not just matters of cosmic imbalance. The Bible condemns all worship of creatures, including nature spirits, ancestors, or images of deities. The Christian gospel offers release from the bondage to the spirit world in which religious Daoists usually live.

Confucianism is the philosophy of life taught by Confucius, another sixth century B.C. figure, in China. It is primarily a code of conduct for individuals and the society they comprise, rather than a set of doctrines about gods or worship practices. The fundamental premise of Confucianism is that there is a proper way in which all persons should act, depending on their station in life and the specific relationship of the moment. Thus, a prince lives under different expectations than a common worker, and both of them are obligated to act differently towards an older man than a younger one. The onus to set the right example lies with the prince; if he will set the proper example, his subject will follow him in proper behavior, and a perfect society will result. The highest Confucian virtue is filial piety, the unconditional obedience of children to their parents. Even though many Confucian ideals are outdated, the attitude of filial piety persists prominently among traditional Chinese, Japanese, and Korean people today.

Response to Confucianism: Christians can resonate with the Confucian commitment to a life of virtue, though they will take exception to the way it puts forms ahead of sacrificial love. Even more importantly, the Bible teaches that perfection is unattainable for human beings and that our greatest need is inward reconciliation with God.

Shinto is the national religion of Japan, worshiping spirits and deities. The *Kojiki*, the Shinto myth, serves to legitimate the claims of the emperor of Japan as divine, a claim now officially renounced. Shinto shrines, marked by the traditional *torii* gate, are colorful ceremonial centers.

Response to Shinto: Shinto illustrates two problems commonly addressed by the Bible: ritualism and escape into myth. By contrast, the Bible offers salvation grounded in the historical Christ, whom we can receive by faith.

Are the Teachings of Jehovah's Witnesses Compatible with the Bible?

Robert M. Bowman Jr.

Jehovah's Witnesses (JWs) claim to regard the Bible as the absolute word of God and to base all their beliefs on it. In fact, the teachings of JWs are contrary to the Bible.

The Bible. JWs use a doctored version of the Bible called the New World Translation (NWT). The JW leaders who produced the NWT were not biblical scholars, and it shows. The most obvious difference between the NWT and other Bibles is its use of "Jehovah" in the NT. JWs claim that the NT originally used the Hebrew name YHWH and that apostate scribes put "Lord" (Greek, *kurios*) in its place. There is no historical or manuscript evidence for this claim.

The Father, Son, and Holy Spirit. JWs teach that the Father alone is Jehovah, the almighty God; that the Son, Jesus Christ, is "a god" (their translation of Jn 1:1) inferior to the Father; and that "holy spirit" is an impersonal force emanating from God. The Bible, on the other hand, teaches that the Father, Son, and Holy Spirit are each God (Jn 1:1; 17:3; 20:28; Ac 5:3-4; 2Co 3:17-18; Ti 2:13). The Son made everything (Heb 1:10-12) and is to be honored as God (Jn 5:23; Heb 1:6; Rv 5:13). The Holy Spirit is a person, called the "Comforter" or "Helper" (Greek, *parakletos*); He teaches, speaks, and bears witness to Jesus (Jn 14:16,26; 15:26-27; 16:13-14).

Death, the soul, and eternal punishment. According to JWs, when human beings die, they cease to exist. There is no intermediate state of the dead and no eternal punishment for the wicked (who are instead annihilated). The Bible, on the other hand, teaches that human beings exist after their deaths as spirits awaiting the resurrection and Final Judgment (Lk 16:19-31; 23:43; Heb 12:9,23; Rv 6:9-11). The NWT mistranslates Luke 23:43 and the Hebrew texts to avoid this implication. The wicked will suffer eternal punishment (Mt 25:46; Rv 14:9-11; 20:10).

Jesus' resurrection and return. JWs believe that God "raised" Jesus from the dead as an angelic spirit, with a so-called spirit body. They deny He will return visibly and personally to earth. Scripture, however, teaches Jesus rose with the same physical body with which He died, though glorified and immortal, and that His body possessed flesh and bones, hands and feet, and even marks of His crucifixion (Lk 23:49; Jn 2:19-22; 10:17-18; 20:20,25; Ac 2:24-32). Though second person of the Godhead, Jesus also as glorified man (Ac 17:31; 1Co 15:47; 1Tm 2:5), will return personally and bodily to the earth (Ac 1:9-11; 3:19-21; 1Th 4:16; Heb 9:26-28).

Salvation. JWs view Jesus' death as providing a "corresponding ransom," releasing all people in principle from the condemnation due to Adam's sin. However, to enjoy everlasting life, JWs believe they must not only accept Christ's ransom but also prove themselves worthy by their works. The Bible's teaching is quite different. Christians are saved by God's grace alone, through faith in Christ, and our good works are the fruit of salvation, not the prerequisite for it (Rm 3:21-28; 5:1-11; Eph 2:8-10; Ti 3:4-8).

Is the Transformation of Jesus' Disciples Different from Other Religious Transformations?

Gary R. Habermas

When discussing the beliefs of Jesus' disciples and their being willing to suffer martyrdom for their convictions, comparisons are often made to other religious persons whose lives were also changed due to their own religious beliefs. Like Jesus' disciples, many have willingly given their lives for their beliefs. Examples include modern Muslims, the followers of various religious teachers, or certain UFO groups. Even political ideas, like communism, have inspired life changes and martyrdoms.

Under these circumstances, can Christians continue to make evidential use of the disciples' transformations, while many other conversions are clearly also apparent? Could contemporary Muslims, for example, claim that they have far more examples of martyrdom in their own faith?

Initially, we need to make a crucial distinction. Transformed lives do *not* prove that someone's teachings are true. However, they *do* constitute evidence that those who are willing to suffer and die for their religious commitments truly believe the teachings to be true.

So can we distinguish between the disciples' transformations and the experiences of others? In general, people committed to a religious or political message really believe it to be true. Of course, beliefs can be false. But in the case of Jesus' disciples, one grand distinction makes all the difference in the world.

Like other examples of religious or political faith, the disciples believed and followed their leader's teachings. But unlike all others, the disciples had more than just their beliefs—they had seen the resurrected Jesus. This is a crucial distinction; their faith was true precisely because of the resurrection.

Let's view this another way. Which is more likely—that an ideology we believe is true, or that we and a number of others saw a friend several times during the last month? If eternity rested on the consequences, would we rather base our assurance on the truth of a particular religious or political view, or would we rather that the consequences followed from repeated cases of seeing someone?

But unlike the world's faiths, which rest on certain beliefs being true, the disciples had both heard unique teachings and seen the resurrected Jesus. Jesus was the only founder of a major world religion who had miracles reported of Him in reliable sources within a few decades. But most of all, He confirmed His message by rising from the dead. The disciples saw Him repeatedly—both individuals and groups. Two skeptics—James the brother of Jesus and Saul of Tarsus (Paul)—even witnessed the resurrected Jesus.

Unlike any other religious teaching, the disciples had not only Jesus' words, but also His resurrection. They knew they had seen Him alive after His crucifixion, and so had others. Some had even seen Him many times. As a direct result, they were transformed to the point of being willing to die not only for their faith, but also for what they had seen with their own eyes. No other religious or political belief can claim both unique teachings and a visible resurrection body.

No wonder the disciples were so sure of their faith! Not only had they been promised heaven, but then they had actually been shown a glimpse of it!

How Does the Bible Relate to Islam?

Barbara B. Pemberton

I slam teaches that throughout history God has sent prophets, from Adam and Noah to Jesus and ultimately Muhammad, all with the same message: there is only one God, and this God desires people to pursue good and to prevent evil. Christians and Jews, whom Muslims call "People of the Book," are believed to be the remaining followers of earlier divine but corrupted revelations. Islam's scripture, the Qur'an, is understood by Muslims to have restored God's original guidance. The Qur'an includes numerous biblical personalities, but recognizes as authentic only three sections of biblical literature: the Torah of Moses, the Evangel of Jesus, and the Psalms of David.

Muslims see many of their beliefs and practices as biblical: the existence of only one God, prophets, heaven, hell, angels, and a day of judgment. They also see the importance of charity, prayer, and fasting in the Bible. Although

Muslims believe that Jesus was only a prophet and not divine, they do believe the accounts of His virgin birth, sinless nature, miracles, and second coming.

The Qur'an accuses Jews and Christians of distorting their earlier revelation by deliberately suppressing the truth or by false interpretation. Muslims charge that the OT and NT contain logical inconsistencies, improbabilities, and factual errors. Charges against the OT include false reports of immorality (David and Bathsheba), missing doctrines (afterlife in the Torah), and incompatibility with science. The Evangel has been corrupted with inaccurate historical references, discrepancies in the gospel accounts, and fabrications (such as the crucifixion). Christians and Jews allegedly suppressed or removed biblical predictions of Muhammad. For example, Muslims say Psalm 84:4-6 is about Muhammad, who overcame his childhood disadvantages by God's grace. Jesus supposedly predicted the coming prophet Muhammad when He spoke of the "Counselor" in John 14:16-18.

Islam rejects the concept of human participation in the process of revelation as seen in the varieties of biblical genres. Jesus' original message is deemed lost. Muslims believe that gospel authors, writing long after Jesus, altered the message to promote their own points of view. Paul is considered guilty of promoting a "mystical" Christ and "false" doctrines such as the resurrection. Another Muslim argument against biblical reliability is the lack of a record that the original texts passed from one generation to the next.

Muslims are, of course, correct that the Bible is older than the Qur'an— but there is not a shred of evidence the Bible has been corrupted. Indeed, the transmission of its text is by far the most accurate of any from the ancient world. The Bible is not compromised by God's using human personalities in its writing any more than when He uses human personality in the spoken word of prophets. Moreover, powerful evidence supports, among other things, the historicity of Jesus' crucifixion and resurrection. Prayerful Christians can help correct Muslim misconceptions about the Bible (e.g., by showing the Bible does not sanction the sinfulness of western culture). Indeed, Christ's followers should befriend Muslims so the Holy Spirit can bring conviction to their hearts through the powerful Word of God (Heb 4:12).

How Should We Relate to Those in False Religious Movements?

Alan W. Gomes

As we witness to those in non-Christian religions we must guard against a formulaic approach that would treat them all as if cut from the same cloth. At the same time, we must not ignore the commonalities underlying religious allegiance, whether Christian or not. So long as we are appropriately sensitive to individual differences, we can identify some helpful strategies for winning adherents of non-Christian religious movements.

Address the Personal Motivations Underlying Religious Commitment. Often, people commit to a religion in order to meet personal needs. In new religious manifestations in particular, there is a focus on the therapeutic transformation of the self. Adherents of false religions often join specifically to address intellectual, emotional, social, and spiritual needs. People are looking for loving relationships and a sense of connectedness; a family atmosphere (particularly attractive for those who lack family or whose family is dysfunctional); a sense of acceptance and self-worth (sometimes by being part of "God's great work" through the cult or false religion); an opportunity to achieve idealistic goals (e.g., doing works of philanthropy and charity); a way to meet deep spiritual longings (e.g., to experience a sense of the "divine" or "transcendent"); and a belief system that will provide answers to life's deepest questions (Why am I here? What is the purpose of life?).

These aspirations are hardly unique to membership in false religious movements, nor is there anything sinister per se in the fact that people have and seek to meet these needs. Indeed, many people become involved in biblical Christian churches for the same reasons—joining our churches, e.g., because of the caring and committed relationships that they experience as part of God's family. The problem with false religions, such as the cults, is that they cannot ultimately satisfy the deepest longings of the human spirit, which only the true gospel can.

One of the most important things we can do in reaching out to those ensnared in false religion is to provide an environment where these spiritual, social, emotional, and intellectual needs can be met. The church should and generally does provide such an environment anyway, but for those emerging from false religions the need is especially acute. Some cults can be very harsh on those who leave, shunning or "disfellowshipping" them. The person who leaves such a group may experience in one fell swoop the loss of his or her entire support system of family and friends. The church needs to be sensitive to this and be prepared to go the extra mile in embracing such individuals, enfolding them into the Body of Christ with loving arms.

Properly Classify, Understand, and Refute the False Belief System. As important as the interpersonal factors mentioned above are, it is also necessary to understand correctly and then refute biblically the false belief system. The first step is to classify accurately the type of belief system in question. A basic distinction should be made between cults of Christianity and religious groups that make no claim of Christian allegiance. A cult of Christianity is a group of people claiming to be Christian, but which denies one or more of the central doctrines of the Christian faith. The Church of Jesus Christ of Latter-day Saints (Mormons), Jehovah's Witnesses, and Christian Science are examples of cults of Christianity. On the other hand, world religions such as

Islam also deny core Christian beliefs, including the doctrine of the Trinity and the deity of Christ. But unlike cults of Christianity, world religions do not claim to be Christian and in fact would explicitly repudiate such a label.

The distinction between cults of Christianity and world religions, is not merely academic. One would approach a cultist differently from a Muslim. For example, one does not have to convince the Mormon that Jesus Christ is the Savior and that Christianity is true. Indeed, the Mormon already thinks Jesus is his "Savior" and that his church is the true restoration of Christianity under Joseph Smith. The task is to show that Mormonism is a counterfeit form of Christianity—"another gospel"—with a false Jesus who cannot save. The Muslim, on the other hand, not only will have faulty views of what true Christianity teaches, but will also need to be convinced that Christianity is the true religion.

We must also understand the non-Christian belief system we are confronting as accurately and in as much detail as is practicable. Failure to do so can quickly short-circuit a witnessing opportunity, for the cultist will soon tune out a Christian who imputes beliefs to the cultist that he or she does not hold. It is important, as Robert and Gretchen Passantino point out, to observe a kind of golden rule when discussing non-Christian belief systems: represent their belief system as accurately as you would have them represent yours. Only then can we hope to be taken seriously as we seek to confront the errors of the cults and false religions with the claims of Jesus Christ.

How Does the Bible Relate to Judaism?

Larry R. Helyer

J udaism should not be confused with the biblical religion of ancient Israel. Early Judaism arises in the aftermath of the destruction of the first temple (586 B.C.). The term Judaism first appears in the first century B.C. (2 Macc 2:21; 8:1; 14:38) to describe the beliefs, customs, and rituals of Jews during the Hellenistic era.

Judaism has developed considerably over the intervening centuries. For example, official Judaism has been a non-sacrificial religion since the destruction of the second temple (A.D. 70). Observance of the mitzvoth (the commandments of Torah) replaces sacrifice, atoning for sin (Tobit 4:6-7,9-11; 12:9-10). Judaism's roots, however, are deep in the OT. The fundamental ideas of modern Judaism, in all its diversity, maintain continuity with the biblical revelation at Mount Sinai. These ideas include ethical monotheism (belief in one God), God's gift of Torah ("instruction") to Israel, and the election of Israel as a light to the nations. A striving for peace, justice, and righteousness for all peoples derives from the Prophets, and a spirituality grounded in everyday life stems from the wisdom and hymnic literature of the OT.

The Torah outlines a way of life for the people of Israel and is nearly synonymous with Judaism. Embedded in the Pentateuch (the first five books of the Bible) are 613 commandments. After the exile, these 613 command-ments were adapted, augmented, and hedged by other laws that became part of an ever-growing oral law (cp. Mk 7:5; Gl 1:14). In time, the oral law was also attributed to Moses. Eventually (c. A.D. 500), the oral law was codified in the Mishnah ("repetition"). This in turn was commented on and augmented in the Gemara ("completion"). Finally, the Mishnah and Gemara were published in two massive works, the Palestinian Talmud (c. A.D. 400) and the Baby-lonian Talmud (c. A.D. 500). Talmud means "learning" or "instruction." For Orthodox Jews, the Babylonian Talmud, some 2.5 million words, remains the authoritative guide for Judaism. The foundation of Talmud, however, remains the Torah of "Moses our Rabbi."

Modern liberal Jews reject the belief that the Pentateuch was divinely inspired and written by Moses. While not treating it as an infallible guide for faith and practice, they nonetheless acknowledge its historical and symbolic role in providing Jewish self-identity.

Modern Judaism maintains continuity with the OT in a number of signifi-cant ways. The annual festivals are primarily those prescribed in the Penta-teuch. The essential ethical teachings of Judaism derive from the Mosaic Law, especially the Ten Commandments. Circumcision, dietary laws, and ritual immersion have their roots in the Pentateuch. The Prophets are appealed to for their emphasis upon social justice and mercy. Throughout the year in syn-agogues, the Torah (Pentateuch) and haphtarah (selections from the Prophets) are read in a lectionary cycle. Most Orthodox Jews still anticipate a personal Messiah and messianic age based upon the Prophets.

For Israeli Jews, the Hebrew Bible (OT) is a national treasure avidly studied in both religious and secular schools. The modern Zionist movement appeals to the Bible as part of its cultural heritage. Archaeology and historical geography of the Bible are national pastimes in Israel. Increasingly, Jewish scholars are also studying the NT as a valuable source for understanding the development of early Judaism.

A key issue distinguishing Christianity from Judaism, though both share the OT in common, has to do with fulfillment. Jesus taught His disciples to read the Scriptures christologically; they speak of Him and His work (Mt 5:17-18; Lk 24:25-27,44-49; Jn 5:39). Judaism denies that Jesus fulfilled the messianic prophecies of the OT. For example, Jewish scholars interpret the so-called "Servant Songs" of Isaiah (42:1-4; 49:1-6; 50:4-11; 52:13–53:12) as referring variously to the prophet himself, an unknown prophet, or, most likely, the people of Israel viewed collectively as the Servant of the Lord. Traditional Christianity, of course, sees these passages as prophecies of Jesus and His ministry (Ac 8:26-35). Orthodox Jews, who still harbor hopes of a personal Messiah, await a Davidic descendant who will rule as king at the end times. Liberal Jews prefer to interpret these passages metaphorically of an ideal age.

Thus a major factor in the parting of ways between Judaism and Christianity centers on the meaning and mission of Jesus. For Judaism, there is no failing, whether collectively or individually, which requires special divine intervention and which cannot be remedied, by the individual, with the guidance of Torah. Salvation consists of faithful, though not perfect, adherence to the mitzvoth. God in His mercy forgives those whose intentions are upright. The NT, however, unambiguously proclaims the finality of Jesus Christ. He is God's last word to sinners (Heb 1:1-3), the Word who became flesh, dwelt among us, and reveals the Father to sinners (Jn 1:1-18). By His atoning death on the cross, Jesus draws all people unto Himself (Jn 3:16; 6:35-40; 12:32).

How Should a Christian Relate to the New Age Movement?

Ted Cabal

Though the vestiges of a biblical worldview are still in evidence, polls reveal that doctrinal beliefs of perhaps a third of Westerners can be characterized as New Age. The ideas of this New Age Movement (NAM) are widely, and often subconsciously, disseminated through numerous television shows and movies. The NAM also has become big-business through its myriads of self-help seminars, journaling/prayer guides (often mimicking Christian tradition), and books.

Adherents of the movement often reject the term New Age due to its various connotations. At any rate, it is better perhaps termed "postmodern religion" in view of the assumptions its shares with philosophical postmodernism. Generally rejecting a scientific or analytic (modernist) approach to life, knowledge is supposedly subjectively constructed and socially determined. Truth is not universal to all humans but may vary according to what works for some and not others. Moral values are not universally objective but only properties of communities choosing to adopt them. Reality is viewed as an evolving unified whole; indeed, they often consider God to be one name for this whole. Biblical Christianity is especially disdained due to its universal truth claims.

Since the NAM is under the authority of no particular religious text, proponents are best identified by various symptoms, such as the following. They prefer the practice of spirituality over organized, classical expressions of religion. No single religious teacher can claim the allegiance of all; claims by Jesus as being "the Way" must be reinterpreted or rejected altogether. Rather than the grace of God revealed in the Jesus of the Bible, "angels," paranormal powers, or even raw human potential serve as "saviors" from the race's predicament. Mixing and matching the objects of worship, it is often not thought strange to identify oneself simultaneously in terms such as Buddhist, Jewish, and Presbyterian. Ultimately the NAM represents a return to polytheism.

How then should Christians begin sharing Christ with those in the NAM? Frequently a truth discussion must pave the way. If objective, universal truth does not exist, then the total claims of the gospel are false. But all people live as if everyday beliefs must correspond to reality (e.g., no one can just choose to live on poison instead of water). Why then should anyone hold that belief in God and the afterlife are somehow different? Incoherence in everyday affairs is viewed as dishonest or irrational. (Imagine trying to say, "Yes, officer, that double-parked car is mine, but it's not mine.") Why then accept claims such as "Christ can be true for you but not for me"?

At first glance, this shoddy handling of truth in the NAM makes it appear more tolerant than Christianity. But actually it condescendingly views the claims of all other religions as wrong, ignorant, and divisive. Only those in the NAM see the complete picture, whereas other religions, fixated on their particular traditional teachings, are unaware of the deep, hidden unity of all religions. But is there good reason to believe many ways to "heaven" exist? How can anyone claim to know this universal truth, especially if there are no universal truths? Earthly roadmaps do not assume just any path can reach a destination. Routes may be chosen by their ease of travel or scenic views, but not all routes lead to the same place.

Is Christian Science Compatible with the Bible?

Robert B. Stewart

Christian Science (Church of Christ, Scientist) is a religion based primarily upon the New Thought metaphysical theories of Christian Science founder Mary Baker Eddy (1821–1910). It is the rebirth of the Gnostic heresy that matter, including disease, is illusory. Still, to the casual observer it often sounds biblical because of Christian Science's propensity to use (while redefining) Christian terms. For instance, one reads Eddy saying in *Science and Health with Key to the Scriptures* that "the Bible has been my only authority," (126:29-30); that "Divine Science derives its sanction from the Bible" (146:23); and also that the Bible is the "inspired Word," and "our sufficient guide to eternal Life" (497:3-4). Nevertheless Christian Science rejects the Bible's plain sense in favor of the spiritual interpretations recorded in Mrs. Eddy's writings, *Science and Health, Miscellaneous Writings,* and *Manual of the Mother Church.* This becomes clear when she states: "The material record of the Bible . . . is no more important to our well being than the history of Europe and America" (*Miscellaneous Writings*, 170).

A brief perusal of *Science and Health* reveals many contradictions between Christian Science and the Bible. Not only are biblical names reinterpreted—"Adam" becomes "belief in original sin," (579:8-9), while "Abraham" refers to "faith in the divine Life and in the eternal Principle of being" (579:10-11)—key doctrines are also denied. The biblical concept of a Triune personal God is replaced by a triple principle of "Life, Truth, and Love" (331:26-27). Sin is denied: "Man is deathless, spiritual. He is above sin or frailty" (266:29-30). Christ's sufficient atonement is rejected: "The material blood of Jesus was no more efficacious to cleanse from sin when it was shed upon 'the accursed tree,' than when it was flowing in his veins as he went daily about his Father's business" (25:6-9). Even Jesus' deity is denied, as they distinguish between the Christ, "the divine manifestation of God, which comes to the flesh to destroy incarnate error" (583:10-11), and the historical person of Jesus.

In summary, by redefining biblical terms Christian Science denies virtually every cardinal doctrine of Christianity as found in the Bible. In no meaningful way can Christian Science be considered compatible with the Bible.

What Are Common Characteristics of New Religious Movements?

Leonard G. Goss

"New religions" or "alternative religions" are breakaways from larger, more traditional religions. They break down into self-improvement groups, Eastern religions or thought systems, unification groups, and Christian deviation sects. Many of these new religions had Christian roots, but have departed from historic biblical Christianity and discarded one or more of Christianity's basic beliefs. What they have left behind is something that decidedly is not Christianity. Jesus said "Beware of false prophets who come to you in sheep's clothing but inwardly are ravaging wolves" (Mt 7:15).

Viewed through the lens of biblical teaching, each new religion abandons orthodox Christian tenants at one point or another (and usually at many different points). Latter-day Saints (Mormons), for example, have parted company with the Christian tradition in multiple ways, but perhaps the most dramatic is their teaching that the authentic church founded by Jesus and the apostles disappeared from human history by the time of Constantine. Hence, the LDS church was founded to once again represent the exclusive truth and to rescue the Christian religion from total apostasy. The Unification Church (Moonies) also departs from biblical teaching and undermines Christian thinking in dozens of different ways, most notably in claiming their founder is God's messiah and messenger who will fulfill the work of Jesus. This is a serious heresy found in many of the new religions, and the apostle Paul warned about following after "another Jesus" who is not the same Jesus revealed in Scripture (2Co 11:4). Other examples are The Way International, a group where the leader's interpretation of the Bible is considered the only valid interpretation and is in fact *the* Word. The Children of God, sometimes called the Family of Love, believes all mainline Christian churches are as anti-Christian as organizations that do not profess Christianity. The basic belief of this sect is that its members are the only true Christians and obedient servants left on earth. Many other new religious groups could be mentioned, but one last example would be Eckankar, one of the mystical new religions, which teaches out-of-the-body travels (bilocation), and replaces Jesus Christ with the group's founder as the incarnation of God on earth and teaches that only through their group can an individual find ultimate truth.

This small sampling of new religions shows how very different these movements can be, and therefore it is not easy to suggest that each cult or new religion looks the same or possesses the same theological, sociological, psychological and moral characteristics. Although each new religious belief system deviates drastically and in individual ways from conventional, historic Christianity, still there are some common characteristics to look for in the new movements. Here is a list of warning signs and danger zones, with some representative groups displaying these characteristics noted in parentheses:

- These groups are almost always outside the mainstream of dominant religious forms and culture, and they display an oppositional style and substance, meaning they are elitist and exclusionist. (Church of Scientology, Global Family, Unification Church, The Walk/Church of the Living Word, The Way International)
- Often there is a "new authority" or new revelation besides the Bible for adherents to find ultimate truths. (Christian Science, International Community of Christ/the Jamilians, Jehovah's Witnesses, Mormonism, Unification Church)
- On the other hand, some groups do not claim to have a new, extrabiblical revelation. Instead, they claim "all we use is the Bible." But the Bible is reinterpreted to justify and defend false teachings. (Alamo Christian Foundation, Children of God/Family of Love)
- The group is comprised of lay people; there are no paid clergy or professional religious functionaries. (Fundamentalist Army, Jehovah's Witnesses, Mormonism)
- The group is gathered around a central figure who is a prophet-founder "chosen" by God to deliver a special message to the modern world that is not found in the Bible, or has not been known to genuine Christians throughout all church history, or to recover the teaching of the ancient church that has been lost through the centuries. (Christian Science, The Farm, Jehovah's Witnesses, Scientology, Unification Church)

- This leader is usually a charismatic figure, and often the style of their leadership is authoritarian. (Children of God/Family of Love, Church of the Living Word, Yahwism)
- Often the group teaches that the Bible foretold the coming of its particular group or leader. (Branch Davidians, Children of God/Family of Love, The Farm, Jehovah's Witnesses, Mormonism, Unification Church, The Walk/Church of the Living Word)
- Serious adherents to the new religion think of their belief system as the last bastion of God's work on earth. They are God's "final and last group" and they play a central role in the last things. The truth of all things spiritual is exclusive with them and the world is doomed without them. (Jehovah's Witnesses, University Bible Fellowship)
- Nearly all new religions perceive they are being persecuted. (Alamo Christian Foundation, Healthy Happy Holy Organization, the Truth Station, Unification Church)
- There are some very predatory and destructive groups engaging in recruitment of new members with vigor, zeal, and high pressure, often deceiving recruits or not revealing their whole theology. (Alamo Christian Foundation, Unification Church, the Way International)
- Sanction of wayward and rebellious members characterizes many of the alternative religions. (Church of Armageddon, Divine Light Mission, Jehovah's Witnesses, People's Temple)
- For most, God is a force or power, not a person who relates to the creation. (Christian Science, Unity School of Christianity)
- The majority of these groups are fixated on eschatology (end times) and they are usually apocalyptic in their teaching. (Branch Davidians, Children of God/Family of Love, Jehovah's Witnesses, People's Temple)
- The average lifestyle of members is highly legalistic. (Alamo Christian Foundation, the Christ Family, Church of Armageddon, Maranatha Christian Church)
- In many alternative religions, there is a notion that communal organization is necessary to fulfill the human calling. Therefore, there is usually a tightly maintained autocratic organization which governs both spiritual and everyday life. Some dictate modes of dress, length of hair, the type of personal adornment that is permitted, and sometimes even marriage partners. (Alamo Christian Foundation, Forever Family/Church of Bible Understanding, Church Universal and Triumphant, Forever Family/Church of Bible Understanding, The Walk)
- Some engage in strange rituals and mindless chanting. (Church Universal and Triumphant, Penitentes/Brothers of Our Father Jesus)
- They emphasize secondary issues and minor points of theology. (Christian Science, Jehovah's Witnesses)

- Members are very often taught that they can have direct revelations and visions from God. (Mormonism, Swedenborgianism, Unification Church)
- There is the standard claim they are compatible or in harmony with the Bible and traditional Christianity, but in fact these movements reduce and discount the Bible or otherwise add to the revelation of Scripture. (Christian Science, Jehovah's Witnesses, Mormonism, People's Temple, Unification Church)
- They have usurped traditional Christian vocabulary, but they redefine and reinterpret terms and concepts from the Bible—making their words do "double-duty"—in order to defend aberrant doctrines. Their language is pliable and has no fixed meaning. (Christian Science, Mormonism, Unity School of Christianity)
- In every case, there is a denial of at least one central truth of Christianity, such as the work of Christ on the cross, the authority of the Scriptures, salvation by grace through faith, the bodily resurrection, the doctrine of eternal punishment, etc. (Alamo Christian Foundation, Branch Davidians, International Community of Christ/the Jamilians, Jehovah's Witnesses, Mormonism, Swedenborgianism—the Church of the New Jerusalem, Unification Church, Unitarian Universalists)
- The central axis of all new religions is that they deny both the doctrine of the Trinity and the Incarnation. (Anthroposophical Society, Children of God/Family of Love, Christian Science, Eckankar, Jehovah's Witnesses, Mormonism, United Pentecostal Church, The Way)
- They recognize Jesus as a great teacher and leader, an avatar, a wise man, even as the most important of God's created beings—but none of them believe Jesus is both fully human and fully divine. (Unification Church, The United Pentecostal Church, The Way International)
- Many teach a works salvation system whereby members must ultimately save themselves. (Jehovah's Witnesses, Mormonism)
- They emphasize experience over basic Christian doctrine. (Alamo Christian Foundation, Children of God/Family of Love, Divine Light Mission, est, Lifespring, Mormonism, Urantia, The Walk/Church of the Living Word)
- These groups are often mystical and individualistically oriented. (Church Universal and Triumphant, Foundation of Human Understanding, New Testament Missionary Fellowship)
- Some cults and new religions dabble in the occult and spiritism. (Anthroposophical Society, Children of God/Family of Love, Mormonism, Unification Church, The Walk)

These erroneous beliefs mislead countless people, sometimes people we know and love. We must equip ourselves to expose the error in a loving manner.

Christians must recognize that our spiritual enemy is not the cult or new religion but rather, Satan (2Co 11:12-15).

How Does a Christian Converse With a Buddhist?

Ravi Zacharias

Attraction to Eastern spirituality, and particularly Buddhism, is very real because the human spirit craves spiritual answers. Thus, whenever a Christian converses with someone of another faith, one must attempt to reveal the hungers of the human heart and how Christ alone addresses them.

Gautama Buddha taught that we should free ourselves from illusions of selfhood, God, forgiveness, and individual life hereafter. Focus should center in a life wherein good deeds outweigh the bad. Buddha believed all life was suffering, and to escape from rebirth we must understand our nature. Extinguish hungers, detach from desires (namely, relationships), and we will then offset all impure acts and thoughts. That is the Buddhist's hope.

But Buddhism's attraction provides no real answers. The self—which is undeniable and inescapable—is lost in Buddhist philosophy, and the hungers of the soul are brushed away. Everything is in our care. All losses are ours. There is no other to whom we can go, not even a self to whom we can speak. Yet Buddhism's denial of a personal god is unable to prevent its practitioners from smuggling in a worship in which a personal being is addressed. The isolation within drives the self to a transcendent personal other.

Buddha considered life to be a payment for previous lives. Each rebirth is due to karmic indebtedness, but without the carryover of the person. In contradistinction, Christianity sees the individual self as distinctive and indivisible. God's love is personal. Jesus brought God's offer for true forgiveness and eternal life while affirming each individual as uniquely created in God's image. For Jesus, suffering is only symptomatic of the life unhinged from right relationship with God. We have broken away from God, from our fellow human beings, and even from ourselves.

In contrast to *karma*—where sin is nothing more than ignorance or illusion—Christ's forgiveness can provide true appeal for the Buddhist. The Gospel proclaims we have come apart from within, and to this brokenness Jesus brings the real answer. In finding true relationship with God, all other relationships are given moral worth. God, who is distinct and distant, came close so that we who are sinful and weak may be forgiven and made strong in communion with God Himself, without losing our identity. That simple act of communion encapsulates life's purpose. The individual retains his or her individuality while dwelling in community.

Moreover, Christ does not prescribe extinguishing one's self—which is not possible—but rather prescribes no longer living for oneself. Hungering after righteousness is good and brings God's fulfillment. Everyone who has surrendered all at the feet of Jesus can confess with the Apostle Paul, "I know the One I have believed in and am persuaded that He is able to guard what has been entrusted to me until that day" (2Tm 1:12). Jesus Christ Himself guards all our purposes, loves, attachments, and affections when they are entrusted to Him.

The Uniqueness of Israel's Religion

E. Ray Clendenen

B iblical scholars have been jubilant over the discovery of law tablets and other literature from the ancient Near East as well as structures such as multi-chambered temples. Such discoveries have done much to help us understand the cultural and literary climate in which Israel and their canonical literature arose and developed. But with these advances comes a nagging question. Why would a religion based on revelation have so much in common with religions that are only products of human imagination?

In the first place, paganism is a corruption of an earlier pure religion. The worship of the only true God did not develop from animism to ethical monotheism according to an evolutionary scheme as modernists claim. The Bible teaches that paganism began to develop when sin corrupted the worship of the true God (Rm 1:18-23). Thus, some of the similarities between paganism and biblical faith could result from a common memory (however faulty) of early events and an earlier legitimate worship that lingers in human personality and culture.

Second, the nations, peoples, and cultures of the world, in spite of their rejection of God, have not developed independently of the Lord's supervision (Dt 2:5,9,19; Am 1:3–2:15; 9:7). On the contrary, their course of departure has been within divinely decreed limits, and they have been included from the beginning in God's redemptive purposes (Gn 12:1-3). Thus, just as God prepared the Hellenistic world for the proclamation of the gospel, so also He prepared the ancient Near East culturally for the revelation of the divine name in Israel. That is, the forms that Israel shared with the surrounding peoples were products of God's common grace, though perverted in the nations' case (and frequently in Israel) by paganism.

Third, however the forms of paganism arose, when God began revealing to the Patriarchs and early generations of Israel how He was to be worshiped, it would be only reasonable that He would employ forms which would have some meaning to them. That would mean using familiar events, symbols, and practices that could be redirected and filled with new meaning. Thus, while the *forms* of Israel's faith shared many elements with their pagan neighbors, the *substance* or heart of Yahweh worship could diverge drastically.

Old Testament faith had five main distinctives. First and foremost, it was to be monotheistic and exclusivistic. Cities in the ancient Near East were often filled with temples to various gods. Each of Babylon's nine city gates was dedicated to a different god. Practitioners of other religions often expended great effort either identifying their gods with those of other nations or demonstrating the subordination of other gods to their patron deity. But Israel's God demanded not a special place in a pantheon, but exclusive allegiance. In the context of ancient Near Eastern polytheism, the call of Deuteronomy 6:4 to the worship of Yahweh as the one true God would have seemed revolutionary.

Monotheism also differed from polytheism in the nature of worship itself. Polytheism by definition precluded wholehearted devotion and loyalty to one god. If divine power existed in many gods, none could possess unlimited wisdom or power, and the activities of one god could often be counteracted by the activities of another. The divine will was thus fragmented so that a person could never be safe and secure from divine displeasure and punishment since the will of one god may very well conflict with that of another. But if there is only one God, we can be wholehearted in our devotion to Him, as Deuteronomy 6:5 goes on to demand.

The second distinctive was that the God of Israel was transcendent and self-sufficient. He was not the personification of nature with a sovereignty limited to the earth, the heavens, or the underworld. He did not need to be tended or fed in His temple like a Babylonian or Egyptian god. Nor did He need other divine or human assistance through cultic rites to maintain cosmic and political order and agricultural productivity. Egyptian temple rituals were the means by which the people contributed to holding the forces of chaos at bay, and Canaanite fertility rites ensured continuing agricultural and human productivity.

Yahweh is rather the transcendent One who created an inanimate universe of nature out of nothing and who continually maintains and controls it for His glory. "The profoundest insight of Hebrew religion," John Oswalt declares, may be that "Whatever God is, he is not the world around us." This means that magic has no part in biblical worship.

The third distinctive is that although He is transcendent, He has not kept His character or His will hidden like the gods of other peoples. T. Jacobsen describes the Babylonian god Enlil: "Man can never be fully at ease with Enlil, can never know what he has in mind. . . . In his wild moods of destructiveness he is unreachable, deaf to all appeals." Where the other peoples had to search continually for the divine will through divination, try to awaken divine interest through bodily mutilation (1Kg 18:26-29), and avoid misfortune through incantations and the wearing of amulets, the Lord had revealed His will in His written Word (see Dt 4:6-8).

The fourth distinctive was the nature of the relationship between God and His people. Israel's relationship with Yahweh was based on divine election in which God established in history a covenant with His people. No other ancient people in that part of the world had a covenantal relationship with their god. The Bible presents mankind as the "crown of creation" and the natural world as theirs to oversee and enjoy. But the foreign gods were primarily feudal gods of the land, which they had created for themselves. People were little more than serfs, a necessary nuisance seldom receiving more than a brief expression of pity or remorse for their grievous situation. But the Lord had formed a people, bound them to each other and to Himself by covenant, and pledged to shepherd them faithfully forever by His grace and to guard jealously their relationship to Him.

Finally, while the Lord ordained the use of ritual in worship, He abhorred ritual that aimed at divine manipulation. The only actions that pleased God were those that arose from the heart (Hs 6:4-6), and true worship was to be accompanied by joy in the Lord (Dt 12:12,18). Thus biblical religion gives at the same time a higher view of humanity and a higher view of God—omnipotent, undivided, purposive, merciful, uniformly righteous, and deserving of our undivided love. Israel was to be a kingdom of priests, singing to the Lord and declaring His glory among the nations day after day (1Ch 16:23).

What Is the Christian Identity Movement?

R. Alan Streett

The Christian Identity movement (CI), formerly called British or Anglo Israelism, teaches that God respects persons based variously on their bloodline or nationality. Many of these groups are anti-Semitic, claiming that white Anglo-Saxons constitute the Israel of God and that ethnic Jews are the children of the devil. Also, all CI sects make a distinction between Israel and the Jews. They base their beliefs on one of two theories: 1) the ten lost tribes theory or 2) the serpent seed theory.

According to the former theory, after the fall of Israel (the northern kingdom consisting of ten tribes) in 722 B.C., the tribes migrated westward into Europe and eventually to America. None returned to their homeland. They assimilated into the culture and hence lost their identity. They now constitute the Anglo-Saxon peoples of the world. The southern kingdom, consisting of two tribes (Judah and Benjamin), fell to Babylon in 586 B.C. After captivity, many returned to their homeland. According to the CI theory, they became known as Jews. They were responsible for the death of Christ, and therefore are the targets of God's wrath.

The lost tribes theory may sound plausible to a biblical novice, but Scripture proves the theory to be bankrupt (see Ezr 3:1; 6:16-17; Lk 1:54,67-68,80;

2:36; Jn 3:1,10; Ac 2:14,22,36; 5:21; 13:24, which indicates that Israel returned to its homeland). Peter says Israel crucified Jesus (Ac 4:8-10). There are no lost tribes. James addressed all 12 of them (Jms 1:1). After the Babylonian captivity, the terms Israel and Jews are used interchangeably. No longer is the nation considered to be divided. In the NT, Jew is used 174 times and Israel is used 75 times to designate the same people. The Apostle Paul used both Jew (Ac 21:39; 22:3) and Israelite (Rm 11:1; 2Co 11:22) to identify Himself.

Other CI groups look to the serpent seed theory to validate their anti-Semitic beliefs. According to this scenario, the sexual union between Adam and Eve produced Abel, the father of the Israelite or Aryan people. Those in this godly line are God's children by birth; hence there is no need for a new birth. A second union, this time between Eve and the serpent produced Cain, who became the father of the Jews. After the great flood, his descendants cohabited with beasts, producing a mongrelized race of people, now consisting of Semites, Asians, and Africans. They are the enemies of God.

The problems with this theory are obvious. First, Israel traces its origin to Jacob, not Abel, when the former's name was changed to Israel. Second, Abraham, not Cain, is called the father of the Jews. Third, all people must be born again, for all have sinned and fallen short of God's glory (Rm 3:23). Fourth, Jesus reminded the woman of Samaria that "salvation is from the Jews" (Jn 4:22). Fifth and most importantly, Jesus was a Jew from the tribe of Judah; thus, according to this theory, He would be the enemy, not the Son of God.

Both the ten lost tribes and serpent seed theories are convoluted attempts to provide theological and scriptural support for anti-Semitism.

SECTION 10

Evangelism

How Should a Christian Relate to a Scientific Naturalist?

J.P. Moreland

" I'm too scientific for religious superstition. Science is the only way of gaining knowledge of reality and it tells us the physical world is all there is." This claim, espoused by many scientific naturalists, is called *scientism*, the view that science is the very paradigm of truth and rationality.

There are two forms of scientism: strong and weak. *Strong scientism* implies that something is true if and only if it is a scientific claim that has been successfully tested and used according to appropriate scientific methodology. There are no truths apart from scientific truths, and even if there were, there would be no reason to believe them.

Weak scientism allows for truths apart from science and grants them some minimal rational status without scientific support. Still, weak scientism implies that science is the most authoritative sector of human learning.

If either variety of scientism is true, drastic implications result for theology. If strong scientism is true, then theology is not a cognitive enterprise at all and there is no such thing as theological knowledge. If weak scientism is true, then the conversation between theology and science will be a monologue with theology listening to science and waiting for its support.

What, then, should we say about scientism, and what should Christians say to those who hold this belief?

Note first that strong scientism is self-refuting. Strong scientism is not itself a proposition *of* science, but a proposition of philosophy *about* science to the effect that only scientific propositions are true and/or rational to believe. And strong scientism is itself offered as a true, rationally justified position to believe. Propositions that are self-refuting do not just happen to be false but could have been true; they are necessarily false—it is not possible for them to be true. No future progress will have the slightest effect on making strong scientism more acceptable.

Two more problems count equally against strong and weak scientism. First, scientism does not adequately allow for the task of stating and defending the necessary presuppositions for science itself to be practiced. Thus, scientism shows itself to be a foe and not a friend of science. Science cannot be practiced in thin air. It has many assumptions, each has been challenged, and the task of stating and defending these assumptions is a philosophical one. The conclusions of science cannot be more certain than the presuppositions it rests on and uses to reach those conclusions.

Strong scientism rules out these presuppositions altogether because neither the presuppositions themselves nor their defense are scientific matters. Weak scientism misconstrues their strength in its view that scientific propositions have greater intellectual authority than those of other fields like philosophy. This would mean that the conclusions of science are more certain than the philosophical presuppositions used to justify and reach those conclusions and that is absurd.

Here is a list of some of the philosophical presuppositions of science: (1) the existence of a theory-independent, external world; (2) the orderly nature of the external world; (3) the knowability of the external world; (4) the existence of truth; (5) the laws of logic; (6) the reliability of our cognitive and sensory faculties to serve as truth gatherers and as a source of justified beliefs in our intellectual environment; (7) the adequacy of language to describe the world; (8) the existence of values used in science (e.g. "test theories fairly and report test results honestly").

Second, there are true, rational beliefs in fields outside of science. Strong scientism does not allow for this fact, and it is therefore to be rejected as an account of our intellectual enterprise.

Moreover, some claims outside science (for instance, "Torturing babies for fun is wrong," or "I am now thinking about science") are better justified than some claims within science (for example, "Evolution takes place through a series of very small steps"). It is not hard to believe that many of our currently held scientific beliefs will and should be revised or abandoned in one hundred years, but it would be hard to see how the same could be said of the extra-scientific propositions just cited. Weak scientism does not account for this fact.

In sum, scientism in both forms is inadequate and it is important for Christians to integrate science and theology with genuine respect for both.

Intellectuals Who Found God

Chad Owen Brand

C.S. **Lewis (1898–1963).** Lewis's parents taught him the proper faith and religious life of an Englishman, but troubles awaited the young man. His mother died when he was a boy, after which his father sent him to boarding schools. Though early on he tried to be a good Christian, he came to resent religion and developed instead a fascination with myth and fantasy literature. His great concerns were with whether Christianity was unique and how it could solve (or not solve) the problem of evil. When he entered Oxford in 1917, Lewis was a convinced agnostic. He had sought through logic to debunk religion in general and Christianity in particular. Yet, his favorite authors—Dante, MacDonald, Herbert, Plato, Milton, and Virgil—were all people who held some sort of religious understanding of the world. In reading George MacDonald and through personal acquaintance with J. R. R. Tolkien and Owen Barfield, he eventually abandoned his nontheistic view of the world. In 1929 he threw in the towel and conceded that "God was God" and he knelt and prayed—perhaps the "most reluctant convert in all England."

Aurelius Augustine (354–430). Augustine was born at a time when Christianity was just beginning to become a dominant faith in the Roman world. Though his mother was a strong Christian, she did not have him baptized as an infant. By age 15, Augustine had abandoned the faith of his childhood and had adopted the cult known as Manicheeism.

His biggest problem with Christianity was its failure, in his opinion, to deal adequately with the problem of evil. If God is all powerful and all good, how can evil exist, and exist so prevalently and powerfully in the world? The Manichees taught that two spirit beings exist, the one good and the other evil. This explains, so they believed, how one can find a mixture of both good and evil in the world. For a decade or so, the young Augustine, eventually a professor of rhetoric at several Roman universities, believed this to be a better solution. But eventually the young intellectual came to realize that this "solution" was unsatisfactory, since it provided no way to understand the "one" side of the problem of the "one and the many."

Augustine despaired, and began reading skeptical philosophers, such as Cicero and Porphyry, those who taught that "everything is a matter of doubt." Perhaps there is no solution. Yet here, at the end of hope, Augustine was transformed. He heard the preaching of the famous Ambrose and began reading Scripture. Ambrose's apologetics helped Augustine understand that the Bible really did present the great solution to the problem of evil.

Though his intellect was satisfied, his heart, filled with sin and with no answer to the problem of sin, was still empty. Augustine read Paul's words in Romans 13:14: "Put on the Lord Jesus Christ, and make no plans to satisfy the fleshly desires." The key to life lay not in trying to live the moral life, but in putting on Christ, the Christ who satisfies both the intellectual and existential dilemmas humans face. Augustine's writings went on to lay the foundation for the political and intellectual developments of the next 1,500 years in the Western church.

Alexander Solzhenitsyn (1918–2008). Solzhenitsyn was born in 1918 into the new Russian Revolutionary system. In 1945 he was arrested for writing disparaging comments about Stalin in his letters, and was sentenced to a "mild" eight years in the Soviet Gulags (labor camps). Upon his release he was exiled to the desert in Kazakhstan and then in 1974 was exiled to the West. During this period, Solzhenitsyn became an orthodox Christian. He came to recognize that only Christianity provided both a realistic understanding of the human condition of sin, coupled with the one solution to the human condition that makes any sense. His writings on the Soviet Gulags and on Russian history have become classics that have given the West a truly clear picture of life in the repressive Soviet system.

Francis Schaeffer (1912-1984). Schaeffer grew up in a liberal Protestant home. As a teenager he began to read the Bible and was surprised to find that it contained answers to life's greatest problems. He gave his life to Christ and, contrary to his family's wishes, determined to enter Christian ministry. In 1948 he and his wife, Edith, moved to Switzerland. There they gave their lives to talking to and witnessing to young people, mostly disaffected youth from America and Western Europe.

Schaeffer was never afraid to confront modernity and postmodernity on their own grounds. His writings demonstrate a dialogue with the key intellectual and cultural developments of the last two centuries. If there is anything one can learn from Schaeffer, it is that one can face the best (and worst) that the nontheistic world can offer, and still have confidence that God is there and that He is not silent.

J. S. Bach (1685–1750). Bach is one of the most gifted musicians of all time. The sheer amount of work he turned out is almost unbelievable, amounting to nearly a thousand compositions, many of which have now been lost. He set the Christian faith to music in a way that no one before or since has done. He read the Bible faithfully and sought to give accurate presentations of its truths not only in lyric but in musical composition as well. Bach also demonstrated that one could serve God by producing music that was not specifically Christian in orientation, such as his Brandenburg Concerti, but which, by their very structure, still demonstrated his conviction that God has made a well-ordered universe. Bach's commitment to Christ can be seen in that he told his students that unless they committed their talents to Jesus, they would never become great musicians.

Lewis Wallace (1827–1905). Wallace was a Union General during the Civil War. Later he sat on the court-martial which dealt with the Lincoln assassination conspirators, then became governor of the territory of New Mexico. His life began to change when he had an extensive conversation with the well-known infidel scholar, Robert Ingersoll. In the conversation he was unable to refute Ingersoll's arguments. So, he set himself to learn everything he could about the life, setting, and historical context of Jesus Christ. Wallace was not over-awed by the reputation of Ingersoll, but believed that investigation of the facts of the gospel message could lead one to the truth about Jesus Wallace's investigations led to his writing the novel *Ben-Hur.*

In the novel, a Jewish man named Judah Ben-Hur encounters Jesus and hears him say, "I am the resurrection and the life." Later Ben-Hur returns to Rome and gives all his wealth to promote the Christian faith.

Does the Bible Teach That Everyone Will Be Saved?

Gregory Alan Thornbury

The Bible plainly teaches only those who personally, consciously and explicitly confess Jesus Christ as Lord possess eternal life. All others will face the holy and just wrath of God in hell throughout eternity.

Throughout the NT, the biblical writers uniformly describe a coming fixed and final divine judgment. Revelation 20:11-15 describes this scene in which all persons, both living and dead, will stand before God to be "judged according to their works." Further, the text says: "Anyone not found written in the book of life was thrown into the lake of fire." The "book of life" lists all those who have believed and obeyed Jesus Christ, who said:

> I will give water as a gift to the thirsty from the spring of life. The victor will inherit these things, and I will be his God, and he will be My son. But the cowards, unbelievers, vile, murderers, sexually immoral, sorcerers, idolaters, and all liars—their share will be in the lake that burns with fire and sulfur, which is the second death (Rv 21:6-8).

This passage reveals central truths concerning who will be saved. Redemption comes by grace through faith in Christ apart from individual merit. Those who have not believed are deemed faithless and will receive a just and endless punishment in hell.

During His earthly ministry, Jesus talked more often about final judgment than He did about heaven (see, for example, Mt 25:41; Lk 16:23-31). He also warned anyone who rejected Him during this lifetime: "Just as the weeks are gathered and burned in the fire, so it will be at the end of the age" (Mt 13:40). Throughout the NT, the apostles consistently echoed their Lord's theme (see 2Th 1:5-9; Heb 9:27; 2Pt 3:7).

Despite repeated scriptural emphasis to the contrary, universalists commonly raise three objections to the *exclusivity* of the gospel.

All religions are equally true; therefore everyone will be saved. This claim is easily disproven. For example, a Hindu might say all religions lead to God while a Christian asserts that Jesus is the only way to the Father. In order to stay true to his conviction, the Hindu must say that the Christian's exclusive claim is wrong. But once he has said this, he has violated his dictum that all religions are equally valid. The two beliefs cannot both be right. Therefore it cannot be concluded on this basis that all persons will be saved.

God will give all human beings an opportunity to accept the gospel after death. Despite a lack of biblical evidence in its favor, this view teaches that God will give a final chance for people to repent after death and before the judgment. On the contrary, the Scriptures clearly indicate that once a person dies, it is too late for them to repent and turn to God (Mt 25:35-46; Lk 16:19-31). "It is appointed for people to die once—and after this, judgment" (Heb 9:27).

What about the "man on the island" who has never heard the gospel? It would not be fair for God to send such a person to hell for not believing in Jesus. This argument from emotion is often heard and is particularly dangerous. If it were true that God is obligated to save everyone who has not heard the gospel, then we might be better advised to recall all missionaries and stop proclaiming the gospel. Of course, the Bible does not countenance such a God-dishonoring approach. The "man on the island," like all people, is in desperate need of the good news about the forgiveness of sins through Jesus Christ.

What About Those Who Have Never Heard About Christ?

Chad Owen Brand

Human beings as a lot are incurably religious. The problem is that since these same human beings are also infected by sin, they tend not to desire to honor and glorify the true God, who is righteous and holy. Rather, they tend to make gods for themselves which are pleasing to them or which satisfy some sense of what they think a god ought to be. As John Calvin said, the human mind is a factory for idols. Such gods, concocted by the rationale of humans apart from special revelation, are invariably out of touch with the truth (Rm 1:18-32).

What hope is there for those who do not live in predominantly Christian parts of the world? Historically, Christians have argued that their hope lies in the mission impulse of the Christian church. From the earliest days of Christianity, Jewish Christians began to spread the message to the Gentile world (Ac 10-11). Christians such as the apostle Paul made it clear that it was not good enough even to be a Jew, since the hope for salvation rests in affirming Jesus as Messiah (Php 3:7-11). In the early centuries of the faith, Christians spread the message to Africa, northern Europe, the British Isles, and the Asian sub-continent, all because they believed that this message was the hope of salvation for the world.

It is obvious to anyone that vast numbers of people in the world today either have never heard the gospel, or they have only heard it in a cursory manner. What hope do such people have? The Bible makes it clear that there is no salvation in any name other than that of Christ (Jn 14:6; Ac 4:12). That means that one must believe specifically in Jesus in order to be saved (Rm 10:9-14). Does this mean that most people ever born will spend eternity in hell? If so, is that a problem for the Christian faith?

A couple of proposals have been offered to respond to this difficulty. Some have suggested that God will evaluate all people according to the "light they have." That is, if someone is a Hindu, or a Muslim, or an ancient Aztec, God will only judge them according to their response to the religious information they have at hand. The problem is that the Bible regularly condemns idolatry. Scripture even indicates that idolaters know intuitively that there is something wrong with their idolatry (Rm 1:19-20). The other problem is that many actions of religious people are terrible. Hindu Kali worshipers murdered travelers and Aztecs sacrificed young women to their god. Another proposal is that God will simply save all persons by His power. The difficulty here is that it ignores the issue of free moral agency, as well as the fact that the Bible indicates that some will eventually go to everlasting punishment (Mt 25:46).

Christians must hold that faith in Christ, and *only* faith in Christ, is the avenue to salvation. But having said that, God will judge those who have heard the truth and yet rejected it more severely that those who have never heard (Lk 10:14). There is also the hope that in the future the church's message of salvation will cover the entire earth.

What About Those Who Have Never Heard About Christ?

William Lane Craig

The conviction that salvation is available through Christ alone permeates the NT (see, *e.g.*, Ac 4:12; Eph 2:12). This raises the troubling question of the fate of those who never hear the gospel.

What exactly, is the problem here supposed to be? The universalist alleges that the following statements are logically inconsistent: (1) God is all-powerful and all-loving. (2) Some people never hear the Gospel and are lost.

But why think that 1 and 2 are logically incompatible? There is no explicit contradiction between them. If the universalist is claiming that they are implicitly contradictory, he must be assuming some hidden premises that would bring out this contradiction.

Although universalists have not been very forthcoming about their hidden assumptions, the logic of the problem would suggest something akin to these points: (3) If God is all-powerful, He can create a world in which everybody hears the Gospel and is freely saved. (4) If God is all-loving, He prefers a world in which everybody hears the gospel and is freely saved.

But are these premises necessarily true?

Consider 3. It seems uncontroversial that God could create a world in which everybody hears the gospel. But so long as people are free, there is no guarantee that everybody in such a world would be freely saved. In fact, there is no reason to think that the balance between saved and lost in such a world would be any better than the balance in the actual world! Hence 3 is not necessarily true, and the universalist's argument is fallacious.

But what about 4? Is it necessarily true? Let us suppose for the sake of argument that there are possible worlds that are feasible for God in which everyone hears the gospel and freely accepts it. Does God's being all-loving compel Him to prefer one of these worlds over a world in which some persons are lost? Not necessarily, for these worlds might have other, over-riding deficiencies that make them less preferable. For example, suppose that the only worlds in which everybody freely believes the gospel and is saved are worlds with only a handful of people in them. Must God prefer one of these sparsely populated worlds over a world in which multitudes believe in the gospel and are saved, even though other persons freely reject His grace and are lost? Thus, the universalist's second assumption is not necessarily true, so that his argument is doubly invalid.

As a loving God, God wants as many people as possible to be freely saved and as few as possible to be lost. His goal, then, is to achieve an optimal balance between these, to create no more of the lost than is necessary to attain a certain number of the saved. It is possible that in order to create this many people who will be freely saved, God also had to create this many people who will be freely lost.

It might be objected that an all-loving God would not create people whom He knew will be lost, but who would have been saved if only they had heard the gospel. But how do we know there *are* any such persons? It is reasonable to assume that many people who never hear the gospel would not have believed the gospel even if they had heard it. Suppose, then, that God has so providentially ordered the world that *all* persons who never hear the gospel are precisely such people. In that case, anybody who never hears the gospel and is lost would have rejected the gospel and been lost even if he had heard it.

Thus, it is possible that: (5) God has created a world that has an optimal balance between saved and lost, and those who never hear the gospel and are lost would not have believed in it even if they had heard it.

So long as 5 is even possibly true, it shows that there is no logical incompatibility between an all-powerful, all-loving God and some people's never hearing the gospel and being lost.

Can the Gospel Be Presented Across Cultures?

John Mark Terry

E vangelical Christians respond to this question with a resounding yes. The Bible includes many passages about cross-cultural evangelism. In the Great Commission (Mt 28:18-20) Jesus commanded His disciples to evangelize all the nations of the world. The word translated "nations" is the Greek word *ethne,* which is the root word for the English word *ethnic.* Thus Jesus instructed the apostles to make disciples of all the ethnic groups of the world. At His ascension (Ac 1), Jesus reiterated the command, instructing the apostles to witness even to the "the ends of the earth" (Ac 1:8). Clearly the Bible reveals God's concern for all the cultures of the world.

Jesus Himself is the supreme example of cross-cultural ministry. He left heaven to minister on earth. He was God in the flesh, the one incarnation who set the example for incarnational missions. In a similar way, Christians today should incarnate the gospel among the cultures of the world. Jesus also demonstrated His concern for reaching other cultures by witnessing to the Samaritans, an ethnic group despised by the Jews of His day (Jn 4).

Peter, the leader of the early church, offers another example of cross-cultural ministry. Like most Jews of his day, he avoided contact with Gentiles. But through a vision God showed Peter the error of his prejudice, and Peter traveled to Caesarea to witness and stay in the home of Cornelius, a Roman army officer (Ac 10).

Paul provides a third example of cross-cultural witness. Though he had been raised to segregate himself from Gentiles, Paul met the Lord Jesus on the road to Damascus, and Christ called him to be a missionary to the Gentiles (Ac 9:15). Paul devoted the rest of his life to planting churches among Gentiles.

So, the Bible reveals the answer to the question before us. Yes, the gospel can be presented across cultural boundaries. Any doubt to the contrary is based upon the false contemporary assumption that at least some vital worldview beliefs (such as the gospel) are incommunicable to other cultures. But not only is this philosophical assumption unproven, it is unacceptable for one who follows the teaching of Jesus and His apostles.

Does the Old Testament Teach Salvation by Works?

E. Ray Clendenen

A ccording to Gn 15:6, Abram did not buy righteousness with his faith. Rather, God gave Abram righteousness, which means right standing or acceptability before God. The biblical message is clear and consistent in both testaments that the curse of condemnation and death that rests on everyone because of Adam's sin (Rm 5:12-21) cannot be removed and exchanged for righteousness through any amount of good deeds that one might do. The exchange can only be affected by God as a free act of His grace in response to a person's faith (Hab 2:4; Rm 1:16-17; 4:1-25; Gl 3:6-9).

The operative key to the exchange is not the quality or degree of faith but rather God's grace; faith is not a means to earn acceptance with God. The Apostle Paul considered Abraham a model of transforming faith even though the content of Abraham's faith was different from Paul's. Abraham simply trusted God and His promise to give him a son and then through that son vast descendants. Presumably Abraham would have supplemented God's promise here with that of Genesis 12:1-3, trusting that his offspring would be vast not only in number but also in significance, bringing blessing to the world. The content of Abraham's faith was not inconsistent with that of Paul, only less specific. Also, Abraham believed what God *would do*, and Paul believed what God *had done*.

Finally, the NT explains that faith itself cannot purchase or serve as the foundation for acceptance with God. Only the cross of Christ can purchase our salvation. But since the eternal and timeless God is sovereign over events, He could apply the work of Christ to OT believers in response to their faith even though they had no specific knowledge of Christ.

Don't Christian Missionaries Impose Their Culture on Others?

Philip J. Sampson

M any people believe Christian missionaries impose their culture on others. Missionaries allegedly soften up native peoples by weakening their cultural resistance, leaving the field open for colonists and Western capitalism. Mission has been described as enslavement or even genocide, and the gospel as the "everlasting story of the West against the Indians."

Such extreme accusations alert us that we are entering a world of stereotype and caricature. We first find them in the nineteenth century, and stereotypes of missionaries became widespread in the mid-twentieth century, with the recognition that some cultures can oppress others. This insight was selectively applied to Christian cultures of the West, especially as supposedly spread by missionaries.

Most caricatures have a basis in fact, however flimsy, and some missionaries have fit aspects of the stereotype. The NT church faced similar issues (Ac 15; Gl 2) when the apostles rejected the imposition of traditions upon new converts. The fact that Scripture records such disagreements is strong witness to its historical reliability. It's also a scriptural warning to churches to be vigilant against imposing local customs on other people groups. The stereotypes assert that missionaries have consistently ignored this warning. Have they?

Missionaries cannot avoid taking their own culture with them; but they can avoid imposing it on others. As Henry Venn remarked in 1868, long before the twentieth century secular discovery of pluralism, the "marked national characteristics" of the church will be its "perfection and glory." Indeed, at a time when anthropology was mired in scientific racism based on evolutionary ideas, missionary scholars, such as James Legge, Robert Morrison, and John Farquhar insisted on the value of native cultures.

Examples abound of missionaries recognizing cultural diversity and pioneering its study and preservation. This isn't surprising, as missionaries often lived alongside native people, and learned their language in order to translate the Bible. From José de Acosta in Latin America to William Carey in India, from Jacob Grigg in Africa to John Smith in Jamaica, missionaries have helped preserve cultures and native languages. Linguist Mary Haas has estimated that 90 percent of the material available on Native American languages is missionary in origin. Some missionaries courageously identified with native peoples. For example, Samuel Worcester went to prison for his defense of Cherokee rights.

Stereotypes of missionaries aren't only factually inaccurate; they can also be unjust towards black and Asian peoples. The stereotype of Christianity as white and Western misrepresents the church's origin and has long been out of date. The period of Western dominance ended many years ago when the church's centers of gravity moved to Africa, Asia, and Latin America.

Moreover, we do no favors to native cultures in saying a few missionaries easily overpowered them. This stereotypes native cultures as weak and easily dominated, and obscures the violent oppression some native peoples have experienced at the hands of non-missionaries. Stereotypes which treat Christianity as Western and native cultures as weak are ethnocentric at best, unintentionally racist at worst.

All cultures, developed and developing, fall short of the biblical standards and need the gospel. We shouldn't fear justified criticism. But to be just, criticism should be informed and fair. Stereotypes of missionaries are neither.

Can a Christian Have Assurance of Salvation?

Chad Owen Brand

S cripture teaches that Christians are saved by God's grace, a grace they access by placing faith in Jesus Christ for the forgiveness of their sins (Rm 3:21-26; Eph 2:8-9). It also teaches they can persevere in that faith since they are "protected by God's power through faith for a salvation that is ready to be revealed in the last time" (1 Pt 1:5). But can they know with assurance they truly do belong to the Lord and in the end will be resurrected to eternal life? The answer is yes.

The NT writers were absolutely convinced assurance is available to believers. Paul wrote in Romans 8:1, "Therefore, no condemnation now exists for those in Christ Jesus," and then concludes that remarkable discussion with this statement in Romans 8:38-39: "For I am persuaded that not even death or life, angels or rulers, things present or things to come, hostile powers, height or depth, or any other created thing will have the power to separate us from the love of God that is in Christ Jesus our Lord!"

John is also convinced that believers can have assurance. "This is how we are sure that we have come to know Him: by keeping His commands" (1Jn 2:3). And again, "We know that we have passed from death to life because we love our brothers. The one who does not love remains in death" (1Jn 3:14).

How can we receive this assurance? Just as medical technicians test "vital signs" to look for indicators of health, so there are several "vital signs" in Scripture for spiritual health. (1) The Bible says we are to examine ourselves to see whether we are in the faith (1Co 9:24-27; 2Co 13:5). There is nothing wrong and everything right with a Christian stopping from time to time and asking the question, "How am I doing spiritually?" I am not looking for perfection at such times, just signs that God is making a difference. (2) Are we walking in obedience to God? Those who love Him obey Him (1Jn 2:3). This is an objective test. Again, we are not looking for perfection, since becoming like Christ is a process that lasts a lifetime (Rm 8:29-30; 1Jn 3:2). The question we ask is this: is obedience to him what I want more than anything else? The answer is known to each of us. (3) Do I have a sense that I truly belong to the Lord and He to me? Scripture teaches that if we are Christians, we have the indwelling Holy Spirit (Rm 8:9), a Spirit who "testifies together with our spirit that we are God's children" (Rm 8:16). It is this same Spirit who enables us to cry out "*Abba*, Father" to our Father in heaven (Rm 8:15; Gl 4:6). I have known people who speak of God as "The Man Upstairs," but the Christian refers to God as "Father—*my* Father." The sense that God is our Father is a sign that we belong to Him.

Scripture gives both objective and subjective vital signs. When it comes right down to it, as John Calvin once noted, assurance comes with faith. If I am trusting Jesus alone for salvation, that brings assurance with it.

What Does the Bible Teach
About Human Beings?

Russell D. Moore

According to the Bible, one of the most powerful apologetic arguments for the Christian faith is humanity itself. The Scriptures tell us that the wonder of the human body points to the creativity and genius of the Creator God in a way that should evoke both fear and awe (Ps 139:14). The human exercise of dominion over the created order is reflective of God's kingship over the universe (Gn 1:26), a kingship that is fully realized in the mediation of Christ Jesus (Eph 1:10). Man is created male and female in the image of God for a one-flesh union resulting in offspring, a union that pictures the archetypal reality of the Christ/church relationship (Eph 5:22-33).

The Bible tells us that the human conscience testifies to the content and the rightness of the law of the Creator. Although human beings sought to define good and evil apart from the authoritative Word of God (Gn 3:16), God nonetheless planted within all children of Adam a witness to His standards of good and evil. The very fact that fallen humans acknowledge any standards of morality indicates that there is a transcendent code of law, somewhere above mere social constructs (Rm 2:12-16). Moreover, as the Apostle Paul points out, this conscience points beyond itself to a day of reckoning. When humans make moral choices—or make immoral choices using moral arguments—they are tacitly acknowledging that they know of a day in which God will judge all the secrets of the heart (Rm 2:16).

Regardless of how often fallen humans seek to classify themselves as merely biological, they know on the basis of their common rationality, morality, and search for meaning that this is not the case. No matter how many times Darwinism, for example, seeks to speak of humans as one more kind of animal and no matter how many times evolutionary psychologists seek to explain our behavior on the basis of a bestial past, human beings just know it isn't so. We know there is something distinctive about us—which is why the Bible calls on us to appeal to the minds and consciences of unbelievers, even though the minds are blinded (2Co 4:4) and the consciences are often calloused (1Tm 4:2).

The biblical witness about human beings stands therefore in stark contrast with other belief systems. Unlike some Eastern religions, the Bible does not present the life of a human being as a cycle of incarnations nor does it affirm, with Mormonism, the preexistence of disembodied human spirits. Unlike many nature religions and various forms of neopaganism, the Bible does not present humanity as part of the larger life force of nature. Unlike Islam, the Bible affirms the freedom and responsibility of human beings as moral creatures before a God they image. Unlike many psychological theories, the Bible does not reduce human motivations or actions to the interactions of unconscious desires, habitual patterns, or the firing of neurons. Unlike both Marxism and libertarian capitalism, the Bible presents the longings of the human heart as far more than material. Unlike Gnosticism, feminism, or misogynistic belief systems, God's good creative purposes are seen in the goodness and permanence of sexual differentiation, in the equal worth of the sexes as image-bearers (Gn 2:27), and in the protective sacrificial headship of men as fathers of families and leaders of tribes (1Co 11:3).

In contrast to rival belief systems, the Bible presents human beings as distinct from a nature they are called to govern (Ps 8:5-8), free to act according to their natures (Jos 24:15), responsible for actions before the tribunal of Christ (Rv 20:12-13), and created for conformity to the image of Jesus as joint-heirs of a glorious new creation (Rm 8:17,29). The doctrine of the image of God grants value to every human life, regardless of its vulnerability or stage of development (Gn 9:6), and it stands in eternal hostility to any form of racial bigotry or nation-state idolatry (Ac 17:25-27).

The Bible's truthfulness about human depravity contrasts strongly with more anthropologically optimistic belief systems, such as Mormonism, Scientology, or progressive secularism. Human sin is an apologetic issue since a Christian framework explains fully how educated, rational, loving persons can bring forth cruelty, violence, and hatred. The biblical teaching on sin also answers what may be the most persistent charge against the truthfulness of Christianity: Christian hypocrisy.

Likewise, the prevalence of world religions and ideologies, which is often used as an objection to Christianity, actually serves as an apologetic argument for Christian claims. The Bible tells us that the universal instinct to worship and to interpret reality is grounded in the revelation of God and that the universal suppression of this truth leads to multiform idolatries (Rm 1:18-32). We should not be surprised then that literally every human civilization in history has had some practice of worship, but also that cults, world religions, and even secular ideologies often ape and mimic some aspects of Christian truth. Nor should we be surprised, as the ancient book of Ecclesiastes illustrates, when the human quest for sensual gratification, material abundance, or the wielding of power apart from the Creator's purposes leads to despair.

Does the Bible Teach that Humans Are More Than Their Bodies?

J.P. Moreland

Throughout history, most Christians have believed in the souls of men and beasts. Animals and humans are composed of an immaterial entity—a soul and a body. The main biblical emphasis is on the functional, holistic unity of a human being. But this unity includes a dualist distinction of body and soul. The human soul, while not by nature immortal, is nevertheless, capable of entering an intermediate disembodied state upon death and, eventually, being reunited with a resurrected body. By contrast, animal souls do not reflect the image of God and most likely do not survive death.

There are two main lines of argument for dualism: biblical anthropological terms and biblical teaching about life after death.

Old Testament anthropological terms. Biblical anthropological terms exhibit a wide field of meanings, and care must be taken to interpret each occurrence in its context. The two most important OT terms are *nephesh* (frequently translated "soul") and *ruach* (frequently translated "spirit").

Nephesh sometimes refers to God as an immaterial, transcendent self, a seat of mind, will, emotion, etc. (see Jb 23:13; Am 6:8). It is similarly applied to humans (Dt 6:5, 21:14; Pr 21:10; Is 26:9; Mc 7:1). It also refers to a vital entity that makes something alive (Ps 30:3; 86:13; Pr 3:22). Finally, *nephesh* refers to the continuing locus of personal identity that departs to the afterlife at the last breath ceases (Gn 35:18; cp. 1Kg 17:21,22; Ps 16:10; 30:3; 49:15; 86:13; 139:8; Lm 1:1). Death and resurrection are regularly spoken of in terms of the departure and return of the soul. Indeed, the problem of necromancy throughout Israel's history (the practice of trying to communicate with the dead in Sheol; see Dt 18:9-14; 1Sm 28:7-25) seems to presuppose the view that ancient Israel took people to continue to live conscious lives after the death of their bodies.

Ruach, frequently translated "spirit," sometimes signifies a vital power that infuses something, animates it, and gives it life and consciousness. Thus, the *ruach* in man is formed by Yahweh (Zch 12:1), proceeds from and returns to Him and is that which gives man life (Jb 34:14). In Ezekiel 37, God takes dry bones, reconstitutes human bodies of flesh, and then adds a *ruach* to these bodies to make them living persons (see Gn 2:7). There is no *ruach* in physical idols and, thus, they cannot arise and possess consciousness (Jr 10:14; Hab 2:19). *Ruach* also refers to an independent, invisible, conscious being as when God employs a spirit to accomplish some purpose (2Kg 19:7; 22:21-23). In this sense, Yahweh is called the God of the vital spirits of all flesh (Nm 27:16; cp. 16:22). Here, "spirit" means an individual, conscious being distinct from the body. Moreover, *ruach* also refers to the seat of various states of consciousness, including volition (Dt 2:30; Ps 51:10-12; Jr 51:11), thought (Is 29:24), emotion (Jdg 8:3, 1Kg 21:4), and one's moral or spiritual condition (Pr 18:14; Ec 7:8).

The Old Testament on Life After Death. The OT depicts individual survival after physical death in a disembodied form. The dead in Sheol are called *rephaim.* Old Testament teaching about life after death is best understood in terms of a diminished though conscious form of disembodied personal survival in an intermediate state. First, the OT depicts life in Sheol as as lethargic, inactive, and resembling an unconscious coma (Jb 3:13; Ps 88:10-12; 115:17-18; Ec 9:10; Is 38:18). However, the dead in Sheol are also described as being with family, awake, and active on occasion (Is 14:9-10). Second, the Hebrew Scriptures clearly teach the practice of necromancy (communicating with the dead) as a real possibility and, on some occasions, an actuality (see Lv 19:31; 20:6; Dt 18:11; 1Sm 28; Is 8:19). Third, according to the OT, the *nephesh*—a conscious person without flesh and bone—departs to God upon death (see Ps 49:15).

New Testament Anthropological terms. Several NT passages use *pneuma* (spirit) or *psyche* (soul) in a dualistic sense. Hebrews 12:23 refers to deceased but existent human beings in the heavenly Jerusalem as "the spirits of righteous people made perfect." In Revelation 6:9-11 refers to dead saints as the "souls" of the martyrs who are in the intermediate state awaiting the final resurrection (Rv 20:5-6). Several texts refer to death as giving up the spirit (Mt 27:50; Lk 23:46; 24:37; Jn 19:30). Matthew 10:28 says, "Don't fear those who kill the body but are not able to kill the soul; rather, fear Him who is able to destroy both soul and body in hell." In this text, "psyche" seems clearly to refer to something that can exist without the body.

New Testament teaching on the Intermediate State. Certain NT passages seem to affirm a disembodied intermediate state between death and final resurrection. First, there is the transfiguration passage (see Mt 17:1-13) in which Elijah (who never died) and Moses (who had died) appeared with Jesus. The most natural way to interpret this text is to understand that Moses and Elijah continued to exist—Moses was not re-created for this one event—and were made temporarily visible. Thus, the transfiguration passage seems to imply a disembodied intermediate state.

In Luke 23:43, Jesus promised the thief on the cross: "Today you will be with Me in paradise." The term "today" should be taken in its natural sense, namely, meaning that the man would be with Jesus that very day in the intermediate state after their deaths.

In 2 Corinthians 5:1-10 and Philippians 1:21-24, Paul referred to a state after death and prior to the resurrection in which conscious disembodied ("naked," "unclothed") existence in God's presence.

In 2 Corinthians 12:1-4, Paul admitted that, during a visionary experience, he did not know whether he was in his body or temporarily disembodied. Because Paul understood himself as a soul/spirit united to a body, the latter was a real possibility for him.

Isn't Christianity Intolerant?

Paul Copan

U nless we're talking about language development, it's a good idea to understand words before we use them—especially when they may be emotionally charged. One commonly used—and abused—word describing Christians is *intolerant*. Of course, some prickly, pugnacious persons call themselves Christians but deny this by their lives. True Christianity shouldn't be equated with abuses committed in Christ's name. Without compromising their convictions, all Christians should—as much as possible—live at peace with everyone (Rm 12:18).

Today, people assume *tolerance* means "accepting all views as true." And because genuine Christians don't accept all views as true, they're charged with being intolerant.

Whenever you hear Christians criticized as intolerant, ask, "What do you mean by 'intolerance'?" True tolerance doesn't mean accepting all beliefs—the good and the goofy—as legitimate. After all, one who disagrees with Christians doesn't accept Christianity; he thinks Christians are wrong! Historically, tolerance has meant putting up with what you find disagreeable/ false. You put up with strangers on a plane who snore or slurp their coffee. Similarly, you put up with another person's beliefs without criminalizing him.

Tolerance differentiates between beliefs and persons. While disagreeing with certain beliefs, we can show respect to persons holding those beliefs, since all humans are made in God's image and inherently deserve respect. Furthermore, Christianity's truth doesn't imply that non-Christians are 100 percent wrong. Christians can agree with non-Christians about, say, certain ethical truths and scientific findings. All truth is God's truth. Truth is more basic than tolerance since tolerance itself presupposes belief in truth.

Tolerance operates at different levels. What can be tolerated in one area may not be tolerated in another. I'll tolerate certain behavior of other children that I won't tolerate in my own. Christians shouldn't tolerate adultery within the church (ecclesiastical intolerance), but this doesn't mean we seek to have the adulterer imprisoned (legal tolerance).

Condemning arrogance, Christianity emphasizes grace and humility. Some "Christians" think they're superior to non-Christians. But this violates the spirit of the gospel. We gratefully receive God's kind gift of salvation, being like beggars telling other beggars where to find bread. Unlike the manager of some exclusive country club, God lovingly invites everyone to participate in His family—and not at the expense of truth.

Author Index

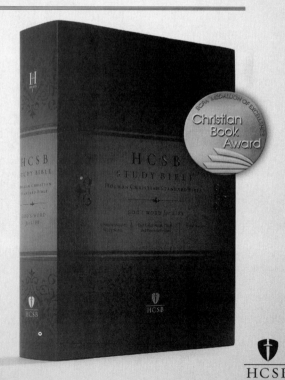

KNOW
WHY YOU BELIEVE

In response to a postmodern culture bent on challenging everything Christians believe, the *Apologetics Study Bible*, the *Holman Quicksource Guide to Christian Apologetics*, the *Holman Quicksource Guide to Understanding Creation*, and the *Apologetics Study Bible for Students* submit complete evidence, historical fact and supporting arguments to bring the truth to light.

Now available online and in bookstores everywhere.

ApologeticsBible.com

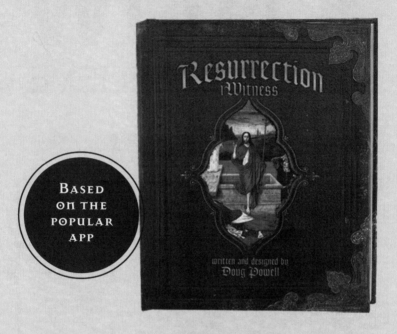